Praise for *From*

"Travis Collins has written a much-needed introduction to the growing Fresh Expressions movement in North America. My prayer is that the Lord will use *From the Steeple to the Street* to inspire hundreds if not thousands of new fresh expressions across the United States and around the world. I highly recommend this book for anyone from any denomination or background wishing to reach their community for Christ!"

Rev. Dr. Winfield Bevins
Director, Asbury Seminary Church Planting Initiative
Author of *Plant: A Sower's Guide to Church Planting*

"When I read Travis Collins's work, I know I will experience a mixture of laughter, furrowed brow, and tears. He inspires me to dream new dreams, challenges me to think and re-think, and he moves me deeply. As someone who loves the inherited church, I am grateful for this important book that connects the steeple with the streets where real people live. Blending excellent theology and missiology with an honest description of America in the twenty-first century, Travis brings to life some tantalizing new possibilities for the American church. In these pages you will find helpful deep background work alongside very practical ways of bringing ideas to life. We need it all, and I am grateful to have this excellent resource to help guide us toward a season of relevance and vitality."

Bill Wilson
Director, Center for Healthy Churches

"We live in a time when so much of what is being written is simply an attempt to describe the difficult days ahead for the local church in North American. When you look at all the descriptions and statistics printed, it is truly disheartening. It seems as if everyone is out to describe the water in which we are all drowning. Personally, I don't find that very helpful, much less encouraging. In *From the Steeple to the Street*, Travis Collins is offering a constructive, deeply spiritual approach in the Fresh Expressions movement that could potentially revitalize any local church. Fresh Expressions is an approach that is not dependent upon style, denomination, size, or any of the other restrictions. It is a free movement of the Spirit of God in the life of any local congregation that is willing to support and encourage the spiritual pioneers within its community. I highly recommend Travis Collins's new book to everyone looking for a sense of direction in a foggy time. Collins is offering to us a fresh, encouraging insight into what the church movement is becoming."

John Upton
Executive Director, Baptist General Association of Virginia

"One of the ways we have come to define fresh expressions is 'putting the church Jesus loves closer to where the people Jesus loves actually are.' *From the Steeple to the Street* is not only a comprehensive overview of this modern day mission movement, but it lays out a clear path for churches and leaders to get out of their building and into the world in concrete ways. With this book in hand, church leaders will have an essential tool for joining the mission of God in innovative ways.

Chris Backert
National Director, Fresh Expressions US

FROM THE STEEPLE TO THE STREET

INNOVATING MISSION AND MINISTRY
THROUGH FRESH EXPRESSIONS OF CHURCH

TRAVIS COLLINS

 Seedbed

All Scripture quotations, unless otherwise indicated, are taken from the Holy Bible, New International Version®, NIV® Copyright © 1973, 1978, 1984, 2011 by Biblica, Inc.™ Used by permission. All rights reserved worldwide.

Scripture quotations marked KJV are taken from the *Holy Bible*, King James Version, Cambridge, 1796.

Printed in the United States of America

Cover design by Nikabrik Design
Page design by PerfecType, Nashville, Tennessee

Collins, Travis.
From the steeple to the street : innovating mission and ministry through fresh expressions of the church / Travis Collins. – Franklin, Tennessee : Seedbed Publishing, ©2016.

xii, 263 ; 22 cm.

ISBN 9781628243000 (paperback : alk. paper)
ISBN 9781628243017 (Mobi)
ISBN 9781628243024 (ePub)
ISBN 9781628243031 (uPDF)

1. Emerging church movement. 2. Missional church movement. 3. Pastoral theology. 3. Christianity--21st century. I. Title.

BV601.9.C64 2016   266
2016932680

SEEDBED PUBLISHING
Franklin, Tennessee
Seedbed.com

to the Pioneers

CONTENTS

PART THREE: FRESH EXPRESSIONS (NEW FORMS) OF CHURCH

PART FOUR: A WAY FORWARD

FOREWORD

The Fresh Expressions movement, which began in the United Kingdom, has proved to be a surprise gift of God to the world church. Something which began with a report to the governing body of the Church of England,[1] and which then became an initiative of a number of denominations in partnership,[2] is now seen as a movement of the Spirit shared by partnerships of churches in a wide variety of nations and contexts.[3]

Fresh expressions of church are appropriate to diverse national contexts because what began in the UK is not a franchise to be licensed, or a model, or set of models, to copy. This is not *The Empire Strikes Back*. It is a set of principles for cooperation with the God of mission. Its purpose is to plant new churches or congregations which are both authentically expressions of the church of Jesus Christ, and contextually appropriate. Authentic church has to be contextual church. Contextual church has to be authentic church. The underlying theology and praxis is about incarnational mission through discerning the leadership and activity of the Holy Spirit. The Fresh Expressions movement is about planting new communities of faith through contextual mission.

In Western contexts at least, this is a time when fewer people would consider joining a church, however attractive. It is a time of rapid and discontinuous change when many tried and tested approaches to evangelism are less fruitful. It is a time of increasing cultural diversity, when franchise or formulaic approaches to church planting fail to reach large sections of society. One size cannot fit all. It is not, however, a time to lose confidence in the gospel. Nor is it a time to jettison all historic and traditional approaches to church. But it is a time to practice the new alongside the old. My challenge to any church, however fruitful its model of mission and ministry may be, is "Who will never be reached if you only do this?"

In the UK, fresh expressions of church have proved to be a fruitful way to draw into Christian faith and discipleship many people who had no previous explicit faith or church connection. It has also drawn back many others who had previously given up on the church. It is a flexible, resource-lite praxis of mission, which is well within the reach of most churches, however small. It has proved effective in rural, urban, and suburban contexts. It has also been instrumental in identifying many new missional and pioneering leaders, most of them lay. It has created new ecumenical partnerships in mission, with shared training courses for practitioners and each denominational partner benefiting from the lessons learned by the others.

This book by Travis Collins is the fruit of our sister movement in the United States. It gathers and shares their learning. It has been a delight to watch the same principles we have been learning take appropriate root across the Atlantic, and to recognize the same authentic marks of the missionary Spirit at work. I have learned from it and recommend it warmly.

Bishop Graham Cray
Chairman of the Mission-Shaped Church working party
formerly Archbishops' Missioner and
leader of the UK Fresh Expressions Team
currently Advocate for Pioneer Ministry and
Fresh Expressions of Church in the Diocese of York

INTRODUCTION:
A TENT REVIVAL CHURCH

In 1911 a little boy named J. D. was born in a coal mining village in western Virginia. Soon his family moved to Sand Mountain, Alabama, where J. D.'s father became a sharecropper.

He quit school after the sixth grade, and when the Great Depression hit, J. D. fought and partied his way across the South. When I knew him he had a gold tooth where the original had gotten knocked out in a fight.

About 1946, J. D. was married with a son and a daughter. At his place of work, however, he met a woman with whom he became romantically involved. They ran off together, J. D. abandoning his wife and kids, with Maude abandoning her husband. J. D. sent a little money back, to help support his son and daughter, but not much. His wife and children were devastated. I spoke with his daughter six decades after he left home, and she wept as if it had happened the day before our conversation.

J. D. and Maude were married and moved to Anniston, Alabama.

Somewhere around 1950 a church in Anniston decided to hold what they called a "tent revival." They rented a vacant lot downtown, put up a carnival-like tent, invited a traveling evangelist, and planned a series of services.

J. D. had not been in churches except for weddings and funerals and was not a follower of Jesus by even the greatest stretch. On a survey Maude would have checked "Christian," but she hadn't darkened the door of a church in years. She loved J. D. but found it hard to live with him. He had a good heart but also had a foul mouth, crude manners, and an inordinate affinity for alcohol.

Then, somebody in that church that was holding a tent revival invited J. D. to a service. Since his friend invited him, and since going to a tent wasn't exactly like going to a church, J. D. considered it. When J. D. mentioned it to his wife, Maude, she thought it couldn't hurt.

So they went. And something happened. That fire-breathing, pulpit-pounding, Bible-waving preacher spoke of sin and salvation in language that grabbed J. D. by the heart and wouldn't let him go.

J. D. and Maude kept going back, night after night, and then after the service one night, J. D. couldn't sleep. He didn't know what was going on inside him but, knowing it had something to do with that tent revival, he called Barto, his brother-in-law, who was a pastor. Although it was the middle of the night, Barto, a pastor with big hands, broad shoulders, and a tender heart, drove over to J. D. and Maude's house. There, Barto explained what it means to be changed, saved, "re-born," to become a follower of Jesus. They knelt in the living room and J. D. threw himself on the mercy of God. He prayed through his tears for God to forgive him and change his life. God answered his simple prayer and J. D. became a moral, ethical, loving husband and devoted follower of Jesus. He was radically changed.

I have a personal interest in that story. The strapping pastor who drove over in the middle of the night and prayed with J. D. was Barto Mason, my uncle, and one of my heroes.

J. D., the man with the rough history whose life was transformed, was my father. Maude was my mom. I know God can do anything, but it frightens me to think of who, what, or where I'd be (and even *if* I'd be) had my father not had that life-transforming experience. That was a defining moment in my life, although it happened nine years before I was born.

As corny as it sounds and as preachy as it sounds, there are lots of J. D.s all around us. As we will see, a tent revival is not exactly a fresh expression of church. But fresh expressions of church are like a 1950 tent revival in that they engage people that churches as we know them probably will not.

If we will be willing to re-imagine church, to take the church Jesus loves to the people Jesus loves, and welcome new forms of church alongside us, perhaps one day someone will tell stories about their parents who found Jesus through our missional church or a new form of church which God birthed through us.

Part One

YOUR CHURCH

Chapter 1

IF YOU'RE DISCOURAGED, YOU'RE NOT ALONE

More and more of your neighbors think less and less about your church. Some people in your community have dismissed the church because they've been hurt, angered, or shamed by the church. It is just as likely, however, that people in your community are simply indifferent toward the church. For whatever reason, becoming part of your church is of no interest to millions of North Americans.

For one, your rituals (even your "contemporary" rituals) seem odd to them. And many just don't see that your church would be a helpful addition to their lives. People are so busy that they are going to invest their time only in activities they perceive to be of real benefit, and countless people simply perceive that the church offers no value to them. What is more, most people genuinely want to involve themselves in organizations that make a real difference in the world, and embarrassingly few consider the local church to be one of those organizations.

The church in the Western world is facing startling challenges, the likes of which have not been faced in several hundred years. Many consider the church to be part of a bygone era. Hence all the statistics you keep hearing about plummeting church attendance, congregations closing their doors, and so on.[1]

It's Not Just Churches That Are Losing Members

If it's any consolation, the church is not the only volunteer organization on the decline. In his book *Bowling Alone*, Robert D. Putnam noted the decline in community activities across the board. From the VFW to the NAACP to whatever acronym your church goes by—people are just not joining and participating like they used to. "Somehow in the last several decades of the twentieth century all these community groups and tens of thousands like them across America began to fade," Putnam observed. He continued:

> For the first two-thirds of the twentieth century a powerful tide bore Americans' ever deeper engagement in the life of their communities, but a few decades ago—silently, without warning—that tide reversed and we were overtaken by a treacherous rip current. Without at first noticing, we have been pulled apart from one another and from our communities over the last third of the century.[2]

So what happened? Among other things, commutes got longer. Wives started working full-time. Americans started watching more television. We became more individualistic and religion got "privatized." Schedules became far more complex. All that and more—factors beyond your control—work against participation in your church.

Not only are people not "joiners" much anymore, it seems no one wants to serve as an officer or on a committee even in the few organizations with which they do have some affiliation.[3] (Ever wonder why it's harder nowadays to get volunteers at church?)

Enter the Nones

Of course, with each generation we know that corporate religious participation is dropping. And, as Putnam put it, "compared with older generations—even when those older generations were the same age as the X'ers are now—they [the X'ers] are . . . less likely to attend church."[4]

You have probably heard a good deal about the rising number of the "nones" (those who, in polls and on surveys, check "none" under religious affiliation). The masses are becoming more "none"—more secular and/or more individualistic, less likely to believe in one particular religious view or to believe there is Truth with a capital "T." The authority of the Bible is not even an option for consideration in many circles, and ministers are more tolerated than appreciated.

In his book, *The Next America*, Paul Taylor listed the following as top four reasons for the rise of the "nones."

1. Backlash from the entangling of conservative Christianity and conservative politics that have painted Christians as anti-this and anti-that and multi-phobics.
2. Married people are more likely than unmarrieds to attend church, and people are marrying later than ever.
3. People are less engaged with their community overall.
4. When a nation is healthy and prosperous, the population tends to become less religious. While some might debate our national economic strength, the nation is relatively sound. "Gradual secularization is to be expected in a generally healthy, wealthy, orderly society."[5]

So the decline in religious affiliation cannot be attributed to any single factor. There is more to it than the apathy engendered by liberalism or the anger provoked by fundamentalism. There is more to the steady fall in church participation than poor strategies and weak leadership. Societal shifts, demographic changes, and dramatically different weekend schedules also have become formidable obstacles to church growth.

And, of course, the issue is not just "church growth." The matter is more ominous than a mounting scarcity of nickels and noses. The percentage of those who so much as check "Christian" on European and American surveys is trending dramatically downward. The 2015 Pew Research report told us that the percentage of Americans who describe themselves as Christians fell about eight points—from 78.4% to 70.6%—between 2007 and 2014.

Please understand, this Fresh Expressions movement is about the Great Commission and the Great Commandment. It is about loving God and loving people and "going into all the world." It is not another church growth methodology.

At the same time, we believe the church is *the primary partner of the missionary God*,[6] and thus is of immeasurable and eternal importance. That is why this Fresh Expressions movement concerns existing, and new forms of, *church*.

The Church's Future in Question

Jesus still remains a popular figure in North America, even among those who do not associate with Christians. For Jesus' approval rating, we can be grateful. Yet, we cannot pass off as inconsequential the fact that so many have a fondness for Jesus that does not equate to a fondness for His church.

What's more, even a number of *believers* who aren't giving up on Jesus *are* giving up on the *church*. Many see the church as more distracting than helpful in their quest for real, Christ-centered spirituality.

The alarming trajectory of the North American church is not only about the people no longer in the pews. This is also about the people who are no longer in the pulpits. There are lots of gifted, called young ministers who don't want to be stuck running the machinery of large, inherited churches. Long-established church cultures, histories of conflicts, and complex governance structures hold little attraction for many young pioneer-types.

With so many deciding to absent themselves from church participation and church leadership, the future of the Christian faith in North America has been questioned. For multiple reasons this is a critical time for the Christian faith in North America.

But aren't there lots of megachurches nowadays? Yes, but mega-exceptions to this downward trend in church involvement are just that—exceptions—and perhaps temporary. The church is inching ever closer to the periphery of American culture.

It is hard to imagine the Christian faith flourishing with such a weakened church. It is true that many people are privately, individually, loving Jesus "in their own way." This privatized, individualized, customized approach to the Christian faith, however, is both unsustainable and unbiblical.

It is unsustainable in that no movement can survive without some sort of structure, some sort of corporate underpinning. It is unbiblical in that, for one, we were intended to follow Jesus as a community, not as lone rangers. Furthermore, this personalized faith has often resulted in a sentimentalized Jesus. Without the mutual accountability of a genuine Christian community, we are prone to embrace only those parts of the Bible that are palatable to our tastes.

In short, we now find ourselves in post-Christendom;[7] the Christian faith has lost much of its influence on North American culture. Jim Kitchins put it like this: "It's as though we began our ministries playing a game of football in a football stadium, but when we came out of the locker room after halftime, the field has been rearranged for baseball."[8]

A Time of Opportunity

It is naive to pretend the church is as strong as it used to be. However, it is irresponsible to issue morose prophesies of an absolute and irreversible demise of the church and the faith in the West. It would be head-in-the-sand-ish to think it is business as usual. It would be chicken-little-ish, however, to assume the news is all bad. The stage has been set for innovative expressions of church. The door has been opened for the Holy Spirit to blow through in a new way.

There is a bright side even to all the bad news. If we understand ourselves to be in a missionary culture, and act accordingly, this is actually a time of great opportunity. There is a story, as an example, attributed to Bill Parcells, the famous NFL football coach. He seems to have told a story about two salesmen who were sent to Australia to sell shoes to the Aborigines. After arriving, one called back to his boss and said, "There are no opportunities here; the natives don't wear shoes." But the other called back and said to his boss, "There are a lot of opportunities here. These people don't have any shoes!"

We can read the alarming statistics as a sign that North Americans "don't *wear* shoes" or that North Americans "don't *have* shoes." Leonard Sweet declared, "Christianity is now such a nonfactor in the wider culture that people are becoming open to it as if for the first time . . ."[9]

Thinking and Acting Like Missionaries

Lesslie Newbigin named North America "the most vital missionary frontier of our time."[10] The terminology is key here. We live on a missionary frontier, and perceptive Christ-followers on a missionary frontier think differently than people in a primarily Christian society. It's time we think like missionaries to a post-Christian culture, not chaplains to Christendom.

While any potential strategy for addressing the crisis of North American faith is welcomed, most of the strategies offered are simply tweaks of this, modifications of that, and fine-tuning of the other. We have come to a time when deeper questions must be asked, more profound issues must be addressed, and new forms of church must be launched.

The time is ripe for just such re-dreaming. When all is well, innovation is a hard sell. But with signs of decline all around, there are going to be more people open to innovation than in a long time.

We have entered (albeit unwittingly) a new context—a context that demands our best thinking and, what's more important, a radical dependence upon the Spirit of God.

Chapter 2

WHEN A CONTEMPORARY SERVICE, A VISION STATEMENT, AND A STRATEGY TEAM AREN'T ENOUGH

Vision statements have brought clarity to churches struggling for direction and identity.

Traditional worship services have helped us value rich, sacred traditions; profound hymn texts have helped us celebrate the transcendence of our Creator.

Contemporary worship services have engaged spiritual seekers, reengaged people who'd been gone from church for years, and salvaged those who were on the verge of walking away by helping us celebrate the imminence of our Lord.

Christian concerts and Christian novels have strengthened Christian hearts.

Christian schools have educated Christian minds.

Sunday school lessons and neighborhood Bible studies for stay-at-home moms and dads have provided strength for the journey.

Preachers, whose rhetorical skills would have made Aristotle proud, have comforted, exhorted, taught, and cast vision for the people of God.

Church architects have created majestic space . . . then later created space that wasn't so religious-looking that it threatened people . . . then most recently have created space that looks much like what we imagine ancient worship spaces to have looked . . . each time helping new generations and varying personalities connect with the Divine.

As valuable as those contributions are, however, they are not enough for a new world.

That leaves church leaders wondering how to do church in this emerging milieu. With church participation waning, leaders are, understandably, seeking answers.

Any church leaders worth their salt are wrestling with ways to make their congregations more effective. From worship styles to governance to discipleship models—all of us who care about local churches are trying to figure those things out, and appropriately so. However, we have to acknowledge that those questions arise from a paradigm that is rooted in an understanding of church that probably has more to do with European modernity than with global post-modernity. The societal shift is not complete, of course, so making our present model of church better is an honorable task. We simply need a new, additional model that will be somehow balanced with the present one. While adjusting our present model, we also have to build and add a new model for a world that is still materializing.

The Viability of the Institution . . . and the World Beyond the Institution

Leaders of local churches intuit that nickels and noses are insuf-ficient measurements of a congregation's effectiveness. Yet, they do have the responsibility to help ensure their church's future. In fact, concern for the future viability of one's church is something we would expect from good leaders.

A genuine desire to reach young adults, for example, is imper-ative. The church *needs* young adults; not to think about ways to engage young adults would be irresponsible. It is unwise for leaders to ignore the future needs of their congregations.

There simply has to be more to church than making sure we can pay the bills tomorrow and that our descendants will have a place to do church exactly like we've done church. The mission of God certainly does not negate the need for a focus on institutional viability. The divine mission, however, is far, far bigger than institutional concerns.

Furthermore, if we are not careful we will obsess over ourselves to the point that we forget our reason for being. Indeed, "if left unchallenged, institutional dimensions of church life will inevitably pull the church into a vortex that will not only suppress the message but in the process destroy the spiritual legitimacy of the church itself."[1]

Church leaders bear the responsibility to consistently call the attention of the church to realities beyond the bubble that church life can become. Yet that kind of leadership is difficult and often costly. Countless leaders have paid a high price for attempting to keep people outwardly oriented. The leader's love for people beyond the church circle can be misconstrued as apathy toward people within it.

Yet that is the call of the missional leader within a local congregation. Without leaders courageously agitating for an outward orientation, the congregation will succumb to the overwhelming pull inward. The inward pull has to be stubbornly resisted. Not with a callous disregard for the pastoral needs of members of the church family. Of course not. But with the loving tenacity of a good shepherd-leader who gently turns the chin of the congregation and points people's gaze beyond the building.

Better tactics?

Western culture is transforming so rapidly and diversifying so widely that it is naive to think one particular tactic will suffice. For instance, it wasn't so long ago that churches were assuming (wrongly) that if they just added a contemporary worship service they would reach young adults and not-yet-Christians. That new worship service seemed to be the silver bullet. While many of us find contemporary worship really meaningful, it never has been the panacea that it was often portrayed to be.

In many ways, discussions about tactics are insufficient. Necessary, of course. Admirable, yes. But inadequate for a new world.

Our new world needs additional, other, complementary forms of church, not merely improvements to church as we know it.

The world certainly needs existing churches that radically rethink how we do church. The world needs existing churches who change their metrics, who structure themselves like mission outposts, who listen to their neighbors instead of the latest church growth guru, who think like cross-cultural missionaries.[2] And the world needs existing churches that, in addition to all this, are willing to champion, and bring alongside them, new forms of church.

Excellence is not enough

I have often found myself in spectacular spaces during Sunday morning worship services where the music is superb. Marvelous choirs and kickin' bands have raised the proverbial roof. My spirit has soared and my mind has wondered, "How do they get such wonderful music in a church?"

Yet, in many cases, I have looked around those same sanctuaries and worship centers and noted lots of empty pews. These are churches with credentialed, gifted ministers and passionate, happy members . . . in awe-inspiring facilities, with music that is breathtaking and programs that run like well-oiled machines . . . with vision statements that can be seen on the wall and roadside digital screens that can be seen for miles . . . and yet there are fewer in their gatherings this year than last, and that has been the case for the last two or three decades.

So what do we do? What do we add? What do we enhance? Who do we hire?

Gone are the days when the loudest subwoofer money can buy, a creative drama team, and the hippest website in town can be counted on to bring in people who need Jesus. Gone are the days (if there ever were such days) when hiring a pastor who is thirty-five, with two children and a winsome spouse, will attract those elusive young adults that everyone from Madison Avenue to First Church is after.

Yet people who care about the future and the effectiveness of their congregations are constantly thinking about helpful strategies. Upgrading the facilities, enhancing the worship experience (better sermons, better music, better media, better lighting, better amplification), improving the programs, hiring the right people, continuing education for the ministerial staff, improving the way people are welcomed—any good pastor and leaders are thinking about those things. Offering better service and ministry to people is commendable, even if it is prompted by the fact that the new church down the road is enticing our present and prospective members. And, if we are quite honest, we have to admit that the possibility of having our members migrate to another congregation keeps us on our toes.

Yet, how shallow would our experience be if the Christian faith were limited to competition between churches? Surely, if I may borrow a common phrase, Jesus died for more than that.

Securing what we have, making sure the offerings come in, and winning the head-to-head competition with the church down the street—all those goals are less inspiring than ever. Even casual Christians are increasingly aware of how shallow are the aspirations that, frankly, have driven much of church life. Thinking Christians certainly will not settle for trivial pursuits.

Moreover, the enhancements that we typically attempt (facilities, programs, and so on) are less and less effective in our efforts to make inroads into the homes and lives of people who need Jesus. There is such a widespread disconnect between church and culture that even creative new ideas often come up short. The downturn in church participation among North Americans makes the typical improvements inadequate.

That is not to say that improvements are unimportant or a waste of time. They are simply not enough.

I love the fact that churches such as Willow Creek helped the rest of us see the importance of excellence in all we do. Yet, more excellent preaching, programs, and performance are not going to overcome the great cultural divide between most of our churches and most of our fellow North Americans.

Only so much a church can do

Let's not run off too quickly to reinvent every congregation. Let's remember that even the most conventional church has qualities that still are meaningful to postmoderns and other emerging North Americans—things like mystery and roots and liturgy. The fact that many existing churches have multiple generations is another appealing quality.

Furthermore, there is only so much an existing church can do without violating its identity. As much as we might like to think a church can reinvent and repurpose itself, the kind of changes required to become germane to people really far from God are often impractical.

The answer, then, is for existing congregations to be the very best they can be, given who they are, where they are, and what they have . . . *and*, in addition . . . to start, and advocate for, fresh expressions of church.

The Reachables

Missiologist Alan Hirsch suggested that only 40 to 50 percent of the American population is reachable by church as we know it, and he believes that number is decreasing. If he is right, that means 50 to 60 percent are not going to come to our churches no matter how well we do things.

The following is from Alan Hirsch and Dave Ferguson in their book, *On the Verge*:

> Until recent years . . . most people were within the cultural orbit of the church and open to being influenced by the ideas that energized the church. However, this has definitely begun to shift in the last fifty years. It is our opinion . . . that the prevailing, contemporary church-growth approach to church will have significant cultural appeal—marketability, if you will—to about 40 percent of the American population. . . . This means that the prevailing models of evangelistic churches could likely max out at around 40 percent of the population, perhaps 50 percent at the very best.[3]
>
> Around 60 percent of America's population (much higher in Europe and Australia) is increasingly alienated from the

prevailing forms of church. In missionary terms, it means they are culturally distant from us.[4]

We could debate the percentages offered by Hirsh and Ferguson, but in doing so we would miss the critical and unequivocal point: Those people who are merely in need of a clear gospel presentation . . . those people who would come and be part of our churches if we only issued a culturally appropriate invitation . . . those people who would really "dig" church if only our music more closely resembled what they listen to on the radio . . . are fewer than many of us seem to realize.

The following, from Paul Taylor's secular book, *The Next America*, supports the claim that only a minority of North Americans would be interested in us if we just did the things we are doing better.

> Another common misperception is that religiously unaffili-ated Americans are "seekers" who haven't yet found the right church for them. In fact, very few are in the market. Leaving aside atheists or agnostics, just 10% of those who describe their current religion as "nothing in particular" say they are looking for a religion that is right for them; 88% say they are not.[5]

That means there are few people within the reach of your church who are in search of an excellent church program or facility. So here is the sobering news: you can start an innovative new worship service, hire a pied-piper-like youth minister, and redecorate the children's wing . . . and most still aren't going to come.

Megachurches and New Models

We've noted that megachurches are reaching lots of people, and they are providing meaningful experiences for lots of worshipers. However, there are at least three problems with counting on megachurches to reach unbelievers. One, even with their large crowds, there are countless people whose lives they will not touch (remember, probably 50–60 percent of the population are not reachable via any of our prevailing models of church, whether megachurches or smaller churches, contemporary or traditional, etc.). Megachurches, one could argue, have simply become effective in reaching the declining population of people who are attracted to church as we know it. Two, lots of the people (though, of course, not all the people) they reach are merely relocating from one (probably smaller) congregation to another. Three, although God is using the talented leaders of megachurches, their skillsets are exceptions to the rule. Most churches are not blessed with such wonderful communicators, artists, financial resources, and infrastructures.

So, if those megachurches are the exception, and if they have the capacity to reach less than half the North American population, then we need other approaches. Instead of holding up the "megas" as models (models few will be able to imitate), why not figure out new models? Why not plant new forms of church alongside our present churches?

Church Planting and New Lanes

New congregations often result in the transformation of lives, the rescue of families, and the shaping of communities for the better. Nevertheless, church planting (as sometimes practiced) is being questioned as a viable option for post-Christendom. The following is what I mean by church planting "as sometimes practiced":

- There is a gregarious church planter.
- The new church plants spend lots of money on buildings and salaries.
- They utilize marketing strategies that would make used car salespeople blush.
- They claim to be targeting unchurched people but, in reality, attract churched people looking for a more satisfying experience.
- They require lots of resources and yet many of them never get off the ground.
- They take advantage of suburban sprawl (or, as of late, urban renewal).
- They produce replicas of attractional churches.

In fairness, most of us could point to several effective new churches that these caricatures do not represent. There are lots of church planters and new models of church planting that go far beyond the stereotypes. It is thrilling to see so many new church planters with a sacrificial willingness to invest themselves in communities, often difficult communities, for the sake of the gospel.

Yet, there is a reason for the stereotypes: far too many church plants fit them. The realities behind the stereotypes are still common. Those realities have caused numbers of people to question church planting as an effective strategy.

David Fitch described a meeting with denominational leaders in which someone declared, "We will spend no more money on traditional church planting. The failure rate is over ninety percent. No one is willing to give us funds for this kind of effort anymore."

Fitch reported that there was widespread agreement on that. These are sobering words.

Fitch continued,

> The landscape has changed for church planting. . . . For years, to expand their reach into new neighborhoods and population groups in North America, denominational groups would send small groups of people into a locale, set up a worship service and provide a list of support services for families. They would announce their arrival with some advertising, then wait for people to gather at a public "launch" service. A new church would be born. There are now, however, fewer and fewer Christians even remotely interested in another local "franchise" of a church. . . . What used to work in starting new churches now fails. We need a new practice of church planting for the challenges of a post-Christianized society.[6]

Of course there is still a place for conventional church planting, just as there is still a place for traditional, inherited churches. The answer is not the abolition of all we know. Fitch is simply suggesting "a new practice of church planting for the challenges of a post-Christianized society."

Another, complementary answer is diversification. Warren Bird and Ed Stetzer posited that one new way to look at church planting is to think of various checkout lines.

> Our present system for starting new churches is like the checkout line at Walmart. But the store has only one lane open, and it's terribly backed up. Furthermore, this open lane is one that requires full-time church planters with up-front money. So now is the time to think about "new lanes." Those lanes need to be different such as one that gives permission to laypeople to start new churches. Another lane could be for bivocational church planters. There are many more lane possibilities, but the first step is for more attention to changing the idea that one lane is sufficient![7]

The good news is that new lanes are opening up.

Learning together

One of the beautiful things about all these new lanes is that we are learning together. The weaknesses of emulating so-called heroes have been exposed, and there is a real sense of following the Holy Spirit *together*, without competition, sans the idolization of this or that model. It is refreshing, quite frankly. And, interestingly, following the Spirit of God seems to have become more popular than following human models and human idols.

No doubt we will misfire and misstep. We will misread the times and misunderstand the promptings of God's Spirit. Some experiments will disappoint. Some will flop. Some will be disastrous even. But we will experiment and open new lanes and learn as a team of holy conspirators, not self-centered competitors.

Fresh expressions of church

Which brings us to fresh expressions of church. Fresh expressions of church fit well the concepts of variation and cooperation.

A fresh expression is a form of church for our changing culture established primarily for the benefit of people who are not yet members of any church. Fresh expressions of church are even more likely than megachurches and typical church plants to engage people who have no history with, or affinity for, "church." Although intentions are good, and while there are numerous exceptions, many megachurches and church plants reach people disenchanted with their churches or perhaps church dropouts. Fresh expressions of church, on the other hand, have proved to be particularly effective among those who have no connection to the Christian faith. They also are *so* different from known forms of church that most long-time church members don't feel comfortable there.

The Fresh Expressions movement, then, offers a valuable, viable, and replicable new approach for the present North American context. Glenn Hinson noted, "From his disciples to our own day we who believe have tried to figure out how best to bring to expression in our times and circumstances what he, still living among us, wants."[8] Hinson's words illustrate beautifully that a fresh expression of church is simply an attempt to "bring to expression" the kind of church that will fulfill our Lord's purposes in each new generation.

This conversation is about more than merely adding one more tool to the toolkit. It is about a fundamentally new way of being church. New objectives. New ways of measuring effectiveness. It is about the missional conversion of existing congregations and the birthing of new forms of church for people unlikely ever to make their way inside the buildings of an existing church.

A welcomed option

For church leaders who have spent most of their lives emulating megapastors, appeasing fickle worshipers, and struggling to keep their heads above water, this is a welcomed option.

The church as an institution is critical, for as an institution, the church embodies and perpetuates the life and teachings of Jesus. However, there are lots of ministers who started out believing they were going to change the world and ended up just keeping the ecclesiatical "machine" operating.

This idea of new forms of church begun by existing churches returns the conversation to purposes worth the sacrificial investment of time and energy. Beginning a fresh expression of church out of and alongside your church could breathe new life not only into your church, but also into *you*. Starting a fresh expression of church could be the answer to your innate sense that a contemporary service, a vision statement, and a strategy team aren't enough.

Chapter 3

MISSIONAL PASTORS ARE IN GREAT DEMAND

L ots of the conversations about fresh expressions of church, understandably and appropriately, center around pioneer-types. We extol the innovative, entrepreneurial, courageous souls who, by the power of the Holy Spirit and little else, bring to life amazing things from scratch. We marvel at their grit and ingenuity.

Of course those pioneers deserve every word of encouragement, every journal article, and every accolade they receive. Theirs is a rare, lonely, and daunting calling. It is remarkable how God uses those present-day apostles. Soon we will talk about those heroes (and I don't use "heroes" lightly).

However, first I want to ask for a round of applause for missional pastors of inherited churches. These are the people with their feet . . . and hearts . . . in multiple worlds. Their job descriptions are astonishingly broad.

These missional pastors navigate complex congregations through hot-button social issues and shepherd families through divorces and deaths. They hold the hands of the elderly and bless the arrival of the young. Emergencies torpedo their golf outings and nasty letters ruin what otherwise would have been good days. The demands of creatively communicating biblical truths every week are grueling. Many of them are painfully aware that this year's worship attendance average is lower than last year's, and know there are fingers of blame pointed in their direction.

Yet these missional pastors tenaciously encourage distracted congregations to look outside their walls. They model personal evangelism and compassionate ministry to the marginalized. They fight for money in strained budgets for the homeless ministry. They plead annually for people to support the fund for international missionaries.

They hear stories of congregations that have cast off the shackles of traditionalism and wonder how they could stretch their congregations in that direction. They pray earnestly for spiritual renewal that will impact their cities. They patiently and lovingly lead their congregations toward a new worldview.

It does not come without personal cost, and it does not come quickly. Yet, eventually, they not only lead their church to pursue missional activities, they help the congregation to orient itself outward. With time, their church becomes a church whose identity and organization reflects its role in God's mission to the world. With time, people see themselves as envoys of God's kingdom, agents in God's mission to the world, instead of church customers.

Of course not all pastors are *missional* pastors. Some pastors think little of the world beyond their church's walls. They are NMPs (non-missional pastors).

Some of these NMPs are more interested in the liturgical colors than in the reading levels at the local elementary schools. They craft eloquent sermonic works, but no one can remember them pleading from their hearts for new disciples.

NMPs' desire to please every church member trumps their desire to hear "well done" from the Lord of the mission.

They either don't believe in, or don't care about, the lostness of people without Jesus, and so evangelism is of no interest them.

Let me not be too hard on all non-missional pastors. Some have the gift of shepherding and find it hard to stretch themselves toward missional leadership. Some have beat their heads against irresponsive walls so long they have merely grown tired. Some are so embroiled in petty conflicts, and so drained by malicious assaults, that they have no energy for anything else.

And let me not in any way disparage the role and duties of the pastor in caring for the flock. An unequivocal calling of the local pastor is to the sick, the dying, and the hurting. "Missional" is not the descriptor for a person who is so singularly focused on projects outside the congregation that he or she does not represent Christ in the lives of the congregation. The appropriate descriptor for the pastor who callously ignores the needs of the congregants is "negligent," not "missional."

Truly missional pastors are both *missional* and *pastoral*. They pray for church members as the apostle Paul prayed, "I pray that your partnership with us in the faith may be effective in deepening your understanding of every good thing we share for the sake of Christ" (Philemon 6). Missional pastors understand that to be ingrown is to become flabby and weak as a congregation. Missional pastors love their congregations and know that turning their attention outward will be healthy *for the people of the church* as well as for those with whom they will interact.

An Encouraging Word

Too much of the missional literature ignores or even dismisses the role of pastors in existing churches. A strength of the Fresh Expressions movement is our encouragement of those pastors. If the faith in North America has a future, God will use missional pastors in existing congregations, not just pioneers who are beginning new forms of church.

As one who has spent a long time as the pastor of local congregations, I was encouraged when I read the following from entrepreneurial Christian leaders Hugh Halter and Matt Smay. Maybe it will encourage you, too.

> The hundreds of pastors with whom we've shared our story love unchurched folks as much as our edgiest church planters, but

they are also responsible to keep a church structure afloat. . . .
I used to judge these leaders as weak, or unwilling, or even
worse, unloving toward the harvest field. But now I've come to
believe that they are just as important as the brave, arrogant,
pioneer pastors. . . . Is it possible that God doesn't need nor ask
everyone to start something new? Is it possible that God needs
millions of leaders to care for a host of Christians who won't
be able to make the turn into new forms of church? I think so
. . . I think we must.[1]

The Best and Brightest?

It has been suggested that the emphasis on church planting and
new forms of church has the potential for damaging existing
congregations through neglect. And, according to Ed Stetzer and
Warren Bird, some seminary professors are now concerned that
their brightest students are only wanting to plant new churches.

> A recent conference of the largest seminaries in the nation
> expressed concern that so many of the best and brightest were
> going into church planting that few were left to lead struggling
> established churches. That's quite a shift. One conference filled
> with church planters recently had a main session entitled,
> "Church Planting Is for Wimps: Try Revitalizing a Church."
> That's quite a change.[2]

I understand why the call of many young ministers is to the
frontier—to something that feels more worthy of their efforts than
the bureaucracy of an existing church. An entrepreneurial spirit,
typical of growing numbers of young adults,[3] also shows up among
those called to ministry.

On the one hand, we should celebrate that the spotlight on
new forms of church has brought some ministers out of the proverbial woodwork. Many were not at all interested in serving churches
they knew, but stories of unconventional church have ignited a
passion in them. These entrepreneurial ministers have been encouraged to respond to God's call by new opportunities that seemed

less restrictive, less political, and less administrative than existing congregations. For that we can be grateful.

On the other hand, we will have erred if we imply that the most gifted and most devoted are starting new churches instead of leading existing congregations. God's mission to the world has not bypassed inherited churches, and these congregations of seasoned Christ-followers (at least many of them) are poised to offer themselves and their resources in significant ministry. To ignore the missional capacity of local churches, and the significance of local pastors, is a strategic error of eternal proportions.

Petrine Apostleship and Pauline Apostleship

Dick Scoggins, Tim Catchim, and Alan Hirsch have noted in Galatians 2:8-10 two distinct, yet equally important, apostolic giftings. They call them "Petrine apostleship" and "Pauline apostleship." These are two complementary breeds of apostles: Petrine apostles (leading God's people to be missional) and Pauline apostleship (advancing the edges of the kingdom).

Pauline apostleship was a calling "to the Gentiles" while Petrine apostleship was a calling to "Israel and the Jews of the diaspora."[4] This is a powerful reminder of the Pauline apostolic calling to extend the kingdom of God to the frontier, and the equally apostolic Petrine calling to turn the orientation of existing congregations outward. In the words of the authors:

> . . . a good portion of the work that is needed in Western contexts is corrective and relates to internal, more distinctly reformational issues that are likely to be more the jurisdiction of the Petrine apostle. Although the Pauline apostle is likely to extend Christianity and start new movements on new frontiers of the church, the Petrine apostle is likely to be the one to remissionalize the church as we now experience it.[5]

Later we will talk about the Pauline apostles—the pioneers, entrepreneurs, trailblazers who, to borrow a theme from C. T. Studd, are more at home within a yard of the gates of hell than within the sound of chapel bells. However, here we focus on those who follow more in the footsteps of Peter and help the people of God realize their missionary opportunities. They have to be pastoral, patient, and persuasive in order to nudge their churches out the doors. The Petrines have organizational astuteness as well as the skills and demeanor to navigate change. Although they get frustrated with the "machinery," they appreciate its value and the people who created it. "Therefore, if Pauline apostles are classic entrepreneurs, Petrine apostles can be described as intrapreneurs."[6]

Complex organizational realities and competing political realities don't rob Petrine apostles of their joy. (Not completely, at least.) The needs of the world outside the church, and the potential meaning and joy that come from being a missional church, keep the Petrine apostles in the proverbial game. Petrine apostles will be misunderstood by both the old-schoolers within the traditional church as well as the spiritual swashbucklers outside it. From the one side will come unwarranted complaints that the Petrines only care about the new and creative ministries. From the other side will come unfair accusations that, if they had missional hearts, the Petrines would be out on the front lines instead of in an established church. They miss out on the hero status bestowed upon the pioneers, and suffer from charges of neglect from people who crave more attention. They are disparaged by tradition-bound pastors who view the Petrines' creativity as frivolity, and, on the other hand, are dismissed by pioneers who assume the Petrines are motivated by fear or money or another one of the unseemly reasons why someone would want to draw a salary from a church.

The ones called to love God's sons and daughters as they are, and to draw out from them a God-given passion for those yet outside the family, are Petrine apostles.

An important aspect of the Fresh Expressions movement is the synergy between the core and the edges—the partnerships of established churches and fresh expressions of church, and thus the partnership and mutual appreciation between Pauline and Petrine apostles.

"Patient in One of Those Old Churches"

Many years ago, at a time when I was a discouraged missional pastor, I thought about leaving the church I was serving to go start a new church. Then I read this:

> Our experience leads me to say that if you want to be part of a church that is radically different from anything you've ever known, then plant one—start one. You can create new programs, new rules, and new structures. And you'll have about a one-in-five chance that it will survive. And if that's your call, go for it. There's a lot of nobility in planting churches. It's happening all over the countryside.
>
> But if you are willing to be patient in one of those old churches (like ours) that is pretty high up the S-curve, then put your head down and go to work. Be patient, be prayerful, seek allies, build alliances with other generations. You'll probably have to convince a lot of people, and they'll come dragging their feet like the members of our Discovery Group. But as time passes, somehow the Spirit of God will grab at hearts, and you just may see a miracle—a hundred-year-old church that acts with the spirit of an enthusiastic teenager. That's what happened to us.[7]

You don't have to plant a new church, or new form of church, to be missional. In fact, to leave an established church for the so-called front lines might be a violation of your call. If deep in your heart you sense that the Lord of the mission has you in a servant-leadership role in an inherited church, then remain there with conviction and *be missional*.

There are countless congregations, of course, who are in a long-term, steady, maybe even precipitous, decline. Yet, the Holy Spirit still lives in those temples; He has not abandoned His people. So maybe God is giving you one of the most difficult, most potentially rewarding, roles of all—to stoke the embers, to facilitate genuine revival, in a challenging, existing church. You can be a missional pastor.

Hugh Halter and Matt Smay defined *missional leadership* as "culturally savvy, deep in character, clear in calling, and committed to incarnational ways of life and church."[8] Maybe God created you to exercise missional leadership in what many would consider an unlikely setting—your church.

Chapter 4

TAKING THE CHURCH JESUS LOVES CLOSER TO WHERE THE PEOPLE JESUS LOVES ACTUALLY ARE

The world is increasingly more divided—segregated into countless subcultures. So . . . one-size-fits-all church is perhaps less effective than ever. Identifying with people's interests and respecting the complexity of their lives is part of what it means to incarnate the gospel. That's where fresh expressions of church can play a vital role in God's mission of redemption.

Chris Backert, the Fresh Expressions US National Director, defines fresh expressions of church as "taking the church Jesus loves closer to where the people Jesus loves actually are." This missional movement is about an incarnational approach to the planting of new faith communities—having gospel conversations, making disciples, and establishing churches in ways that are at home among particular populations of people. This is a welcomed approach for the many who recognize the growing gap between the *churches* they know and the *people* they know. Countless people are simply unreachable by church as we know it, and that truth weighs heavily on the hearts of devoted Christ-followers. People are looking for a way of being church for the de-churched (those who've left the church) and the unchurched (those who have no tie to, or history with, any congregation). As an example, Reggie McNeal wrote,

A research scientist at a major university told me over lunch about his efforts to convene his colleagues around spiritual discussions in the research department where he works. "Not one of these people is going to church," he said. "Most of them are working on Sunday. If we don't find a way to be the church where they are, they will never experience it."[1]

Combining Worlds

The early churches met largely in homes and were at the intersection of work, family, and leisure networks. Somehow we modern church people have been guilty of segregating the church from the center of everyone's life. Over time we placed the church in one compartment of people's lives and the rest of their lives in a separate compartment; the sacred and the profane have become two distinct worlds for most of us. The Fresh Expressions movement, as an attempted reflection of the Incarnation, is about putting the church back into the heart of life.

Liberation

One of the magnificent characteristics of this movement called Fresh Expressions of Church is that it is beautifully liberating. The only parameters are provided by Scripture and our best interpretations of the holy texts. Fresh Expressions means the dissolution of categories.

That doesn't mean anything goes. This is not twenty-first century ecclesiological licentiousness. It is, however, a movement toward more freedom for living out the biblical definition of church. The Fresh Expressions movement allows us to move in multiple directions at once, taking the church beyond its walls . . . and into new, meaningful wineskins. After all, "Jesus didn't put a sign on a palm tree and say, 'All those willing to be disciples meet here at 1:00 p.m. on Sunday; refreshments will be provided.'"[2]

The Organic Church movement associated with Neil Cole is not exactly a Fresh Expressions movement. There are, nonetheless, many similarities. Note, for example, that Cole's philosophy resembles the Fresh Expressions mantra of "taking the church Jesus loves closer to where the people Jesus loves actually are."

> Instead of bringing people to church so that we can then bring them to Christ, let's bring Christ to people where they live. We may find that a new church will grow out of such an enterprise, a church that is more centered in life and the workplace, where the Gospel is supposed to make a difference. What will happen if we plant the seed of the Kingdom of God in the places where life happens and where society is formed? Is this not what Jesus intended for His Church? What would it be like if churches emerged organically, like small spiritual families born out of the soil of lostness, because the seed of God's Kingdom was planted there? . . . We believe that church should happen wherever life happens. You shouldn't have to leave life to go to church.[3]

Too Many Churches Already?

There are street corners in North America with churches on every quadrant. Methodists, Episcopalians, and Baptists square off like Walgreens, Rite-Aid, and CVS. Lots of communities have "church rows"—streets lined with churches of various stripes. The omnipresence of church buildings has caused some to claim "Enough is enough." Some would suggest we have enough churches to call a hiatus on church planting.

Yet God seems not to be on board with the idea of a hiatus. He continues to call out new church planters, even to "traditional" church planting. And new churches, even replicas of the inherited model, still witness more conversions than well-established churches.

Beyond that, whether or not we need more buildings with steeples and columns and lots of committees, we do need more *new* kinds of church. We need churches enmeshed in the lives of people who need Jesus.[4]

Attractional/Extractional

Most of our existing churches are attempting to attract people to life within their walls. One of the weaknesses of this attractional model of church is that it extracts new believers, potential missionaries, from their long-time environment.

Imagine with me a congregation that has gotten outside its walls, handed out water on hot days, held car washes and other "servant evangelism" events, and met and befriended people. One of the men from the church meets Tommy, a gregarious leader in the community, and invites Tommy to worship and Bible study. Tommy accepts the invitation and, surprisingly, feels at home. With time, Tommy becomes a follower of Jesus and is baptized into the church family.

The church's ministers have read somewhere that if Tommy doesn't get plugged in quickly he will drift away, so they look for a spot to fill with Tommy. There is an opening on the Recreation Committee, so they ask him to serve. Tommy feels an obligation to his new church, so he agrees.

The chairman of the Rec Committee loves meetings, and they meet once a month. Besides that, there are the regular volleyball tournaments, the Upward basketball league, and the monthly church-wide fellowships the committee has to plan and oversee.

Tommy is now really busy at the church. Besides his Rec Committee work, he goes to Wednesday night Bible study, attends choir rehearsal, and never misses the Tuesday morning men's prayer breakfast at the local coffee shop.

"Where's Tommy?" ask his former friends in the neighborhood. "He joined the church," answers one of Tommy's old pals. "We don't see Tommy 'round here no more."

Tommy, a man who could have introduced many of his friends to his new life in Jesus, is too busy at church to hang out with his buddies any longer.

Of course that's a somewhat hyperbolic story, but, in some ways, do we not do that to people? And do we really want to fill our churches' programmatic committees with people who could be changing their neighborhoods? Certainly there is an important place for those who run the infrastructure of complex churches, but saddling new believers with programmatic responsibilities so that they are isolated from the people whom they have long known, and who are potentially far from God, seems like a bad strategy.

Doing church in Tommy's world among Tommy's friends with Tommy as a key leader . . . now that's a different story. That would be a fresh expression of church!

Trending toward Incarnation

A church's context does matter, and in some places traditional models are more effective than in others. Rare is the context, however, where doing what we've always done will yield new outcomes. Churches shaped by Christendom will be increasingly irrelevant in post-Christendom. Impactful congregations will assume a missionary posture. Incarnation, not attraction and not domination, is now the hope of the North American church.

This is hard to grasp for people who live in areas of the country where knowledge of church culture is still high. What they must recognize is that, no matter where we are in North America, the number of people *outside* the church who understand life *inside* the church is declining rapidly. The attractional model of church ("Let's do everything with excellence and we will attract people") still has legs, but those legs are growing shorter by the day. We are constantly trending toward the necessity of an incarnational approach to evangelism and new church starts.[5] After all, "lost people do not spend their hours trying to figure out how to get to church, or what kind of church they would like."[6]

Relevance or incarnation?

There is lots of talk nowadays about being relevant. We want to speak the language of, know the trends of, and quote the heroes of, pop culture. We want to be in on the latest memes and up on the latest vernacular. And that is not a bad thing; relevance is not unimportant.

Yet the deeper issue in the starting of new forms of church is not relevance; the issue is incarnation. When people from inherited churches, with long histories in the Christian community, seem not to be connecting with people outside their walls "the problem is not that they are irrelevant, but that they are not incarnational."[7]

Incarnation is not just a matter of tweaking our delivery method. It's about planting new forms of church in bowling alleys, fitness centers, restaurants, recording studios, VFW halls, homes, and workplaces. It's about planting new forms of church among students, artists, scientists, the homeless, people who are deaf, rock climbers, rockabillies, and bodybuilders. It's about entrepreneurial models that house multiple businesses in a building that also houses worship and is a platform for ministry. It's about serving people, listening to them, and figuring out by the leadership of God's Spirit what form church would take if it were planted in a particular context.

Incarnation is about more than hosting a businessperson's prayer lunch or starting a "Faith at Work" class in the church building, for example. It's about more than a church in a fishing village hosting dinners for the fishermen in the church fellowship hall and bringing in Christian professional fishermen to speak. A truly incarnational approach would try and figure out how to be church of, with, and for those businesspeople and fishermen *in their worlds*.

Will incarnation mean the reinvention of the American church?

Lots of us talk about single digit church participation in Europe and warn that the US is headed inevitably and quickly in that direction. "Not so fast," wrote futurist Paul Taylor.

Those who worry that America is headed toward a European future of institutionalized secularism and empty cathedrals would do well to reflect on the resilience that religion in the US draws from this genius for tolerance and reinvention . . . our organized religions have always understood they need to adapt to survive. The fact that "nones" are on the rise indicates that religious institutions have some work to do. In modern times, American religion has become "more personalized and individualistic, less doctrinal and devotional, more practical and purposeful," in the words of sociologist Alan Wolfe.[8]

Taylor suggested that if the American church will recognize the growing need for "personalization" and "individualization," without drifting into relativism and consumerism, we might just witness something surprising. If Taylor's predicted reinvention results in more incarnation, the future of the church could be strong.

A Peek into the Future

Reading the predictions of futurists strengthens the case for fresh expressions. New forms of church will have an adaptability, a malleability, that will be difficult for existing churches. Here we will rely heavily on the work of David Houle as reflected in his book *Entering the Shift Age*. Houle wrote,

> The Transformation Decade, 2010–2020, will be a time when an incredible amount of change will occur. Most of humanity's institutions and ways of thinking will change their nature, character, form, or shape. A fundamental reason that this will happen is that legacy thinking will fall away, collapse, or be rendered obsolete. What do I mean by "legacy thinking"? Legacy thinking is viewing the present and future through thoughts from the past.[9]

Legacy thinking means that, if encouraged to think about new forms of church most of us will, at least at first, simply imagine new and improved versions of the churches we know and love. That legacy thinking is helpful for the revitalization of existing congregations, but terribly limiting as we consider a new church in a new world.

The Fresh Expressions movement is a natural fit for the new world on the horizon. Without the shackles of previous models, yet with roots deep in the pages of Scripture, this movement fits what is coming. Consider, for example, where church happens.

As the concept of "place" is rethought, fresh expressions of church can adapt and provide community without the centrality of a building. Consider the following observations about "place" from Houle:

> We are losing the need to be any place, as long as we are connected.[10]
>
> . . . by 2020 we will be able to carry holographic communication capability with us. . . . As with several of these transformative technologies, second-generation augmented reality will further alter the way we think about . . . religion.[11]
>
> We will be in a physical place but will be taken to such fully multi-sensorial space that while our biological processes will be in one place, our neurological and sensory processes will be of another space.[12]

I cannot even begin to imagine all that these technological advances, and others as revolutionary as these, will mean for churches. I don't know what implications there are here for our earlier conversation about incarnation. What, I wonder, does incarnation look like in a world in which *place* is so radically redefined?

It seems obvious that fresh expressions of church will be much more able to adapt to this revolutionary technology than will building-based churches. Fresh expressions of church are well-suited for this kind of experimentation on the edges of church life.

(These conversations, by the way, make the debate over traditional vs. contemporary worship seem embarrassingly provincial, do they not?)

Chapter 5

THE MIXED ECONOMY: INHERITED CHURCHES AND FRESH EXPRESSIONS OF CHURCH

I believe I have seen the future of the church in North America. Prominently located on the main thoroughfare of Sheffield, England, is the cathedral. That cathedral (unlike so many in England) is active and vibrant. It supports strong worship services, a big music ministry, the works.

Just down the hill from that cathedral, on a back street, is the Print House. It is called that because of the previous use of the building in which it is located. This Print House is a fresh expression of church.

The casual, open space of the Print House is large enough to contain forty or so people. On the third floor is office space, corners of which are rented out to small businesses needing offices or cubicles, providing contacts with the community and a revenue stream for the new church.

These two approaches to church—the cathedral and the Print House—bear little in common. Yet each has engaged a segment of the population that the other almost certainly would not. They are complementary and supplementary expressions of church. In England, leaders utilize a phrase coined by Archbishop Rowan Williams—the "mixed economy"—to describe the roles and relationship of these two congregations and those like them—an emerging partnership between churches that have been around for a long time and new churches that look very different.[1]

Moreover, the future of the Christian faith is bright with strong inherited churches and vibrant new churches. "Christian management guru Ken Blanchard observes that it is commonly asked, 'Which approach is better—improving what is or creating what isn't?' The answer he gives is 'Yes!'"[2] The Fresh Expressions movement is about improving what is and creating what is not yet!

Alongside

Fresh Expressions is about a new form of church *coming alongside* those congregations we know and love; not about replacing them. The phrase, "mixed economy" (some prefer "mixed ecology"), reminds us that inherited churches and fresh expressions are complementary, not in competition. In today's diverse cultures, God's church needs both our inherited approaches and novel approaches. Those novel approaches are what we're talking about when we talk about fresh expressions of church.

God's Spirit is alive and well in present churches of all ages, shapes, and sizes. So Fresh Expressions is about new forms of church *coming alongside* (not supplanting) existing congregations. Many in the Fresh Expressions movement use terminology of "modalities" (established centers of church life) and "sodalities" (flexible missionary endeavors) to describe the unique roles of existing and new forms of church.[3]

As critical as our present congregations are, there remain untold numbers of people who desperately need Jesus. So, somewhat lightly tethered to present congregations there can be innovative expressions of the body of Christ to engage people your church wants to engage but simply cannot. Alongside the steeple churches we need creative, simpler, more intimate groups that have the potential to exhibit all the elements of church.

Luke Edwards, pioneer of a fresh expression of church in Boone, North Carolina, declared, "The traditional church has to get over its fear of new forms of church. And new forms of church have to get over their fear of the traditional church. We have to work together to make each other better. We bring different people into the Kingdom of God. And that's what matters."[4]

The philosophy of Fresh Expressions is that these new and novel faith communities are enriched by learning from and building on church tradition, "not by rubbishing and leaving it."[5]

Not Merely Coexisting

These are not merely coexisting forms of church, but mutually dependent and mutually supporting forms of church. It is true that, in many cases, these fresh expressions of church have operated apart from existing forms of church as self-contained entities. While we celebrate any new church that engages new people, we have to caution that parallel-and-independent is not the optimal scenario. Both the inherited church and the fresh expression of church get the most out of this when there is a collaborative, mutually beneficial partnership.

One of the advantages of the mixed economy of church is that it provides a connection from the heart of the inherited church to the edges of what God is doing, and vice versa. Thus it is imperative that we keep these fresh expressions of church in the stories of, and in partnership with, established churches—linked in as many ways as are possible and helpful.

Optimal Situation

The optimal situation (from a Fresh Expressions perspective) is an existing church with a missional pastor sending out a handful of apostles from its membership to begin a new form of church among a particular subculture. In such a situation the existing church offers prayerful support, encouragement, counsel, and mentoring. The existing church is rejuvenated by the intentional efforts to evangelize the world and thrilled by the stories that the apostles from among them tell. The new form of church has a clear connection to the Christian family outside itself and is resourced and cheered on by the more established congregation. The inherited churches and the fresh expression of church are complementary, not in competition.

However, not all fresh expressions of church fit this optimal model. Some of these new forms of church are begun independently by pioneers, without the assistance of existing congregations. Some of the pioneers were previously part of existing churches but launched out solo. Some of the pioneers were actually on staff at existing churches and responded to this missionary call with the blessing of, but without formal support from, their congregations.

What many of us consider the first fresh expression of church in history—the church of Antioch—sprang up rather independently. The church of Jerusalem did not intentionally, strategically, send out its most apostolic members with the goal of planting a new form of church to reach new people. God's Spirit surprised the Jerusalem Christians with an unexpected (fresh) expression of church up in Antioch.

Nevertheless, we should not minimize or ignore the advantages that come from a cooperative venture between pioneers and established congregations. Those advantages are significant.

Unintentional Fresh Expressions of Church

On the banks of the Rappahannock River in Virginia, there is an example of an unintentional fresh expression of church. By "unintentional" I mean no one (neither a congregation nor a pioneer) set out to start a new form of church.

Local residents asked Nita May if she and her husband would let them join in the next time Nita and her husband, Wayne, hosted the young adults from their church for a worship service on the river. From that request has sprung a marvelous new form of church that has resulted in numerous new believers and beautiful baptisms. Nita and Wayne did not set out to start a church; they were responding to an invitation from people who had no church to start something among them. Fresh expressions like this do not have a formal tie with an existing congregation.

Yet, however they begin, fresh expressions of church rely on the traditions of inherited churches as important starting points, or frameworks, for how they will be church in a new way.

Furthermore, the best and most complete fresh expressions of church nurture some sort of relationship with at least one existing congregation, whether or not they came out of a particular congregation. There is much to be gained for both the new and the inherited congregations from such a relationship.

Not Easy

East End Fellowship grew out of a passion people of Third Presbyterian Church (now known as Third Church) of Richmond, Virginia, had for residents of Church Hill, once a really tough neighborhood, in Richmond. Third Presbyterian's Young Adult Minister, Corey Widmer, became increasingly involved in outreach to Church Hill, which meant Third was getting less and less of his time. Of course that meant that Third, the original congregation, would be unable to attract as many young adults to themselves.

Yet, Third Presbyterian had a sense of call to ministry in Church Hill, and sent financial resources, as well as bright young adults, to the work there. The eventual result was East End Fellowship, a fresh expression of church.

Steve Hartman, pastor of Third Presbyterian Church at the time, described that congregation's decision to invest in East End Fellowship. "It's hard to give ourselves away," Steve admitted.

It *is* hard to give one's self away. Understandably hard. Yet that is the essence of mission. Certainly, movements of mission outside the church usually generate movements of renewal inside the church. Yet there is no denying the sacrificial nature of investing in ventures that will not result in direct return for a congregation.

Full participation in the mission of God will require Christians to think more about the kingdom of God than about their local churches. While all of us want our congregations to flourish, there is a higher calling—invitations into the kingdom.

Phyllis Tickle had this to say about the church in Jerusalem (inherited church) and the church in Antioch (fresh expression of church).

The differences between inherited and fresh expressions were never entirely resolved. Tensions remained. And save for one small purse in a time of great need, Jerusalem never received any direct benefits from Antioch. What benefited . . . was and is the kingdom.[6]

We need more churches who are willing to give themselves for the sake of the kingdom of God.

Mecessary (Messy, but Necessary)

Admittedly, this relationship between inherited churches (congregations as we know them) and fresh expressions of church is fraught with potential conflict. Even a cursory review of church history reveals that the relationship between existing and emerging forms of church has often been tense. Monasteries and missionary societies have often challenged the assumptions, stretched the resources, and tested the patience of existing congregations and church structures.

In a later chapter we will explore in more depth the relationship between the first-century churches in Jerusalem and Antioch. That story is a story of conflict, suspicion, confusion, open conversation, negotiation, compromise, and resolution. Many contemporary stories of fresh expressions of church include those same elements. Traditional congregations struggling to survive, for example, could see the fresh expression of church as competition. Skeptics could see fresh expressions of church as a passing fad or even a distraction. Or full-time pastors could feel threatened by an emerging form of church that they fear holds no place for them.

On the other hand, pioneers of fresh expressions could view inherited churches as stale and passé. Pioneers could see the ministers on staff of existing churches as mercenaries too dependent on their salaries to do anything edgy. Those with a passion for new forms of church could arrogantly assume they, not those old stodgy churches, are "where it's at." Often members of the new form of church will get frustrated with, and feel encumbered by, what they see as too much bureaucracy in the established church.

A mixed economy that works is going to require humility, mutual respect, and an acknowledgment that these new forms of church are here to stay.

Each of these churches needs advocates in the other camp. The new congregation needs champions among the inherited congregation who will legitimize them, translate their mission into language the long-standing Christians can understand, and go to bat for the new form of church when those who have followed Jesus a long time might be ready to write off the fresh expression as a deviation from the faith.

Likewise, the inherited congregation needs advocates among the fresh expression of church to remind the newcomers how valuable are the wisdom, stability, and experience of the more mature congregation. Someone has to warn the newcomers against the arrogant attitude that "finally" this new group got church right after others wandered so long in ecclesiastical darkness.

Given those advocates in each group, the relationships can be beautiful, healthy, and reciprocal. In fact, in a day when the church in North America is splintering, attention to this partnership between inherited forms and new forms of church could be something around which we can rally. This can be one of the most important contributions of the Fresh Expressions movement to the church.

I should note quickly that if an existing church is going to start a fresh expression of church, accountability is very helpful. Control, however, is deadly. There must be enough freedom, under the Spirit, to develop both biblically and contextually. The goal is *high support; low control.*

In our efforts to help new churches, we must not lower the bar. Of course, we also don't want to be like the ancient religious leaders whom Jesus chastised: "You experts in the law, woe to you, because you load people down with burdens they can hardly carry" (Luke 11:46).

Yet, fresh expressions of church actually need existing churches (sometimes called "inherited" churches). Members of those inherited churches often are the ones who invest themselves in these new forms of church. Their ministers often mentor the pioneers who launch fresh expressions. Some congregations actually provide a little funding, or meeting space, for the new ventures. Most pioneers of fresh expressions of church are operating on limited resources— especially those fresh expressions that didn't grow out of existing churches. Existing churches can offer much if the issue is partnership, not dependency. Even when a fresh expression of church does not grow directly out of an existing church, the fresh expression can nurture relationships with more experienced congregations.

God Is Up to Something

Congregations have histories, personalities, expectations, and traditions. Therefore, church leaders can perform a radical church makeover and risk an implosion in the process . . . or a few missional people from within that congregation can begin a fresh expression of church. The latter seems to be a much more feasible option.

Those who are choosing this option are often finding their expectations marvelously exceeded. In the words of Paul Sparks, Tim Soerens, and Dwight Friesen, "God is up to something."

> Our task is not really to present a new "model" of church that competes with the multiple options that exist. For too many years even the best proposals for revitalizing the church have ended up perpetuating the endless splintering of new factions and divides. That's not what we're after.
>
> God is up to something in neighborhoods, on the ground in real places. The church, in all its diversity, needs to figure out how to join in. We think God is putting forth a dare that, if practiced, could both revitalize church traditions, and develop a growing unity among members of various denominational expressions in the parish. More than that, it could help the church learn to give itself away in love to the world around it.[7]

KING STREET CHURCH

Boone United Methodist Church is a strong congregation on the beautiful outskirts of Boone, North Carolina. Boone UMC looks and feels like the typical, vibrant, suburban church. A closer look, however, reveals something extra about this congregation.

The people of Boone UMC were concerned about King Street, the main street of Boone where their building formerly was located. The congregation empowered Luke Edwards, their missions minister, to figure out and lead something down on King Street. Luke sensed a call to start a new form of church.

He began to talk to people on Boone Street. He'd ask questions such as, "If I were going to start some sort of church here, what should I do?" Someone said, "You've gotta meet Elizabeth. She knows everybody."

Indeed she does. Elizabeth is the "person of peace" about which you will read later. She loves Jesus but has been turned off by what she's seen in organized churches. Luke and Elizabeth began to host cookouts in parking lots and open spaces they could find. They met people, listened to people, and served people by providing an opportunity for community.

In time, King Street Church, a fresh expression of church, was born. King Street is actually a network of groups. They meet on different nights at the Boone Saloon, at Porto Fino restaurant, at Luke's house, and at the city jail. (Not many fresh expressions of church are a "network" of groups such as King Street Church, but there are enough of them that this idea is not unprecedented.)

Some of the Boone UMC people help out. Anna, for example, is a young lady who is still deeply involved in Boone UMC, but she has plugged into King Street Church and is leading a single moms' group.

I sat with the group at Porto Fino one evening and thrilled at the engagement of people still on their way toward Jesus. I could not imagine any of them showing up at any of the existing churches in town, but here they were, discussing a gospel parable in honest, vulnerable ways.

King Street is a fresh expression, a new form, of church.

Part Two

THEOLOGY, ECCLESIOLOGY, AND MISSIOLOGY

Chapter 6

THEOLOGY, MISSIOLOGY, AND FRESH EXPRESSIONS OF CHURCH

A beautiful value of theology is that it reminds us to prioritize the grand purposes of God over our concerns (understandable though they are) about the future of our institutions. Thus the purposes, nature, will, and glory of God are more important than the ideas we get from the latest gurus of leadership, church growth, and cultural trends.

How and why we do what we do must reflect the God of the mission, or else we will become so oriented toward strategy that we become too pragmatically minded, so self-directed that God becomes an afterthought, and so disconnected from our divine source that we miss the point. A new form of church that is not rooted in an understanding of, and passion for, our Creator will struggle both for direction and for inspiration.

An absence of theological reflection—the lack of awareness of the theological framework that shapes us—results in a weak foundation. No methodology can overcome a poor sense of rootedness.

Moreover, there is strength in articulation. When one's call wanes, when someone tries to hijack the direction of the faith community, or when a leader finds himself or herself responding unrehearsed to a hot social topic, it is one's prayerfully articulated theology that comes to the rescue. Here we will survey the theological underpinnings of the Fresh Expressions movement.

The Queen Mother . . . Born on the Front Lines

One of the defining questions of Fresh Expressions is a chicken-or-the egg style question surrounding ecclesiology, missiology, and theology. Theology has been called "The Queen of the Sciences"; yet mission has been called "The Mother of Theology." German theologian Martin Kähler coined the term, "Mother of Theology," explaining that "the theologizing of the early church was necessitated by its missionary encounters with the world."[1]

Theology was born on the front lines, not in academic halls. The Christian faith's most important theologian, the apostle Paul, was first and foremost a missionary. His theological reflections, inspired by God's Spirit, occurred on the front lines of the advance of God's kingdom. So Francis DuBose wrote, "Mission does not so much need to be justified theologically as theology needs to be understood missiologically."[2]

Intertwined and Interdependent

The church is always at its best when theology and mission are intertwined and interdependent. It has been such since the beginning—since the years when the earliest of theologies were hammered out in debates and apologetics. Theology was, from the first, not an academic luxury but a missional urgency. Theology emerged from humility, not pomposity; from the edges of the kingdom, not secluded offices.[3]

Coming into Its Own

Somehow, as the Christian faith became more institutional, more cerebral, and more at home in mainstream Europe, the study of mission became a practical wing of scholarship, presumably more suited for those who couldn't hold their own in the more rigorous arenas such as philosophy. And the practice of mission—out there on the margins—was widely assumed to be for those whose skills would not qualify them to serve local parishes. Lots of congregations sponsored missions, mission points, or mission churches, meaning those venues where people gathered for worship but where the ministerial personnel, facilities, etc., were not of the same standard as the "real church." And missionaries were more admired for their valor than appreciated for their acumen.

We still have some vestiges from the day when "mission" meant "secondary, peripheral, less than." Increasingly, however, *mission* is coming into its own . . . again. Ecclesiology and missiology are no longer estranged; they are interdependent in the West as never before. More people seem to be acknowledging that mission is not merely an activity of the church and not merely a subtopic of theology/ecclesiology. Mission is respectable among scholastics. At least there is progress.

Perhaps the reason for the resurging respect of mission is the decline in the number of church members in Europe and North America. Perhaps it is that we have been brought down a notch or two by the fact that people are increasingly hostile to what we believe. It has been helpful that scholars like Darrell Guder and Alan Roxburgh have popularized the term "missional" and in doing so made mission, or missions, fashionable. The church planter is no longer the one who couldn't make it in real church, and the missions professor now has a voice in many seminary faculty lounges.[4]

Probing the Limits

Job, from his own depths, recognized his Redeemer's heights. "Can you probe the limits of the Almighty?" he asked. Of course, he knew the answer: "The Almighty is beyond our reach" (Job 11:7; 37:23). Yet we are compelled to probe and reach. So let's dig into specific theological areas with particular relevance to fresh expressions of church.

Chapter 7

WHAT'S THE TRINITY GOT TO DO WITH IT?

There has emerged a critical recognition that the church is neither the origin nor the goal of Christian mission. So, ecclesiology is not the dominant, driving concept for Christian mission. Perhaps even more interesting, in the emerging missiological paradigm, neither is Christology.

Beyond Christology

The Christian world mission has traditionally been viewed as born in the Great Commission. With Jesus as the Great Commissioner, as well as the Way, Truth, and Life, Christology served as a foundation and motivation for mission.

Yet missiological thinking has largely moved beyond Christology to the Trinity for the inspiration and model for mission. This means, for one, that our concept of mission has expanded beyond (but still includes as predominant) the making of Christian disciples through conversion of people to faith in Jesus. Mission goes beyond making more Christians and establishing more churches.

It is imperative that we not misunderstand that. The ultimate objective of the Christian mission is the genuine, eternal transformation of people through Jesus. "Jesus Christ and him crucified" (1 Cor. 2:2) is still the principal message of the Christian mission.

Jesus is Lord and Redeemer and the *sine qua non* of our mission. A broader understanding of the model and motivation of our mission neither nullifies nor minimizes the Christocentric heart of our mission.[1]

The Christian mission, the *missio Dei*, is unequivocally Christocentric. Yet the mission is best understood as about more than "preaching Jesus." When understood as rooted in, and reflective of, the Trinity, we understand the mission of God more broadly. The Great Commission is now more commonly viewed as an invitation to join in the Trinitarian mission.

Our personal and corporate lives are best founded on a Christocentric, thoroughly Trinitarian, missional theology. Mission at its best is focused on Jesus, empowered by the Spirit, and reflects the Fatherly concern of God for all of creation. A church at its best reflects the open-hearted, inviting fellowship of the Three-in-One.

Piecing Together the Puzzle

Early on, thinking Christians began to piece together a critical puzzle. They read here and there that Jesus is God and that the Spirit is God and they began to think systematically about that. The New Testament was written in different places and years and, of course, by different people. Long before emails and faxes and even printing presses, it took a while for those individual writings to circulate. Eventually, as scribes made copies and individual churches accumulated all the books we call the New Testament, they began to assimilate various texts and themes and they took note: when the Bible speaks of God, it speaks of Father, Son, and Spirit.

Of course the word "Trinity" appears nowhere in the pages of Scripture. Yet it appears as that recurring, implied theme. So there developed early on among Christians the recognition that God is Trinity. There is one God,[2] the church declared, yet God eternally exists as Trinity—Father, Son, and Holy Spirit.

Christian Fathers (early leaders) who gathered from time to time to issue statements about God weren't *defining* who God is for the first time. Rather, they were upholding the understanding (though not yet written and formalized) of God in the decades after Jesus—that God is One, yet in three persons. From the beginning Christ-followers had recognized that somehow God the Father, God the Son (who had become human in Jesus), and the Holy Spirit, all are divine—all are God. They didn't have a formula or formal statement, but they knew and talked about God as, somehow, mysteriously, three persons.

Nicea, Constantinople, and Beyond

The statement issued at the Council of Constantinople in AD 381 (presently Istanbul, Turkey), echoed the earlier Nicene statement about the Father and the Son, and added: *And in the Holy Spirit, the Lord and Giver of life, who proceeds from the Father, who is worshiped and glorified with the Father and the Son.* Traced to the theological articulations at Constantinople is the description of God as "one *ousia* (substance, nature, essence) in three hypostases (Persons, individual realities, or natures)." In that phrase is an attempt to express the inexpressible: God is One, yet Three-in-One. In God, Father, Son, and Spirit are distinguishable as persons, yet are one in essence or being.

Millard Erickson made this captivating declaration: "God is one and yet there are three who are God."[3] We could never unpack that completely, yet it is important that we wrestle intellectually with the nature of God, for that intellectual wrestling is both a form of worship and an important attempt to understand the underpinnings of our mission.

Lesslie Newbigin wrote something equally arresting: "The ordinary Christian in the Western world who hears or reads the word 'God' does not immediately and inevitably think of the Triune Being—Father, Son, and Spirit. He thinks of a supreme monad."[4] Newbigin's words are almost certainly true of most of us. Even many who are trained in the ministerial art—professional churchmen and owners of thick books on theology—ponder too little the majesty and mystery of the Triune God.

Perhaps in reaction to the Muslim claim that Christians are tri-theists, or perhaps more due to our inability to conceive of

Three-In-One, we have had a hard time articulating God in three persons. Our rather intractable conception of God's one-ness has perhaps robbed us of the rich truth of the Trinity. Yet our mission, as well as our theology, depends on our willingness to hang onto the enigmatic tension of Trinitarianism and monotheism.

It is important that we embrace the powerful, paradoxical reality of God in three persons, for the Trinity is foundational for fresh expressions of church.

The *Re-prominence* of the Trinity

One of the most important developments in the history of thought about God is the fairly recent *re-prominence* of the Trinity. Whether one attributes it to Karl Barth[5] or the Great Emergence,[6] or someone or something else, it appears to me that today's best theological and missiological minds are pondering the Trinity like never before in recent history.

Crediting Karl Barth with this rise in prominence of a more fully Trinitarian theology, Van Gelder and Zscheile wrote,

> This conception changed the playing field for thinking about mission by shifting the rationale and agency for mission away from the church and placing them instead within the life of the Trinity. Barth stressed that "the term *missio* was in the ancient Church an expression of the doctrine of the Trinity—namely the expression of the divine sending forth of self, the sending of the Son and Holy Spirit to the world." He then proceeded to connect these movements within the Trinity to the gathering, forming, and sending of the church into the world. Although the notion of *missio Dei* (the mission of God) was not conceptualized until later, Barth's point was that there is mission because God is a sending God.[7]

Thus emerged the critical recognition that the church is neither the origin nor the goal of Christian mission. Rather, the church, as the body and bride of Christ, joins in the life of the Trinity and gains both its mission and its legitimacy from that relationship.[8]

Perichoresis

Perichoresis is a term that communicates the interrelationship and interconnectedness of the persons of the Trinity. Father, Son and Spirit are *for, of, with,* and *in* each other—while distinct from each other.

The perichoretic (interpenetrating each other without losing distinction) relationship of the Trinity is a model for Christian community.[9] Jesus prayed that we would be one, as He and the Father are one. The relationships of Christian brothers and sisters is thus no small matter. What we call the "fellowship" of the church, when at its best, is an echo of the Triune God of the mission. Church communion as it should be reflects the image of the Three-in-One. People who invest themselves in new churches, or new forms of church, as well as members of new monastic communities, are living out the model of the perichoretic Father, Son, and Spirit.

Invited In

This perichoresis is not closed or exclusive. God-in-Three-Persons is inviting, generous, open-handed, and open-hearted. The church is welcomed mysteriously into that relationship of Father, Son, and Spirit. In the words of Samuel J. Stone's hymn, "The Church's One Foundation": "She on earth hath union with God the Three in One." We are not just emulating the Trinity in our fellowship; we actually are gathered to participate in the fellowship and mission of the Father, Son, and Spirit.

When a couple has children, those children are welcomed into the couple's love. The children are not part of the marriage, of course; they are not "third parties" in the nuptial relationship. Yet the children participate in, enrich, and are enriched by their part in the unique connection between their parents. All analogies fall short of full insight into the Trinity, but likewise, the church is invited into the unique connection and love between Father, Son, and Spirit.

And, if we may, let's push the analogy of parents and children a bit further. The church is shaped by its participation in, and what it learns from, the interrelating of the Father, Son, and Spirit, just as children are shaped by their interactions with their parents. The personality of the church is thus clearly rooted in the Trinity.

Furthermore, taking our cue from God-in-Three-Persons, a Christian family of faith exists not for each other or ourselves but for those not yet in the family. The fellowship of a church, like that of the Three-in-One, is to be inviting, generous, open-handed, and open-hearted, always willing to love a new brother or sister.

Church/Mission

Among the implications of this shift to a Trinitarian foundation for mission is a refocus on the point of Christian mission—away from church to the nature of God. As recently as several decades ago, what we called "missions" was commonly understood as being about the extension of the church. More churches, for the sake of more churches, seemed the goal.

The expansion of the church, however, is no longer viewed widely as the point. The point, rather, is increasingly seen as being the nature of the Triune God and the overflow of His nature in the world. That shift clarifies our motivation and our direction.

Our driver is the glory of God rather than the glorification of the church. Moreover, our purpose in mission becomes the purposes of God, and God's broader purposes are not always the same as the interests of local congregations. Besides these, the fuel for the movement shifts from human strategies to the mystical, boundless power of the Holy Spirit.

The goal, then, is not simply to have more churches dotting the landscape. The purpose is God's holistic mission to the world. The church is God's primary people/instrument/plan for the fulfillment of that mission, but not the end of the mission.

So a clear and important theological assumption in today's missional conversations is that Christian mission is not primarily *about* the church, is not ultimately *for* the church, or *an addendum to the study of* the church. Mission is no longer "ecclesiocentric." Mission is now appropriately viewed as rooted in the person and nature of the Triune God Himself. According to Darrell Guder,

"The ecclesiocentric understanding of mission has been replaced during this century by a profoundly theocentric reconceptualization of Christian mission . . . mission is the result of God's initiative, rooted in God's purposes to restore and heal creation."[10]
Mission-Shaped Church declared, "Church planting should not . . . be church-centered. It should not be another device to perpetuate an institution for that institution's own sake."[11]

The church is worth dying for. Jesus, in fact, did. A significant thrust of the Fresh Expressions movement (and lots of ink in this book) certainly has to do with church. Yet the mission of God is bigger than any one congregation, and if our evangelistic efforts are merely for the purpose of propping up a local church, our motives are questionable at best.

Sending

In the conversation about the Trinity, there often arises the matter of *sending*. David Bosch wrote of the Willingen Conference of the International Missionary Council in 1952.

> It was here that the idea (not the exact term) *missio Dei* first surfaced clearly. Mission was understood as being derived from the very nature of God. It was thus put in the context of the doctrine of the Trinity, not of ecclesiology or soteriology. The classical doctrine on the *missio Dei* as God the Father sending the Son, and God the Father and the Son sending the Spirit was expanded to include yet another "movement": Father, Son, and Holy Spirit sending the church into the world. As far as missionary thinking was concerned, this linking with the doctrine of the Trinity constituted an important innovation.[12]

God is the Great Sender. Our legitimacy as new forms of church result from our role as sent ones, ambassadors, apostolic families, rooted in and on mission from the Sending God.

The word "mission" comes from the Latin word *missio* which means "to send," and is related to the Greek word *apostello*, also meaning "to send." No matter where we look in Scripture, God is *sending*. Whether it's Joseph to his brothers, Moses to Pharoah, Jonah to the Ninevites, Gabriel to Joseph, or the sending of the Twelve (Luke 9) or the seventy-two (Luke 10), *sending* is both a recurring theme and a precursor to our mission.

The church, as the "sent ones," thus acts on behalf of, and in keeping with the mission of, the Divine Sender. The sendees are accountable to the Sender.

But sending is not the full story. Michael Moynagh noted,

> Mission is God's self-giving for the sake of humanity. This makes divine giving, not sending, the heart of mission . . . sending should be seen as the eternal giving within the Trinity. Sending into the world is what happens when God gives himself to the world.[13]

Moynagh's insights here remind us that God does not remain in heaven as an uninvolved actor in the world. It would be wrong to imagine the Divine Sender as sitting in a safe and cozy war room while the troops engage in battle. Rather, God *sends* us to *join Him* in the world. He is the General or the King leading the charges of the ones He sent. He is in the proverbial trenches with us. He is the Servant-Leader washing the feet of those to whom He has called. The love of the Three-in-One compels us to go, and compels God Himself to lead the way, into "the roads and country lanes" (Luke 14:23) in the mission of redemption.

Enter Fresh Expressions of Church

Understanding the place of the church within God's mission to the world is essential in grasping the validity of, even the desperate need for, fresh expressions of church.

> Church as the primary partner of the missionary God, then, explains why fresh expressions arise at all. They are not, as some assert, some aberration or simply an expression of maverick selfishness or discontent. At best they are expressions of a missionary God raising up a people who can effect God's

highest intentions and deepest desires for this time and place. Put sharply, if the *missio Dei* in any time and place cannot be pursued with the Church as it is, God raises up a new Church.[14]

Fresh expressions of church, then, take their place in the wonderful saga of church history as new forms of the body of Christ in the world.

Furthermore, the planting of a fresh expression of church is the planting of a potential witness to the Trinity. Both the genuine fellowship of believers in a local church, and the relationship of inherited and new forms of church, reflect (at our best, if in small ways) the beautiful, Triune nature of God.

Chapter 8

LIVING AMONG THE PEOPLE YOU ARE TRYING TO REACH

Pertinence is not a bad idea; relevance is not unimportant. We believe that if our expressions of church are to be fresh, so must our approaches be. Yet the deeper issue in the starting of new forms of church is not mere relevance. The issue is incarnation.

Incarnation is not merely a strategy; it is a mentality. Incarnation is an attitude, a way of thinking about starting a new faith community. Incarnation is a way of viewing the people among whom we are called to minister. It is a sacrificial but appreciative sense of our call. It is a matter of seeing ourselves *with*, *of*, and *among* the community. Not just *to* them.

There is a vulnerability that accompanies incarnation. Incarnation is not safe; incarnation risks. Incarnation bears "the burdens of its neighbors as it participates deeply in the life and struggle of the community into which it is sent and within which it lives. . . . This means surrendering a posture of control, distance and mere benevolence in order to enter closely into relational community."[1]

With all its risks, however, genuine incarnation will result in indigenous, or contextualized, new forms of church. "Whereas the traditional approach to evangelism begins with the current church and asks how people can be encouraged to belong, new contextual

churches go to where people are and ask what church should appropriately look like in their context."[2]

The Incarnation and Bodily Resurrection

Why are we constantly having to explain why the New Testament
says, "Don't eat meat sacrificed to idols," why the dietary laws
of Leviticus do not apply to us, and why Paul told Timothy that
women should not wear braids and jewelry? It is because the
written revelation of God was directed to a certain people in a
certain place—contextualized, if you will. Its deep truths are applicable in all times and places, yet are housed in the language of an
historical situation.

In addition to, and even more weighty than, the contextual
specificities of God's revelation through Scripture, is the incarnation of God the Son, the second person of the Trinity.

God the Son not only entered our world, He fully immersed
Himself in our world. He not only came to live on our planet, He
came to share our tables, walk our roads, enjoy our parties, and
suffer our hurts. Thus, an indigenous church is not only an effective missiological goal, it is a reflection of the incarnation. He who
became flesh, dwelt among us, identified with us, and met us at
the places of our greatest need, modeled the ultimate approach to
making the good news known. The Son was incarnate in a particular place, among a particular people, as a particular ethnic group,
yet was for all the world. He turned His heart toward *pan ta ethne* (all
nations), but first He invested in the house of Israel.

One of the lessons of the divine incarnation, by the way, is the
lesson of patience. After all, the incarnation of God began in the
form of an embryo, not a full-grown man with a full-blown message.
These fresh expressions of church often require a great deal of
forbearance from those trying to do church among people who
aren't interested in church.

Not unrelated to the incarnation is the bodily resurrection
of Jesus. As Jesus took on flesh and blood to enter our world, He

was raised in flesh and blood to transform our world. The physical resurrection of Jesus is not something we should pass over too quickly. By our position on this, our missiology and ecclesiology are formed.[3]

Not only does the resurrection shape our message, it determines our approach. Because Jesus was resurrected physically, there is a flesh and blood nature to the church. Church is real people engaged in a real world, addressing real problems, and proclaiming a real Truth.

The resurrected Jesus ate fish and showed them His wounds. This was no apparition. The resurrection—the genuine presence of the Savior among such broken and disheartened people—is no less a model for the involvement of the church in its neighborhood's most difficult situations than the incarnation itself. The more trendy among us have a point when they insist on "keeping it real."

There is an undeniably practical argument for an indigenous approach. Put plainly, the indigenous approach *works* better than approaches that feel foreign. Yet, more fundamentally important is the example set by our Lord Jesus. When God chose to communicate Himself, whether through the prophets or through His Son, He did so contextually. The key, then, to indigeneity is incarnation—the incarnation of the Son in the person of Jesus, and our incarnation of the gospel via our engagement with specific people in specific contexts.

The church is the body of Christ in the world, and thus the incarnation of the Son in the person of Jesus is naturally our model and inspiration. An appreciation for indigenous communities of faith is a matter of honoring the missionary strategy of Jesus. Jesus, after all, was not only *to* people; He was *with*, *of*, and *among* people.

Missionaries in Our Own Culture

Many of us heard first of "contextualization" or "indigeneity" in a missions class in seminary. Lots of us studied cross-cultural mission with the rather naive assumption that such was applicable only for a foreign land. Now we are realizing the power of contextualization within our own national borders as we cross new boundaries to begin new forms of church. The study of indigenous (contextualized) churches, central to the international missionary movement, now is increasingly helpful in establishing churches that engage the North American population.

Like never before we are called, without leaving our own neighborhoods, to cross cultures for the sake of the gospel. Lesslie Newbigin spoke of being "cross-cultural missionaries in our own culture."[4]

Lessons from Missionary Predecessors

Most of us have images in our memories of Western missionaries to Africa wearing pith helmets, following hired guides through the jungle, and dragging with them a pump organ from back home. (It must have been hard to imagine true Christian worship without an organ.)

There are lots of stories of past missionaries who insisted new Christians in other lands dress like the Brits or the Americans and take Christian names. Westernizing the so-called natives was an assumed goal of the typical foreign missionary of yesteryear. In these and many other ways, courageous, well-meaning ambassadors of the gospel ignored the power of indigeneity.

We ought to be inspired by a courage that enabled those missionaries to leave their homes and risk their lives. The soil of foreign lands is indeed stained with the blood, sweat, and tears of missionary heroes. We ought to be emboldened by a tenacity that kept on preaching, teaching, and doctoring when the resistance was often fierce and the possibility of death hung constantly like a cloud over them.

We can also learn from their strategic errors. The international missionary movement has taught us the limitations of a paternalistic, imperialistic, "do-it-like-we've-always-done-it" approach to church planting. The roots of the Christian faith sink deeper, and the results are more lasting, when an indigenous approach is followed and a church reflects the best of its environment. There is richness, depth, and durability in homegrown, indigenous, contextualized churches.

Indigenous Churches

In 1974 Orlando Costas asked a powerful question: "Can an unevangelized world, caught up in a process of political, social, economic, and cultural awakening, be effectively evangelized by a church that is not indigenous?"[5] The answer was "no" then, and it is perhaps a more emphatic "no" today.

Indigenous simply means originating in, or at least fitting and functioning naturally within, a particular setting or environment. An indigenous (or "contextualized") church, then, is a church that, like an indigenous plant, grows up from, or at least fits naturally within, its context. In an indigenous church, everything from discipleship to service expresses the local culture and reflects the backgrounds and experiences of the participants. The way decisions are made, the way worship is experienced, the biblical truths that are emphasized—all those are contextualized.

The noted anthropologist William Smalley described an indigenous church in these words:

> It is a group of believers who live out their life, including their socialized Christian activity, in the patterns of the local society, and for whom any transformation of that society comes out of their felt needs under the guidance of the Holy Spirit and Scriptures.[6]

Indigeneity is a key to the fresh expressions approach. A major tenet of the Fresh Expressions movement is that church must be at home within a subculture, affinity group, or individualized context. In the words of Michael Moynagh, "If the missionary Spirit is present in a setting, the outcome of the Spirit's work will well up from within that setting. If that includes the birth of a church, it will be a church from inside the context."[7] And Darrell Guder described these new forms of church, of which we speak here, as "post-Christendom Western indigenous churches."[8]

The art of paying attention

Contextualization (indigenization) is an art, not a science. The ones seeking to contextualize the message and the new form of church should do the best they can to understand the context and to live out the truths of the gospel in ways that translate to the people they are seeking to engage.

Pioneers who start indigenous churches have to be keenly aware of what God is doing in the neighborhood or subculture among which they are planting. The effective pioneer recognizes that God is at work beyond the church and looks for those points of contact. It is really helpful if the pioneer is an "insider"—at home in the target subculture. If the pioneer is not an insider, he or she will do his or her best to understand the worldviews, the hurts, the joys, and the dreams of the recipient audience. Cultural norms, social values, even the recreational priorities of the community are studied. Certainly, the opinion makers and influencers are identified and honored. If, among those opinion-makers and influencers there is a "person of peace"—one who is drawn to the planter/pioneer and his or her message—then that person of peace can provide invaluable insights.

One way of looking at indigeneity: the three-self formula

The three-self formula is mentioned often in missionary discussions of indigeneity. This popular idea that indigenous churches are self-governing, self-propagating, and self-supporting was proposed by Sir Henry Venn, chief secretary of the Church Missionary Society from 1841 to 1872, and Rufus Anderson, senior secretary of the American Board of Commissioners for Foreign Missions from 1832 to 1866. Anderson and Venn were interested in the planting of indigenous churches—churches that would be suited for and thrive in their particular contexts. The three-self formula came into prominence in the 1950s during the Mao Revolution in China and the resulting vibrant indigenous church movement there.

By "self-sustaining," Anderson and Venn meant primarily that the new churches would not long be supported by outsiders. The costs of their church would be borne by the people of the church. The new congregations would be financially viable and free of propping up by outside mission agencies or congregations.

If the new church is dependent financially upon the sponsoring church, it will be difficult to grow beyond that dependency into a missional, self-propagating community of faith. Lots of good churches with really good intentions have started new churches and poured so much money into them that that the new churches had a stifling sense of dependency.

By "self-governing," Anderson and Venn meant, simply, that the churches would make decisions for themselves, being responsible only to, and being led only by, the Holy Spirit. Neither missionaries nor sponsoring congregations would, after sufficient time for maturation, meddle in the church's affairs. Of course many of these indigenous congregations would be in denominational systems in which the individual church would submit itself to the appropriate authority of their denominational body, but even that denominational identity would be the choice of the people in that particular congregation.

By "self-propagating," Anderson and Venn intended to communicate that the missionary mandate to "go and make disciples" is applicable even to the mission churches. It was important that the young churches would see themselves as participants in God's mission, not merely recipients of mission efforts.

Although the three-self formula is essential to indigeneity, it is inadequate for describing comprehensive indigeneity. There is a necessary fourth self: a church also must be *self-expressing* if it is to be considered truly indigenous. In the words of Orlando Costas, "The church . . . must *express itself* in concrete historical situations. In other words, the church must always be an indigenous community."[9]

By definition, if a church does not support, propagate, and govern itself according to the patterns which are natural and characteristic of its situation, then that church is not self-expressing and thus not truly indigenous. A community of faith has the prerogative to study the Bible and, through a prayerful process, to formulate its own understanding of God and the Christian life. An indigenous family of faith reflects an appreciation for its own context and a deliberate influence of local customs in addition to biblical standards of belief and practice.

The implications of this four-self formula for fresh expressions of church are clear and important. A fresh expression of church is moving toward maturity when it is free from any outside financial help, when it is free from the control of another church, when it is reaching out in ministry and evangelism and even forming another fresh expression of church, and when its worship, governance, discipleship, and everything that defines it reflects and fits well in its context.

A New Church's Place in the Worldwide Body of Christ

One of the blessings of the broader missional movement is the abandonment of cookie-cutting emulation and rejection of the indiscriminate importation of practices from distant churches. We are learning of the joy (and efficacy) of indigenous church models that are somewhat different than every other model ever promoted. In the words of Graham Cray, "Jesus builds his church in each place, but he does not construct production line prefabs."[10]

Likewise, Steven Croft wrote,

> The essence of church therefore lies as much in its difference as in its similarity. Not difference for its own sake, but the difference that is a natural consequence of being an incarnational community of the Christian Godhead in a particular time and place and set in a particular context.[11]

The look of the future church in North America is still unfolding, of course. No one can predict what the church of tomorrow will look like. One thing seems certain, however: the near inevitability, due to contextualization, that the forms and models of church will vary widely. We already have moved beyond the broad categories (i.e., "contemporary" or "traditional") to describe churches. With the complexity that comes with that, there also comes a richness, and freedom.

In 1938, in the context of a discussion of international missions emanating primarily from Europe and North America, people gathered in Madras (present Chennai), India, and declared,

> An indigenous church . . . is a church which, rooted in obedience to Christ, spontaneously uses forms of thought and modes of action natural and familiar in its own environment. . . . Not unmindful of the experiences and teachings which the older churches have recorded in their confessions and liturgies . . . every young church will seek to bear witness to the same Gospel in new tongues.[12]

Note the warning not to be "unmindful of the experiences and teachings" of the "older churches." That warning is as appropriate today when a North American pioneer forms a fresh expression of church as it was when North American missionaries were planting churches in India in the 1930s. There is much to be learned from those who have been loving and serving God in community before we ever considered our new form of church. Their meaningful experiences inform our practices without restricting them. We don't have to idolize our heritage in order to learn from it.

A church's authority is the Bible, its guide is the Holy Spirit, and its head is Christ. A church—whether a century old and traditional, or a year old and nontraditional—has all the privileges and responsibilities of any other church. Ideally, the indigenous church is aware of the church universal and appreciative of its rightful and unique place within that international body of believers. Yet, that indigenous church does not feel inferior or superior to any group anywhere. It feels it has a place in God's family and in His mission to the world, as do other churches.

Therefore, fresh expressions of church, if properly empowered, will not sacrifice their convictions on the altar of conformity. Fresh expressions of church should be encouraged by the growing focus on contextualization. They need not feel the pressures that many older congregations have felt to conform to a generic model.

Critical contextualization

This is not a naive, sentimental, indiscriminating approach. When a practice or belief, though native to the context, is challenged by the clear message of Scripture, then the Bible, not the context, must prevail. Honoring the context is not equivalent to surrendering to the context. An indigenous church must reflect the valued elements of local culture and also challenge, in appropriate ways, the elements that violate what we understand to be biblical principles. Cross-cultural missionaries should note the following: "Contextualization is when the gospel presented and the response called for, offends for the right reasons and not for the wrong ones."[13]

Indigenous leadership

A major factor in the contextualization of a new church is the strategic intentionality of its founders to encourage and bless local leaders. Passing the proverbial baton, as soon as is prudent, is essential. The apostle Paul's missionary strategy included a reliance upon indigenous leadership (see 2 Timothy 2:2), although the passing of authority to local leaders was not always immediate. When a local church came into being, Paul and Barnabas "committed them to the Lord, in whom they had put their trust" (Acts 14:23). Pioneers of fresh expressions can and must, then, be looking for those spiritual leaders whom God will raise up from among the newcomers.

What we give up

In Philippians 2 we find the powerful *kenosis* passage.

> In your relationships with one another, have the same mindset as Christ Jesus: Who, being in very nature God, did not consider equality with God something to be used to his own advantage; rather, he made himself nothing by taking the very nature of

a servant, being made in human likeness. And being found in appearance as a man, he humbled himself by becoming obedient to death—even death on a cross! (Phil. 2:5–8)

While our small losses can in no way compare to that which was given up in the Son's incarnation, the Lord Jesus modeled for us the importance of sacrifice, even if that sacrifice is our notion of how church ought to look. Lisa Smith is a fresh expressions pioneer in Alexandria, Virginia. She has been willing to re-imagine church, and give up some longstanding traditions, in order to establish and lead an effective, new form of church among artists. Lisa once asked, "What, of what we *call* church, are we willing to give up in order to *be* church?" That is a good question indeed, particularly for people interested in indigenous forms of church.

Starting a new form of church necessitates our willingness to give up lots of wonderful but peripheral things in order to be church effectively in a new context. Programs like Sunday school, musical elements such as choirs, organizational structures like membership rolls, . . . all are most likely not going to be found in a new form of church. Indigeneity requires a willingness, on the part of the pioneers, to give up what we call church.

Contextualization is often uncomfortable for the original group. Many means of expressing the Christian faith in other cultures just don't feel right to those of us who are well-steeped in a particular Christian tradition. The resulting worship forms, the way things are organized, and the way decisions are made, often seem foreign to the one who has crossed the cultural barrier to incarnate the gospel. But as long as the gospel is not being violated, and the Bible's clear message not compromised, we must be willing to let the new entity grow in indigenous ways (ways that fit, that occur naturally and are meaningful in, the particular context).

Context broader than place

This conversation demands we remember that a context is not necessarily limited by geography. If we are planting a fresh expression of church in a neighborhood or a section of the city, then there are fairly simple (not easy, but simple) ways to get to know that area. Prayer walking. Sitting at local watering holes and asking questions. Talking with local leaders, both official and unofficial. Demographic studies, and so on. One can get a fairly good handle on what is going on, and what would fit, in a geographical locale.

However, context is not always geographical. The context might center on a hobby, a vocation, an addiction, or an ethnic connection. That context might have nothing to do with a place. Entering, learning, and honoring such nonphysical communities will require creativity and intentionality. It's one thing to start a new form of church in a physical neighborhood. It's quite another to start a new form of church among, say, the military veterans' community, the arts community, or the gaming community.

As is noted often in this book, having an insider among the host community is critical. Without an insider, penetrating and understanding new contexts is difficult, even for those with a missionary gift that enables them to identify with new cultures.

God Already There

We are called to the world beyond our Christian bubble not because God is missing from it, but because God is active in it! Church can fit and flourish in particular contexts because God is already there at work in those contexts. Contextualization is not just a matter of *praxis*. Contextualization honors the Creator and His people. Starting new forms of church that honor their specific cultures recognizes the prevenient grace and universal presence of God. Missiologist J. C. Hoekendijk wrote, "God is understood to already be present and active in the world, with the church being responsible for discovering what God is doing and then seeking to participate in that."[14]

Chapter 9

WHOLE PERSON/
WHOLE CREATION

Christian mission—whether beyond or within our nation's borders—has traditionally been understood as crossing boundaries (national, linguistic, cultural, etc.) in the name of Jesus to join God in His mission to the world. God's mission to the world prioritizes the transformation of individuals, which results in (1) their eternal redemption from sin; (2) their relationship with fellow pilgrims in the family of God; and (3) their joining God in addressing unfair structures, acts of compassion for the poor and hurting, and care for God's creation.

In some traditions, caring for individuals' physical needs is little more than a hook to secure the opportunity to do the so-called real missionary work—the sharing of the gospel. That, however, is gimmickry, not a comprehensive mission. Furthermore, any approach to mission that simply boasts of decisions—meaning the number of people who raised their hands stating they have prayed a certain prayer—is questionable. Conversely, doing good deeds without somehow articulating the reason for our real and eternal hope is hardly Christian mission (with the exception of those who live in countries in which Christian evangelization is illegal).

A comprehensive mission is love-based, hidden-agenda-less, Christocentric, and attentive to the needs, both physical and spiritual, of the whole person. We turn to David Bosch again: "Neither a secularized church (that is, a church which concerns itself only with this-worldly activities and interests) nor a separatist church (that is, a church which involves itself only in soul-saving and preparation of converts for the hereafter) can faithfully articulate the *Missio Dei.*"[1]

The invitation to personal faith in Jesus, and the invitation into a community of Christian pilgrims, remain primary in the mission. Primary in the mission does not, however, mean the entirety of the mission. Mission is broader than making disciples, though that remains the heart of the matter. Mission is our joining God in all that He is doing in the world, embracing His care for all creation. Biblical Christians are concerned for justice—that all persons be treated fairly, humanely, as if they are the handiwork of the Creator. Biblical Christians will be concerned for the planet in which God obviously delights.

So is Christian mission social action? A ministry of compassion to the poor and sick? Is Christian mission ecology? The effort to join God's Spirit in drawing people into individual, spiritual conversion?

The answer, of course, to all those questions, is "yes." God's mission is broad and holistic. The following elements of Christian mission, which originated in the Anglican Communion, reflect a broadly embraced understanding of the mission:

- To proclaim the good news of the kingdom;
- To teach, baptize, and nurture new believers;
- To respond to human need by loving service;
- To seek to transform unjust structures of society;
- To safeguard the integrity of creation, and sustain and renew the life of the earth.[2]

The Kingdom of God

The central and driving theme of Jesus' life and preaching was the kingdom of God. He came to introduce the kingdom in depth, breadth, and power that could only have been imagined before

Christ Jesus. And He instructed His followers to introduce others to that kingdom. If there is any theme that characterizes the movement of Jesus-followers, it is the kingdom of God.

Lesslie Newbigin spoke beautifully of the breaking in of the kingdom, and "the inexpressible mystery of the event that is the center" of that breaking in: "Christ the sacrifice offered for our sin, Christ the substitute standing in our place, Christ the ransom price paid for our redemption, Christ the conqueror casting out the prince of this world."[3] The kingdom is come in power in Jesus.

The kingdom of God in its fullness awaits the future. But the kingdom of God is not a castle in the air, and we're not supposed to just sit around and wait for it. In this meantime of history we, the King's imperfect subjects, work to unleash His kingdom in limited but meaningful ways. We are to pray and work for the coming of the kingdom here and now, in every nook and niche of creation.

The kingdom of God is about justice, ministry to human needs, and reconciliation. So whenever we work for the fair and just treatment of everyone, whenever we help heal hurts, and whenever we work to break down the walls that still divide us as races . . . the kingdom comes.

The kingdom of God is about changed hearts—meaning people here and around the world who need Jesus are given every opportunity to know and submit to the King. So whenever we have a spiritual conversation with someone, or give money to support missionaries, or otherwise help people along their journey to Jesus . . . the kingdom comes.

The kingdom of God is even about ecology; it involves creation. The Bible says in Romans 8 that the earth has been groaning, waiting for the day when it will be restored. The fullness of God's kingdom is somehow going to mean a new creation. God's covenant was not only with Noah and his descendants, but also "with every living creature that was with you—the birds, the livestock and all the wild animals, all those that came out of the ark with you—every living creature on earth" (Gen. 9:9-10). So whenever we take care of God's creation . . . the kingdom comes.

The kingdom of God is all-encompassing, not limited to the human heart. We are to pray that God's kingdom—His unquestionable reign—will come on earth as it is in heaven. On earth . . . all over the earth . . . in all the earth . . . in every corner, office, factory, forest, and home on the planet.

Social Justice, a Missional Responsibility

Social justice is the attempt to address the needs of people at the structural level—practically speaking, the *source*, if you will.[4]

Perhaps you will remember the catastrophic British Petroleum oil leak of 2010. The drilling rig, *Deepwater Horizon*, was digging an exploratory oil well in the deep waters of the Gulf of Mexico when an explosion took the lives of eleven people and sent oil gushing into the ocean. The devastation was heartbreaking, from the massive loss of marine life to the contamination of the sugar sands of the Gulf's beaches.

People rallied. There were people on the beach shoveling oil and cleaning the birds with dishwashing liquid. Others encircled the oil slick with booms that corralled the tar-like mess.

Yet others were out at the place of origination working frantically to cap and seal the leak at its source.

Some worked on the results while others worked on the cause. Attacking the tragedy from both sides was necessary.

Poverty and injustice likewise have to be attacked from both sides. Some will minister to people who are victims of unfair housing, others will go after the slumlords, or petition local governments to incentivize low-cost housing in attractive places.

Some will minister to those in jails and prisons due to their use of crack cocaine (used often by people who are poor), while those who use more upper-class drugs go unpunished. Others will try to make the punishment fair across the socioeconomic spectrum.

Some are called and gifted to minister in Christ's name to those impacted by societal evils. Others are called and gifted to attack the root causes of those evils.

Social justice—the attempt to address the problem of poverty at the level where policies are decided and laws are made—has been demonized and dismissed by some, even though social justice is a recurring theme of Scripture. Isaiah, Jeremiah, Ezekiel, Amos, Micah, Habakkuk, Zephaniah, Zechariah, and Malachi all would be shocked that the phrase "social justice" has been labeled as somehow unbiblical. It was fairness for the poor, for example, not appropriate punishment for the criminal, that Amos was referring to when he declared, "Let justice roll on like a river!" (Amos 5:24). And the book of Jeremiah goes so far as to say that defending "the cause of the poor and needy" is what it means to know the Lord (Jer. 22:15-16)!

One does not have to give up a concern for evangelism to champion fairness for all people at the structural level. The Christian heart and mind are capable of embracing both causes. We can witness so that people become followers of Jesus *and* work to make sure everyone has opportunities for such basics as good education, fair housing, and impartial treatment in our courts.

What did Jesus do?

The broad sweep of Scripture certainly confirms our call to ministry to the whole person and whole world. Jesus' primary topic, the kingdom of God, reflects God's all-encompassing love.

In Luke 4:18, Jesus clearly speaks of a so-called cultural mandate. Ministry to the captives, blind, and oppressed (both spiritually and physically) was unquestionably central to Jesus' ministry, and must also be to ours. Yet Jesus' priority seems to have been to seek and to save the spiritually lost. That, at least, seems to have been what He saw as the entrance point into the kingdom.

Jesus spoke with particular frequency about the redemption of individuals—about people submitting to the kingdom of God, the kingship, the empire, of God—and being transformed. As soon as Jesus' impending birth was announced to Mary and Joseph, "to save people from their sins" was understood to be His clear mission. In fact, His very name would symbolize that. Luke 24 makes plain the heart of our faith and mission.

He told them, "This is what is written: The Messiah will suffer and rise from the dead on the third day, and repentance for the forgiveness of sins will be preached in his name to all nations, beginning at Jerusalem. You are witnesses of these things." (verses 46–48)

This redemption which Jesus preached, and which begins in the human heart, is transformative. New births result in new structures, for people who have experienced that transformation so radical Jesus called it being "born again" now long for—as a matter of their new nature—the transformation of all people and all society.

Of course, it would be naive of us to think or claim that converts to the Christian faith absolutely and automatically meet human needs and repair unjust human structures. Yet the new birth propels and empowers individuals and congregations to take on the genuine transformation of the world.

New birth, new structures

A requirement for remedying the societal ills of our world . . . as well as the ills of our own lives . . . is changed hearts.

To say that Martin Luther King Jr. had his detractors is an understatement. And many of those who criticized him most vehemently were proponents of civil rights. They agreed with his goals, but believed the nonviolent strategy would not be effective. Roy Wilkins, of the National Association for the Advancement of Colored People, felt that King's strategies were accomplishing nothing. In 1963, Wilkins said to King, "In fact, Martin, if you have desegregated anything by your efforts, kindly enlighten me."

King answered, "Well, I guess about the only thing I've desegregated so far is a few human hearts."[5]

King knew that changing laws alone would not make for a different America. He knew that a changed America would begin with changed hearts.

That is true whether we are talking about racism, oppression, or human trafficking. Such things as the temperance movement and Prohibition in the 1920s remind us that changing laws alone merely drives certain behavior underground. The ultimate answer is changed hearts.

In fact, new structures without new hearts eventually will either return to their previous state of unfairness or morph into something even more unjust, for the root of the problem is our sinful human nature—our innate, overwhelming tendency to do the wrong thing.

Spiritual conversion does not inevitably translate to societal correction. Yet societal correction will not happen without spiritual conversion.

New churches, new world

"What did the New Testament missionaries do? They planted churches," wrote Peyton Jones in his book *Church Zero*. Jones even declared, "The Acts of the Apostles could be called The Acts of the Church Planters."[6]

An apostle was primarily a church planter. New churches were the chief result of the apostolic ministry of our missional predecessors. This is a good and simple argument for the primacy of new churches in the mission of God.

I heard Jake Medcalf, a young pastor who was then doing urban ministry in San Diego, say, "We believe the way to transform neighborhoods is to plant churches."[7] New families of faith are indeed a means toward genuine community transformation.

Fresh Expressions and Holistic Mission

God intends the establishment of churches that are deep in faith and broad in mission. And that is where there is a great opportunity for fresh expressions of church. As has been often observed, it's easier to *create* a culture than to *transform* a culture. The launchers of a new form of church have the opportunity to join God's Spirit in shaping a family of faith committed to the comprehensive understanding of what God is doing in the world and how we can join Him in that inclusive mission.

The thrust of the Great Commission is giving witness to the life-transforming power of the gospel, playing whatever role the Spirit allows us to play in nurturing people into faith in Jesus, then walking with them as fellow disciples as they mature in the faith. Lesslie Newbigin declared, "The calling of men and women to be converted, to follow Jesus, and to be part of his community is and must always be at the center of mission."[8]

New forms of church are able to do just that. Fresh expressions engage people who are far from God, introduce those people to life in God's kingdom, and help them become new apprentices of the Lord Jesus. People in these new churches understand that their mission is bigger than someone's conversion, yet is incomplete without that conversion.

To live as if the mission of God is limited to the private change in an individual's soul is irresponsible. Yet, to live as if the heart of our mission is something other than personal redemption from the power and penalty of what the Bible calls "sin" is unbiblical.

Chapter 10

SALVATION AND EVANGELISM

Words like "salvation" and "evangelism" have fallen out of favor it seems. That is quite understandable, given the manipulative nature of some evangelistic methods and the sometimes shallow interpretation of salvation. Yet the fact that the terms have been counterfeited by some does not mean we all should abandon them.

To speak of salvation is to speak of a spiritual transformation so dramatic Jesus called it the "new birth." There is a spiritual lostness so staggering that Scripture describes some people as "without hope and without God in the world" (Eph. 2:12). Thus we are compelled by grace to engage in evangelism—to facilitate divine encounters—providing space for the Holy Spirit to lovingly nudge people toward faith in Jesus.

It would be tragic for us to miss out on the beautiful experience of witnessing the miracle of genuine and holistic conversion. "Salvation" and "evangelism," then, are words worth reclaiming.

Mission and Evangelism Are Not Synonymous

Perhaps it will be helpful here to note that "mission" and "evangelism" are not synonymous. On the one hand, evangelism (faithfully living out and bearing witness to the good news with the ultimate hope that people make a decision to follow Jesus) is not our only mission, and expanding God's kingdom has to do with more than evangelism. On the other hand, engagement only in a social element of God's mission (feeding the hungry, for example, or fighting for fair salaries) without somehow articulating the good news, cannot be claimed as a full engagement in Christian mission.

Bob Hopkins, whose nontraditional church planting work in England helped launch the Fresh Expressions movement, had this to say:

> This is something we want to be very clear about: evangelism and mission are *not* the same thing. Evangelism is a core feature of effective mission but the mission of God is so much wider. Our call to evangelism is just one part, although a very central part, of God's grand plan to transform and save the whole world. . . . Mission is the totality of God's activity to restore His order (Kingdom) to the whole of His creation. Evangelism is that part which seeks or results in the restoration of God's right relationship with humanity as the good news of Jesus (gospel) is both told and lived out. . . . Mission action . . . could include social campaigning, working for justice, fighting for ecology and seeking to engage in all sorts of social action with no intention of connecting those affected with a knowledge of God's love.[1]

Is Evangelism Passé?

Candidly, evangelism is increasingly portrayed as an idea whose time has passed. Leonard Sweet observed, "Many Christian churches are themselves post-Christian, with meager interest in evangelism, with little faith in the Christian tradition itself, but lots of interest in political activism of the liberal persuasion."[2] In too many cases evangelism is politely tagged on as an obligatory "also" (if it is tagged on at all).

In at least two important works on Christian mission[3] it is declared that *recent rethinking* of the mission of God has resulted in a more holistic view of that mission. That more holistic view is a welcomed development. However, is it possible that one day in the future, missiologists will point to our era and say we lost our evangelistic focus in the name of a more inclusive mission? Perhaps.

This is in no way an argument for backtracking away from a holistic understanding of what God is doing in the world. It is simply a word of caution against following a trend away from the plain reading of Scripture which asks, "What good is it for someone to gain the whole world, yet forfeit their soul?"[4]

And Should We Not Be Talking about Hell?

Hell is another word that is no longer in. Hippies, hula hoops, hot pants, and hell seem to have all gone out of style at the same time. We can tell somebody to knock it out of a baseball or that a snowball wouldn't have a chance in it. We can even give it to somebody. But, with few exceptions, nobody's talking seriously about hell.

Maybe the debate between saving whales and planting churches comes down to this: Do we believe in hell? If we don't believe in hell, then ecological concerns are as easily justifiable as evangelistic concerns.

I'm not talking about brimstone and an inflamed lagoon. I'm talking about an eternal wasteland apart from the loving God, a topic about which Jesus spoke often.

The opening lines of the John Grisham novel *The Testament* are the words of a miserable billionaire. Hear his reflective words as the novel begins: "I'm an old man, lonely and unloved, sick and hurting and tired of living. I am ready for the hereafter; it has to be better than this."

This terribly unhappy man's assumption was that the end of this life would provide relief from his misery. "I am ready for the hereafter," he said, "It has to be better than this."

However, and it's a critical however, the hereafter *does not* have to be better than this!

There is a wideness to God's mercy.

And there is an amazing-ness to His grace.

But there also is a fierceness to His righteous judgment.

The realities of the next world simply have no adequate descriptors, no adequate vocabulary or categories in this world. In an attempt to describe both hell and heaven, the biblical writers, though inspired by God's Spirit, still grasped for words to communicate the incommunicable, describe the indescribable, express the inexpressible, and explain the inexplicable. We only have God-inspired metaphors for realities beyond our language.

Second Thessalonians 1:9 declares that some will be "shut out from the presence of the Lord and from the glory of his might." There are no words even in the most vast, commanding vocabulary to describe such a horror. The symbols of hell in Scripture, as in *gehenna*, are representative of realities for which there are no adequate human descriptions.

In 1741, the fiery preacher Jonathan Edwards proclaimed, "You cannot save yourselves . . . all your (goodness) would (no more) keep you out of Hell than a spider's web would stop a fallen rock." Subtlety was not Edwards's strength. He was right, however, about the "you cannot save yourselves" part. We are in desperate need of the remarkable and eternal rescue that comes through faith in Jesus. That is one of the bedrock messages of the Christian faith.

The Articulation of the Gospel

God's mission is more comprehensive than the securing of people's places in heaven. God is concerned with the whole person and the whole planet. Of course, His mission is broader than what we typically call "evangelism," and does include matters of social ministry and social justice.

However, if everything is mission then nothing is mission. And at the heart of God's mission to the world is the redemption of the lives and hearts of people. God's transformation of a life is holistic, to be sure; yet it begins with His act of pure grace by which our sins are forgiven and remembered no more, we become part of His family, we pass from death to life, our new identities are "in Christ," and we become "new creatures."

The plain reading of Scripture provides us with a description of God's mission that prioritizes proclamation regarding the eternal destiny and ultimate redemption of individuals. (See Acts 26:18; 2 Corinthians 5:20; and Luke 24:46–48, as examples.)

Such is clear from the ministry of Jesus. Though His deep concern for the marginalized is evident, and the exercise of His power to bring down oppressive strongholds is clear, His proclamation of the gospel was paramount. Bob Hopkins noted that

> Even when his disciples were pointing out to him the enormous demands of multitudes pressing for his healing ministry, it was Jesus' affirmation that he had to press on to the next place saying, "Let us go somewhere else—to the nearby villages—so that I can preach there also. That is why I have come." (Mark 1:38)[5]

Acts of compassion, struggles for justice, ministries of presence . . . all are reflective of God's character and key elements to our missions' calling. If God's ultimate desire for humankind, however, is that people cross "from death to life" (1 John 3:14), the Christian mission is not holistic until we lovingly and clearly verbalize the story of Jesus—the gospel—and His invitation to follow Him. Mission without proclamation is truncated, incomplete.

Complete Salvation

A popular topic nowadays is what N. T. Wright called "the nature and scope of salvation." Wright proposed,

> Many Christians in the Western world, for many centuries now, have seen "salvation" as meaning "going to heaven when you die." I and others have argued that is inadequate. In the Bible, salvation is not God's rescue of people *from* the world but the rescue of the world itself. . . . The salvation of human

beings, though of course extremely important for those human beings, is part of a larger purpose.[6]

Just as the kingdom of God is far greater than the human heart or the local church, salvation encompasses more than many of us might initially consider. "Salvation" (Greek *sozein*) is used in reference to the healing of soul, body, and life experience. David Bosch suggested,

> Our reflections on mission in the early church has revealed that salvation was interpreted in comprehensive terms. . . . Luke, for instance, uses "salvation language" in respect of a very wide spectrum of human circumstances—the termination of poverty, discrimination, illness, demon possession, sin, and so forth—or as Scheffler (1988) puts it, in respect of economic, social, political, physical, psychological, and spiritual suffering.[7]

If we define salvation too narrowly, the church sees its work as only "soul winning." Yet if we neglect the personal, eternal, heart element of salvation, then the church ends up with a work that is not so different from that of Goodwill, Big Brothers Big Sisters, the local food bank, or a similar nonprofit that does good deeds.

How we understand salvation will largely determine the level of our commitment to new forms of church, or at least the direction those new churches will take. David Bosch asserted, "How we define salvation determines the scope of the missionary enterprise."[8]

Salvation of Individuals for the Salvation of the World

The running debate over social justice versus evangelism versus social ministry, and its implications for how we understand salvation, is not a mere academic matter. That debate relates to our definition of *salvation*. And how we define salvation will determine the scope of our involvement in God's holistic mission.

Humankind's deepest needs stem from our innate and over-whelming tendency to do the wrong thing. Nothing is more important than sharing the gospel in relevant ways with people who are, in so many meanings of the biblical word, "lost." Of course, fallenness is not limited to the human heart; structures, institutions, families, even creation, are lost as well. Salvation is a broadly used term in the Gospels.

David Bosch wrote, "Salvation in Christ is salvation in the context of human society en route to a whole and healed world."[9] Likewise, N. T. Wright asserted that people are saved "not for themselves alone but for what God now longs to do through them. . . . He wanted . . . to rescue humans *in order that humans might be his rescuing stewards over creation*."[10] Salvation, Wright contended, "is both *for* humans and *through* saved humans, for the wider world. This is the solid basis for the mission of the church."[11]

We are saved not merely for the next world, then; we are saved for this one. We would do well to remember that God sent His Son into the world (this world) so that the world (again, *this* world), through Him, might be saved (see John 3:17).

Let's return for a moment to David Bosch. Bosch understood the centrality of personal conversion to salvation. Two pages after his above quotation he wrote, "We therefore hold on to the transcendent character of salvation also, and to the need of calling people to faith in God through Christ. Salvation does not come but along the route of repentance and personal faith commitment."[12]

Salvation is not limited to the soul and whether "if you died tonight you know where you would spend eternity." Salvation involves the whole planet and the whole person. Nevertheless, if we forget that humankind's deepest need is spiritual redemption we have distorted and limited the meaning of salvation. After all, and again, "What good is it for someone to gain the whole world, yet forfeit their soul?" (Mark 8:36). Holistic salvation is centered in genuine, personal transformation which is, in fact, the most important element to holistic salvation.

Compelled by Grace

All of us desperately need grace. That's why Fresh Expressions is about taking the church Jesus loves closer to where *the people Jesus loves* actually are.

Grace is God's unconditional, undeserved, unlimited, unrelenting love. Grace does not mean our choices are unimportant. Grace simply means that our value in God's eyes, and our place in God's heart, are not determined by our choices.

Anything less than grace is an inadequate motivation for the planting of new forms of church. Humbly dependent on grace ourselves, we are driven to share that grace with others. With no place for either sanctimony or condemnation, ours is to love unconditionally.

Self-aggrandizement, adventure, and disdain for church-as-we-know-it are poor motivations for the work of pioneering. We are at our best when we are overwhelmed by God's love for us and propelled by such a marvel toward the people Jesus loves and their life situations.

Chapter 11

THE SCANDAL OF PARTICULARITY

According to Lesslie Newbigin, "The scandal of particularity is at the center of the question of missions."[1]

It sounds harsh, of course, even to imply that faith in Jesus is the only means of entering into the kind of relationship with God that transforms our lives now and forever. More and more sincere Christ-followers reason that (1) everyone will go to heaven in the end; or (2) all who are sincerely spiritual are saved by Jesus, whether or not they know of Him or explicitly call on Him. They are not without their biblical defense. Jesus' disciple, Peter, for example, declared, "I now realize . . . that God . . . accepts from every nation the one who fears him and does what is right" (Acts 10:35). Yet it seems a stretch to claim that the context and intent of such verses, believed by some to be evidence of broad-spectrum salvation, are sufficient to refute such forthright statements in Scripture as that of Jesus: "I am the way and the truth and the life. No one comes to the Father except through me" (John 14:6).

Both Jesus Himself and God's human spokespersons such as Luke and the apostle Paul addressed a society at least as religiously pluralistic as ours, and they did not hesitate to declare faith in Jesus Christ as the sole answer to humanity's deepest need. Unique among religious figures, Jesus was, in the words of John Stott, "not just another signpost, but the destination to which the signposts had led."[2]

Incarnation

Let's return to the topic of God's incarnation to see how it might inform this conversation about the scandal of particularity.

The late John Hick, a British theologian and philosopher of religion, was one who did not believe in this "scandal of particularity." He wrote a book titled *God Has Many Names*. He was one who would say Jesus was a terrific teacher, a superb sage, and a first-class philosopher. But not God in the flesh.

Yet Hick conceded,

> If Jesus was literally God incarnate, the Second Person of the Holy Trinity living a human life, so that the Christian religion was founded by God-on-earth in person, it is then very hard to escape from the traditional view that all mankind must be converted to the Christian faith.[3]

So, if Jesus really was (is) God incarnate, then it follows logically that He is the means of our salvation. Unlike John Hick, orthodox Christians do believe that Jesus is the incarnation of God the Son, the second person of the Holy Trinity. Therefore it is logical (as well as biblical) to assume that Jesus, and He alone, is the Savior of the world.

What about God's Love?

Before Rob Bell declared *Love Wins*, Phillip Gulley and James Mulholland pondered *If Grace Is True*, a book subtitled, *Why God Will Save Every Person*. Gulley and Mulholland have come to believe that God is going to save everyone. As they experienced the pain of the members of their congregations, and as they pondered the mystery of grace, they arrived at the truth that no one will spend eternity apart from God, and everyone will be welcomed into God's presence forever.

Bell, Gulley, and Mulholland are honest. They raise tough questions. And they seem to have sincere, warm, and admirable hearts. But is their argument biblically defensible?

Newbigin again:

> We must reject the kind of rationalistic universalism that argues from the omnipotence of God's love to the necessary ultimate salvation of every soul. . . . It does not give serious attention to the freedom and responsibility that God has given to the human person. It moves in a different world of thought from that of the Bible.[4]

Gulley's and Mulholland's position comes down to not believing Jesus is who He said He is. They write (in one voice),

> I believe Jesus had a special relationship with God and an important role in human history, though I'm no longer persuaded this requires his divinity. I'm committed to living the way of Jesus, though I no longer insist "there is no other name under heaven given to mankind by which we must be saved" (Acts 4:12). . . . My understanding of Jesus has changed.[5]

Gulley and Mulholland have had a change of mind about Jesus. C. S. Lewis, however, could muster no such change. Lewis could not get around the very exclusive claims of the Bible about Jesus. C. S. Lewis was no right-wing zealot, yet he could not escape the claims of Scripture.

Lewis, in *Mere Christianity*, offered this popular summation.

> I am trying here to prevent anyone saying the really foolish thing that people often say about Him: "I'm ready to accept Jesus as a great moral teacher, but I don't accept His claim to be God." That is the one thing we must not say. A man who was merely a man and said the sort of things Jesus said would not be a great moral teacher. He would either be a lunatic—on a level with the man who says he is a poached egg—or else he would be the Devil of Hell. You must make your choice. Either this man was, and is, the Son of God: or else a madman or

something worse. You can shut Him up for a fool, you can spit at Him and kill Him as a demon; or you can fall at His feet and call Him Lord and God. But let us not come with any patronizing nonsense about His being a great human teacher. He has not left that open to us. He did not intend to.[6]

When we believe Jesus really is God in the flesh, it makes a great deal of difference. First, if Jesus is God then His words are more than just the words of an ancient sage. His teachings are not the same as those of Plato and Confucius. These are God's words, and they are divine truths worth building a life on and trusting with both life and death.

Second, if Jesus really is divine then He has the power to make a difference in our lives—to give us a radical, new beginning.

Third, what people decide to do about Jesus governs the kind of lives we live here and determines our eternal destination.

Reverent, Unassuming, Open-Minded Exclusivism

So, is explicit faith in Jesus the absolute only way to God? Is this exclusivity biblical?

The most biblically defensible stance is a reverent, unassuming, open-minded exclusivism that trusts God to do the right thing and rests in His sovereignty. That is a complicated bundle of words, but this is a complicated issue!

Reverent and *unassuming* seem to be apt terms, for, when all is said and done, this question is unanswerable by humans. Furthermore, while exclusivism is closer to the New Testament message than any other theory, nothing beyond *open-minded* exclusivism is justifiable. Like Paul, we all "see through a glass darkly."

While the New Testament stresses the importance, centrality, and influence of preaching the gospel, it is conceivable that God in His sovereignty would choose extraordinary means, such as angels, visions, or other direct revelations, to communicate the explicit truth about the life and ministry of Jesus, and the importance of His death and resurrection, to people who would not otherwise have heard the gospel. There are various stories of Muslims who have come to faith in Christ by reading the Koran, for example, and of isolated tribes who told stories of their dreams of Jesus even before Christian missionaries arrived. And it is perhaps imprudent to deny the possibility of rare occasions when persons might respond to the light available to them and be saved by Christ though they have never heard the gospel. Because the conversion of people beyond the clear presentation of the gospel is not directly taught in the Bible, however, speculation on such matters must be guarded.

It is rather irresponsible to go farther than Scripture has gone in addressing this subject. While we may leave the question in the hands of God, it is unwise to offer hope where the Bible does not offer hope.[7]

Thus we may maintain tenuous optimism that in unique circumstances and according to God's providence people are saved without explicit faith in Christ. But because the Bible does not plainly cite such a potentiality, it would be presumptuous to embrace that possibility. It is ours to live as if Jesus is the unique door to the kingdom.

Our Missionary Passion

Any position less than exclusivism tends to dampen missionary passion. Newbigin was right: "The scandal of particularity is at the center of the question of missions."[8] This question of Jesus as the way to God will shape how (and maybe *if*) we launch new forms of church. How we answer the question "Is Jesus the Only Way?" could determine whether or not we engage in God's mission at all.

While it is wrong to embrace exclusivism only because it encourages mission, the consequences of being wrong on this issue are sobering. We take upon ourselves an awesome responsibility by endorsing a concept that weakens a passion for the mission of God. David Bosch understood the importance of this issue for the missionary mandate.

Paul refrains from any unequivocal assertion of universal salvation; the thrust toward such a notion is balanced by an emphasis on responsibility and obedience for those who have heard the gospel. . . . The salvation offered by God is thus not universal in the sense that it makes human response inconsequential; "Paul fuses 'qualifiers' onto his statements about salvation such as to those 'who believe,' those 'who are in Christ,' those 'called'" (Senior and Stuhlmueller 1983: 175). There is no talk of surrendering the missionary mandate.[9]

Mystery and Trust

There is mystery here that can neither be explained nor resolved. If God has provided another means to Himself, that is His business. Yet we have to live by what we understand from Scripture, and what I understand from Scripture is that people without Jesus are indeed without God and without hope for this world and the next.

It is true that some of us have a lot easier path to Jesus than do many others. The environment into which we are born largely determines whether we will find it easy or hard to accept the claims of Jesus. And certainly the place on earth where we are born will determine even how much access we have to the gospel. I cannot unravel those mysteries. Yet of this I am absolutely confident: we can trust God to do what is right. The Bible assures us: "He is the Rock, his works are perfect, and all his ways are just. A faithful God who does no wrong, upright and just is he" (Deut. 32:4). And, "Yes, Lord God Almighty, true and just are your judgments" (Rev. 16:7).

One man of whom I know was asked, "Is everyone going to be saved in the end?" He answered, "I hope so." And I do, too! God forbid that I hope otherwise. God forbid that I hope anyone would be eternally separated from God. But to hope it, and to believe it likely, are two different things. While we can content ourselves to trust the Creator to do the right thing, we must not abdicate our clear biblical responsibility to make Jesus known.

God Himself said, "There is a way that appears to be right, but in the end it leads to death" (Prov. 16:25). Jesus is not a way, a truth, or a light among many. He is the very foundation of all that is. He is the architect and builder of the universe. Nothing is, that didn't come from Him. He is presented in Scripture as the only means of rescue from our sinfulness and the means to joining God's mission on earth.

Therefore Pilate's question, recorded in Matthew 27:22, is arguably the most important question ever asked by a human: "What shall I do, then, with Jesus who is called the Messiah?"

Alan Hirsch and Michael Frost put it like this:

> We must affirm, as do the Scriptures, that Jesus is the only way to salvation. It is a given to say that in the ideological/cultural climate of the emerging global culture, this aspect of the Christian claim is under serious threat, and it is not getting any better. When Jesus said in John 14:6, "I am the way and the truth and the life. No one comes to the Father except through me," then once again we must realize that our identities, as well as our mission, are tied to the Messiah. We agree with Peter's confession, "Lord, to whom shall we go? You have the words of eternal life" (John 6:68). We can either deny him or confess him, but we cannot avoid him. And neither can our spirituality avoid the messianic (Christocentric) nature of the New Testament faith. We sink or swim with Jesus.[10]

Chapter 12

THE WIND OF THE SPIRIT

Like the plain-looking cousin of a gorgeous debutante at a fraternity party, the Holy Spirit often gets slighted. "He prefers it that way," many contend, and they note the Spirit's role in pointing beyond Himself to Jesus (John 15:26). Yet to consider a fresh expression of church or any other missional effort without humble reliance on God's Spirit is about as futile as trying to increase one's height by worrying about it (Matthew 6:27).

This is one of the thrilling elements to this fresh expressions story. There is an unscripted, unorchestrated element of Fresh Expressions that defies human ingenuity. There is no charismatic personality, no master plan, no manual sufficient to launch, define, or manage this. It is a work, I believe, of the Holy Spirit. A movement like this is bigger than plans, personalities, and programs. It is nothing less than an act of God—a miracle of His Spirit.

We cannot manage a Spirit-inspired movement. We can only join in the work of the Spirit Who initiated it. We are merely privileged participants in this pneuma-driven mission.

The Very Key to This Movement

Bishop Graham Cray said of Fresh Expressions, "I'm going to give you the key to this movement in four words... Obey the Holy Spirit."

When we obey Him, Cray continued, the following result: (1) new imagination about the church, (2) a new climate of permission from people who might otherwise be resistant, and (3) new resources.[1]

I confess here my tendency to handle things on my own. That short-sighted, self-centered strategy consistently results in three outcomes. One, I tend to give myself credit when things go well. Two, I tend to blame myself when my expectations aren't met. And, three, I get only the results that I can produce by my own power.

One of the things I am learning through my deepening involvement in the Fresh Expressions movement is a desperate reliance on the Holy Spirit. I am learning from deeply spiritual people what can happen personally and corporately when God's Spirit is given the prominence He merits, and when we rely on Him altogether.

I am, in fact, becoming more mystical, more open to the powerful workings of the Holy Spirit. I have seen God's Spirit work mysteriously through ordinary people like me who were extraordinarily available as a conduit of His power. I am convinced that Bishop Cray was right—obeying the Holy Spirit is the key to this movement. As Lesslie Newbigin wrote, "The church is witness insofar as it follows obediently where the Spirit leads."[2]

Redemptive Surprise

The book of Acts is the story of the Holy Spirit's work of redemptive surprise. Ananias and the apostles were surprised God would use someone like Saul. The people of Jerusalem were surprised at how the Spirit instigated such a new form of church in Antioch, and how many of those people from Antioch—so different from themselves—actually turned to follow Jesus. Peter and the "circumcised believers" (Acts 11:2) were surprised at God's inclusion of Cornelius in what had been a narrowly defined family of faith. The Christians in Corinth were surprised that they had not gotten in on all the Spirit had for them (Acts 19). The Holy Spirit was (and is) surprisingly nonconformist.

Alan Roxburgh likewise noted the boundary-busting work of the Spirit in *our* time.

We can understand our own time as one in which the Spirit
of God is breaking the boundaries within which the Christian
movement has operated in the Western context. . . . The good
news is that God is doing something far bigger and more
imaginative than can be placed in these small, parochial
categories. . . . God's Spirit is breaking the boundaries of ecclesial life in the Western churches because they can no longer
contain the ways in which the Spirit is at work in the world.[3]

The Holy Spirit is again doing the work of redemptive surprise.
Surprises, by the way—what Roxburgh calls "the boundary-
breaking work of the Spirit"[4]—are not always welcomed. Surprise
is often accompanied by confusion and conflict. Such was true in
the early days of the church and is no less true today. Thus we have
a responsibility to work for unity when there is not unanimity, and
harmony when there is not unison. And we have a responsibility not
to get in the way of the Holy Spirit as He liberates the church from
its confines.

Beyond Our Control

The hope of the world lies in a movement beyond that which we can
orchestrate, manipulate, or calculate. A true movement resulting
in fresh expressions of church is beyond our imaginations and will
surpass that which we can control. The intellectual, physical, moral,
and spiritual limitations of even the most missional, faithful, and
resourceful Christ-followers render us inadequate for the task of
re-evangelizing an increasingly lost population.

Only the Spirit of our Creator can do that. Only the Holy Spirit can
fuel what Roland Allen famously called "spontaneous expansion."[5]

The power of the Holy Spirit is greater than our finite imaginations. It would be an egregious violation of the essence of Fresh
Expressions to rein in the Spirit in order to overly define and overly
regulate these new forms of church. And it would be wonderfully
liberating and empowering to simply, quoting Graham Cray again,
"obey the Holy Spirit."

Neither Behind Nor Ahead

The Spirit has wandered beyond the walls and wills of churches. That doesn't mean He has abandoned the church as we know it. It does mean the Spirit is bigger than our boundaries and beyond our categories. He is at work in conversations in the park and the coffee shop. He is at work in the factory and the office in the curious wonderings of people. We don't take God to the world; He's long since been there.

The Spirit is ahead of us.

Steven Croft noted,

> Integral to the understanding of earliest Christianity as a fresh expression is the recognition that mission was not conceived as taking the Spirit into new territory, so much as following where the Spirit was leading the way. It was openness to the Spirit moving in unexpected ways that was the key. . . . Christianity as a fresh expression is primarily a matter of keeping up with the Spirit, of following the Spirit's lead.[6]

Dawdling is tragic. Dragging our apostolic feet when the Spirit is moving is indefensible.

Likewise, it would be disastrous for us to get ahead of Him. We rely on the Spirit's timing. Leonard Sweet recalled an old saying of the sea: "'When the wind is not blowing, row.' But be careful," warned Sweet, "when the Winds of God's Spirit are not blowing, don't move."[7]

You probably will remember the story recounted in Numbers 14 about the failed attempt to take the Land of Promise. "Don't try it," Moses warned. "You blew the first opportunity God gave you, and God will not bless this effort." Yet the people stubbornly forged ahead. Alone.

Here is how the story is recorded in Numbers 14:44–45.

> Nevertheless, in their presumption they went up toward the highest point in the hill country, though neither Moses nor the ark of the LORD's covenant moved from the camp. Then the

Amalekites and the Canaanites who lived in that hill country came down and attacked them and beat them down all the way to Hormah.

So, as much as is possible for humans, we must walk in step with the Spirit of God—neither lagging slothfully behind nor bounding arrogantly ahead.

Pleading for the Pumping

Acts 1:14 describes what the disciples did while they waited in Jerusalem for the powerful unveiling of the Spirit's new role: *They all joined together constantly in prayer.*

Our prayers are not mere ritual, not mere catharsis, not mere duty. God is not so callous that He would tell us to pray and then do what He was going to do anyway. We have a voice in heaven, a say-so in what God does or does not do.[8]

What greater motivation could we have? God offers us the opportunity to plead with Him about the actual course of events on earth. There are no guarantees as we usually think of guarantees. He doesn't write us a blank check, but He says, "Know Me, and know My heart. Then ask in harmony with Who I am and I will act." This, I believe, is what it means to pray "in His name" (John 14:14).

Bob Hopkins, whom the Spirit of God has used in the transformation of countless lives across England, is a man unequivocally dependent on the Holy Spirit. Hopkins is a person of ardent prayer. He wrote,

> Prayer is the power behind evangelism. At all times we need to be talking to the Father, looking and listening for His reply, so that it is our relationship with Him that leads the way. Only God has the requisite knowledge, authority, power, and love to transform lives, so it is on God we must rely for our understanding, strength, confidence, and assurance.[9]

Without the "power behind evangelism," there is no evangelism.

Stuart Briscoe wrote about a famous organist who, in the 1880s, traveled the country giving concerts. (Those were the days of the reed organ. Large organs required someone besides the organist to pump air into the organ.) In every venue this famous organist would hire a boy to pump during the concert. After one performance the young pumper said to the organ player, "Well, we had a great concert tonight, didn't we?"

"*I* had a great concert," replied the organist rather arrogantly.

The next night, in the same concert hall with the same boy pumping, right in the middle of the concert the organ faded out. The little boy who'd been pumping the organ, had stopped. The boy grinned, and called to the man at the keyboard, "*We* aren't having a very good concert tonight, are *we?*"[10]

We can study the theory. We can memorize the melody. We can strike the keys. But if God Spirit isn't pumping, if you will, there is no music. Without the miraculous, mysterious blessing of the Holy Spirit, then we are going through the motions, marking time. And the stakes are too high to let that happen.

Chapter 13

WHAT IS A CHURCH?

Some of the most important questions raised by the Fresh Expressions movement center on church: Are these fresh expressions really church, or are they *missional communities* or something like that? And what is the difference? Can uncredentialed laypersons legitimately serve and lead a full-blown church? How should denominations relate to these new churches? And, perhaps most important, What *is* a church?

Someone might argue that fresh expressions of church are a new species altogether, and need a different name than "church." Millard J. Erickson noted that potential.

> If the definition of the church is to undergo frequent change in order to relate it to the modern world, in what sense is there continuity with what has preceded? Or, in other words, why continue to call it the church? What is the common thread identifying the church throughout all the changes? Is it not likely that at some point a different term should be applied? Consider the field of biological evolution. When a new species develops from an existing species, a new name is assigned. Biologists do not apply the old name to the new species. That name is reserved for the members of the old species. . . . Yet it is being argued that while the church is changing and must

change, very radically perhaps, it is to continue to be called the church. But if it is to continue to be called the church, we must know just what it is that distinguishes the church as the church, or qualifies it to be called the church.[1]

So why do we insist on the term, "fresh expressions *of church*?" Are they really *churches*? And how do we *know* whether we can call them churches? Should we come up with a new name besides *church*? Without a clear understanding of church, attempts to decide whether a new form of church (or historic form, for that matter) is church at all will boil down merely to personal, preconceived notions.

One of the unintended (and positive) consequences of the Fresh Expressions movement is that we all have been nudged into a discussion about the biblical essence of church. It is fairly simple to talk about the functions of church and, pragmatic as most of us are, that is where we tend to start (and end). To speak of the functions of the church without a grasp of its nature, however, seems like getting the proverbial cart before the horse.

Neil Cole, in talking about new forms of church, made a provocative statement: "We must lower the bar of how we do church and raise the bar on what it means to be a disciple."[2] In the context of fresh expressions it is hard to even talk about the appropriateness of lowering the bar, or even to consider what that might mean, without a basic understanding of what the bar is. We have to ask, what is a church?

So let's first consider the biblical essence of church and, I hope, settle this matter of whether a fresh expression is, in the biblical sense of the word, a church.[3]

Essence, or Nature, of Church

Our word for "church," according to linguists, is rooted in the Old Testament Hebrew word *qahal*, meaning, "the assembly of God's people."[4] The Greek word in the New Testament, which we eventually translated into English as "church" is *ekklesia*, meaning "called out ones." This word is used to denote both a local congregation and the universal communion of Christ-followers.[5] The *ekklesia*, then, is the community (whether local or universal) of those called by God. God has taken the initiative here, and it by His grace that any are called. That He would call us, by His Spirit and His Word, is a gift of grace.

Rowan Williams, then archbishop of Canterbury, blessed the beginnings of the Fresh Expressions movement in a number of ways. Among them was his reminder of the core meaning of church. He described church in terms of relationships. In his foreword to *Mission-Shaped Church*, he wrote that *church* "is what happens when people encounter the Risen Jesus and commit themselves to sustaining and deepening that encounter in their encounter with each other."[6]

It is in relationships that we discover the nature of church. In the Fresh Expressions movement it is often said that the essence of church is found in the four relationships to which we so often refer: Up, In, Out, and Of. Michael Moynagh, for example, argued persuasively that church is best understood not in terms of its functions, but in terms of its relationships. These relationships, Moynagh contended, are the "defining features of the church."[7]

In Fresh Expressions circles, these relationships are described like this:

UP: Worship of God and participation in the Trinitarian community of Father, Son, and Spirit.

IN: Discipleship and fellowship within the community.

OUT: Loving service to the world through mission, ministry, and evangelism.

OF: Identifying with and participating with the universal body of believers. (The word "catholic," as in "one holy catholic and apostolic" implies an identity with both the universal body of believers today and a place in the line of Christian congregations since first-century Jerusalem.)[8] That identity can be a subtle recognition of the connection to other churches or can be more tangible through affiliation with a denomination or informal partnerships.

Each of these relationships is indispensable. All are intertwined. The whole lot are critical. Without the full complement of these relationships a group of people, as fine a Christian group as it might be, is less than church.

Marks of the Church

The familiar characterization (marks) of the church as "one holy catholic and apostolic" is traced to the Council of Constantinople (AD 381) and the Council's expansion of the Nicene Creed from AD 325. This declaration affirms the unity, sanctity, universality, and missionality of the Christian community. For our purposes here, it will be helpful to dig a bit deeper specifically into the word "apostolic."

For our Roman Catholic brothers and sisters, "apostolic" refers to, among other things, the belief in apostolic succession, meaning spiritual authority that is traced back to the apostles and passed down through the selection of bishops. Protestants view this differently, preferring to affirm that the church is, in the words of Ephesians 2:20, "built on the foundation of the apostles and prophets, with Christ Jesus himself as the chief cornerstone." "Built on the foundation" does not, in the Protestant view, apply to some sort of authority passed down through individuals but, rather, that the mission and message of the apostles are the mission and message of the church in all places and all times.

The early Protestant statement of faith, the Augsburg Confession of 1530, defined the church as "the congregation of saints in which the gospel is purely taught and the sacraments are rightfully administered." Reformed churches soon added to the definition: "Discipline is exercised."[9] While we can appreciate the depth and accuracy of that definition, and the context in which it was birthed, it is inadequate for the purpose of determining whether a fresh expression of church is, indeed, a church.

In the spirit of the Fresh Expressions movement (drawing from the global and historic nature of the faith), we now move to a definition of church and, by doing so, affirm the aptness of defining these fresh expressions as fresh expressions of *church*. We may call a fresh expression a "church," then, if it is a **community of people transformed by the resurrected Jesus, committed to each other, growing together toward the likeness of Jesus, corporately celebrating the glory of our Creator, teaching the Word of God, baptizing and** celebrating Communion, serving the world through holistic mission, and identifying as a member of the universal family of Christ-followers.[10]

Mature Church

Of course a fresh expression of church might not yet be church in its maturity. A weekly gathering of restaurant workers, for example, for the purpose of discussing faith and life, might not yet exhibit the full complement of marks of a church. Yet they have the DNA of church. As a pastor once asked me regarding fresh expressions of church, "Is a sprig not a tree? It has all the makings of a tree," he continued, "but only in a not-yet-mature form!" It's a great observation! Isn't a sprig really a tree in its infancy? His point was clear: a fresh expression of church has all the elements of church in its DNA and simply needs time to mature. Or, as Moynagh likes to say, the shallow end of a swimming pool is still the swimming pool; it's just not the deep end.[11]

Thus, some fresh expressions of church are still developmental—carrying the full potential for church but still in process. We could debate the semantics of whether a fresh expression in its infancy is qualified to bear the name "church," or perhaps should be considered a church-in-progress. Yet the following *is* clear: a mature fresh expression, demonstrating all the marks of a church, is as much church as any inherited, existing, more conventional church anywhere.

Moynagh reminded us that measuring a new church's maturity is not necessarily dependent upon how much it looks like its "mother." He quoted George Lings: "Maturity is not necessarily becoming like your parents. It is growing into what you are." Moynagh continued, "We would expect the birth of a church to bring something new into the tradition, just as children make distinctive contributions to the family and beyond."[12]

It is a grave error, then, to disregard one of these new forms of church as less than church simply because it does not fit our existing categories or conceptions of church. Church is not defined by its structure, its worship style, its day or place of worship, its ministerial leadership's credentials, or by so many of the forms we so often associate with church. Any group centered on the resurrected Lord Jesus and exhibiting the upward, inward, outward, and "of-ward" relationships spoken of here is fully church.

Categorizing Fresh Expressions of Church

Parameters, so long as they are biblical parameters, are helpful. Some traditions are constrained, however, by limited categories. For example, a pioneer of a fresh expression I know went to his denomination to seek recognition as a church. (For many pioneers, of course, it is still important to be legitimized by a denominational body.) But the community of faith this pioneer leads does not fit any of the categories on his denomination's list. Therefore, they still view his group as a "mission point," or an "outreach ministry." They simply have no slot in which to fit his church. So he and the people of the fresh expression miss out on the affirmation that comes with recognition, and the denomination (the biggest loser in the deal) misses out on the opportunity to spotlight and encourage new forms of church for a new world.

Archbishop Williams reminded us of the value of flexibility in our characterizations of Christian communities.

> If "church" is what happens when people encounter the Risen Jesus and commit themselves to sustaining and deepening that encounter in their encounter with each other, there is plenty of theological room for diversity of rhythm and style, so long as we have ways of identifying the same living Christ at the heart of every expression of Christian life in common.[13]

Church and Kingdom

Max De Pree, former CEO of the Herman Miller furniture company, wrote that once he and his wife and another couple were driving along a coastal road in England. They were driving alongside a body of water, but they weren't sure what they were seeing, so they pulled over and asked. Depree rolled his window down and asked a British lady who was walking alongside the road, "Excuse me, ma'am, is that the English Channel?"

The lady glanced over her shoulder at the water and answered, "Well, that's *part* of it."[14]

So take a look at the photos in your church directory. Is that the kingdom of God? Well, that is *part* of it!

The kingdom of God—God's purposeful, effective, and complete reign—is larger than the church, yet the church is the key player in the kingdom. Moreover, the church is the fullest expression of the kingdom in our world.

People should be able to look at a Christian community and, at least, say, "They're certainly not perfect, they're not really my type, and I'm not sure I believe what they believe. But if what they have is half of a glimpse of a believable future, I want to know more."[15]

The church is not the sole proprietor of, yet is far more than a casual participant in, God's kingdom. The kingdom of God is to be modeled in, but not limited to, the church.

The church is

- Mission outpost of the kingdom
- Cornerstone of the kingdom
- Major stockholder in the kingdom
- Base of operations for the kingdom
- Welcomer of the kingdom
- Ambassador of the kingdom
- Best image on earth of the kingdom

Since the 1960s we've been talking about the *missio Dei*, the mission of God. We do that not simply because we want to sound scholarly; the term actually helps us remember two key truths. One, the mission of which we speak is not ours; it's God's. Mission is a reflection of God's very nature, and is neither the idea nor the possession of the church. Two, God is beyond the church. His kingdom is not limited to the spiritual family who represents Him.

Of course, "not limited to" should not be read "completely apart from." The church is God's primary agent of His mission to planet earth. Yet He *is* at work *beyond* the church. Where people of multiple faiths battle human trafficking, for example, or when people of no faith build an orphanage in a war-torn land, there is the kingdom of God. Not in its fullness, I would argue. As someone said, "The Kingdom is not in its fullness without the announcing of the King." Yet God is at work beyond the church. Therefore the church fulfills its purpose not merely by *being*, but by joining God in His mission and, as the new Israel, being a blessing to the world (Genesis 12:2).

The church is both *sent to* the world and *embedded within* it—both a *recipient* of the redeeming work of God's Spirit and an *instrument* of the redeeming work of God's Spirit.

God is at work uniquely, but not exclusively, in and through your congregation. The world beyond the church walls is neither useless, hopeless, nor God-less. We might be surprised to see what God is doing out there—beyond the places we expect Him to work—if we would get out there more often.

Church and Mission

While "mission" and "church" are not synonymous, "church" cannot be described apart from mission. Perhaps you've heard the famous quote by Emil Brunner: "The Church exists by mission, just as a fire exists by burning. Where there is no mission, there is no Church."[16] Mission is not marginal; it is essential to the church's nature.

The centrality of mission seems to have gathered new steam in the last couple of decades. We seem to be experiencing what David Bosch called "an almost imperceptible shift from an emphasis on a church-centered mission . . . to a mission-centered church."[17]

This is a welcomed shift, and a reminder that mission is not something we do as a nice add-on. Church finds its very reason for being in the mission of God.

The Functions of the Church

As we consider what a true church *does*, 1 Peter 2:9–10 is a good beginning point.

> But you are a chosen people, a royal priesthood, a holy nation, God's special possession, that you may declare the praises of him who called you out of darkness into his wonderful light. Once you were not a people, but now you are the people of God; once you had not received mercy, but now you have received mercy.

We are reminded here that the church is a people born out of the mercy of God—called out (*ekklesia*) by God due not to our own merit but as a divine gift.

We also see in 1 Peter 2:9–10 the *priestly* and *missionary* functions of the church. Members of the church ("a royal priesthood") are to be priests to each other and to have a pastoral role in His world. When John Wesley said, "I look upon the world as my parish,"[18] he was reflecting the priestly function of the church in the world. It is our calling to minister to, and mediate on behalf of, God's creation. There is also a missionary function reflected in 1 Peter 2:9, to declare God's wonderful deeds and, by implication here, spread the word that God calls people "out of darkness into his wonderful light."[19]

There have been multiple efforts to unpack the description of the church in the New Testament and, from that, establish the biblical functions of today's church. In his popular book, *Purpose Driven Church*, Rick Warren looked to Acts 2:42–47 and found five functions of the church: worship, fellowship, ministry, evangelism, and discipleship. Those five purposes, or roles, of the church, are widely recognized.[20] A Christ-centered group becomes church, many would affirm, when they fulfill those roles. Without the fulfillment of those roles, we might say, that Christ-centered group is merely a circle of Christians. With the fulfillment of these roles, along with the relationships noted above (up, in, out, and of), a Christian community is *church*.

Fresh Energy, Fresh Initiatives, Fresh Expressions

Before we leave this topic of church, it will be helpful to remember a brief, but important, point: everything novel and creative is not a fresh expression of church.

Our friends in the UK realized that some churches were claiming they had begun a fresh expression of church when, in fact, they had launched a new ministry, or mission project. Leaders of the Fresh Expressions UK movement realized that, while all missional initiatives should be celebrated, it would not be helpful for churches to apply the fresh expressions label too widely.

Therefore, they established three categories as a means of clarifying the meaning of "fresh expressions." Those three categories are: Fresh Energy, Fresh Initiatives, and Fresh Expressions.[21] Loosely defined, *fresh energy* would be a sense of renewal or new excitement in a congregation centered on an outwardly focused theme. A *fresh initiative* would be a creative effort to engage people outside the church's walls, such as a homeless ministry or a food pantry, a Bible study for those in the hospitality industry, or a worship service during the vacation months in a resort area. A *fresh expression* is a new form of *church*. It has the "upward, inward, outward, and of-ward" relationships discussed above. It fulfills the functions of a church (worship, fellowship, ministry, evangelism, and discipleship). It is an ongoing community that a participant would identify as "my church." It is, by the criteria discussed in this chapter, *church*.

It seems clear, then, that fresh expressions of church are genuinely "church." They are not (recalling Erickson's analogy from earlier) a new species in the evolution of Christian community. They are more than a collection of like-minded people with a common purpose. They are churches.

These new forms of church often look very different from our notions of church, but if they bear the biblical marks of church, they are churches indeed.[22] They take their rightful and honorable place in the worldwide fellowship of congregations.

Chapter 14

LUKE, ACTS, AND A BIBLICAL DIRECTION

Some have noted that today's Western cultures look more like the world of the early church than has been true in almost two millennia. Likewise, the Fresh Expressions movement looks much like the early church. Loose, ill-defined organization. Team leadership. Christian faith not the dominant worldview. Passionate believers. New believers, often first-generation believers. Reliance . . . intense reliance . . . on the Spirit of God.

Remember the story of the early church: from a circle of unpolished novices to a band of 120 frightened hopefuls to a church of thousands. From the established Jewish community to a multi-ethnic family of faith. All within a few short years.

These were not progressions, these were quantum leaps. This was not the evolution of the church, it was the explosion of the church. Across cultural boundaries, ethnicities, and centuries-old traditions, the Holy Spirit fast-tracked the church. Things happened in dizzying fashion and the advance of the kingdom could be attributed to nothing less than the combustible power of the Spirit of God.

Two Texts from the Pen of Luke

There are two texts from the pen of Luke (the author of both the Gospel that bears his name and the book of Acts) that are particularly instructive for us in this movement called Fresh Expressions: the sending of the seventy in Luke 10:1–12, and the story of the churches in Jerusalem and Antioch recorded in Acts 11–15.

We begin with the story in Luke 10.

Luke 10

In Luke 10 there is a story that helps us as we think of penetrating a world much different from our church world. There we see Jesus sending out His disciples in teams of two with the purpose of planting themselves among new friends and developing relationships, finding persons of peace, performing signs and wonders in His name, and, sometimes, failing and moving on to the next opportunity.

This is the text.

> After this the Lord appointed seventy-two others and sent them two by two ahead of him to every town and place where he was about to go. He told them, "The harvest is plentiful, but the workers are few. Ask the Lord of the harvest, therefore, to send out workers into his harvest field. Go! I am sending you out like lambs among wolves. Do not take a purse or bag or sandals; and do not greet anyone on the road.
>
> "When you enter a house, first say, 'Peace to this house.' If someone who promotes peace is there, your peace will rest on them; if not, it will return to you. Stay there, eating and drinking whatever they give you, for the worker deserves his wages. Do not move around from house to house.
>
> "When you enter a town and are welcomed, eat what is offered to you. Heal the sick who are there and tell them, 'The kingdom of God has come near to you.' But when you enter a town and are not welcomed, go into its streets and say, 'Even the dust of your town we wipe from our feet as a warning to you.' . . .
>
> Whoever listens to you listens to me; whoever rejects you rejects me; but whoever rejects me rejects him who sent me."
>
> The seventy-two returned with joy and said, "Lord, even the demons submit to us in your name." He replied, "I

saw Satan fall like lightning from heaven. I have given you authority to trample on snakes and scorpions and to overcome all the power of the enemy; nothing will harm you. However, do not rejoice that the spirits submit to you, but rejoice that your names are written in heaven." (Luke 10:1–11; 16–20)

This is an important text for the Fresh Expressions movement. It is descriptive of an approach that can be effective in our own context. We do not assume it is prescriptive; we understand the differences, for example, in travel customs. Yet this text is descriptive in a way that can inspire and instruct us. The underlying principles are instructive as we try to engage people as potentially resistant as those among whom Jesus sent His disciples.

They were to go humbly. Jesus instructed them not to take a lot of stuff with them. This made them largely dependent on the hospitality of those among whom they now would move. This would necessitate conversations in which the disciples would not be *offering* something, at least not at first.

They would live among the people. They would not sit among themselves and decide what "those people out there" need. They would ask questions, seek input, and see people as *people* instead of as a *target audience.*

We can imagine meals together, conversations into the night, each learning about the other. We can imagine relationships taking on greater depth than merely that of guest and host. We can imagine the disciple of Jesus lying down at the end of an evening of discussion and thinking, *I never would have known that! What an interesting insight into this culture. I wonder where the good news of Jesus intersects with the worldview and needs of these people.*

Luke 10 helps us think about what it might be like if we were to actually get beyond the strategic planning meetings of our churches and disabuse ourselves of the idea that we already know what people think and need and how to reach them. Luke 10 speaks of the ambassadors of Jesus actually sitting with strangers to talk.

Many churches I know remind me of a missionary compound that perhaps you can imagine with me—a residential community of missionaries in some exotic, foreign land—surrounded by a high and foreboding wall inside of which the customs seem strange to the locals on the outside.

Imagine it with me: flyers are stapled to the outside of the compound's wall inviting people in to events. Missionaries on the inside maintain a cutting edge website and even tweet about their beliefs and programs. From time to time the bravest of the missionaries actually venture outside the walls and, in a broken version of the local language, invite people to events inside the compound.

Until one day . . . someone has the wild idea . . . that maybe they should move outside the walls and become dependent upon local people—learning the language, receiving hospitality, risking difficult spiritual conversations, actually beginning to feel at home outside the compound walls.

Now *that* is incarnation of the Luke 10 variety.[1]

They would announce the kingdom of God and heal the sick. In Luke 10, Jesus' ambassadors were to articulate a Jesus-centered message. Their very lives were reflections of their time with Jesus. Furthermore, at the appropriate time, in the appropriate way, they would speak of those matters of eternal significance. Not according to some predetermined method, but as a natural conversation. And it would have been a two-way conversation about spiritual matters, not a standardized, memorized, homogenized evangelistic presentation.

They would not simply be present and would not simply do good things. They would speak of Jesus as the answer to humankind's greatest need, and note, in whatever ways outsiders could, the structures they saw as inconsistent with the reign and intentions of God for His world.

They also were to heal the sick. That's where many of us get nervous. There are probably lots of people reading this who are thinking, *I might be open to planting a new form of church but I'm not interested in a healing ministry.*

We are certainly wise to be cautious of the counterfeits, false claims, and abuses. However, to be open to God's miraculous work among us and through us seems only right.

Matthew 8 records this exchange between a leper and Jesus: "'Lord, if you are willing, you can make me clean.' Jesus reached out his hand and touched the man. 'I am willing,' he said. 'Be clean!' Immediately he was cleansed of his leprosy" (vv. 2–3). If we were to pray with sincere hearts, "Lord, if You are willing, we ask that You perform Your miraculous healing," perhaps we would be, as Jack Deere titled his book, "surprised by the power of the Holy Spirit."[2]

They would be willing to fail. Maybe "shaking the dust off your feet and move on" is a way of saying "failure is an option."

I became involved in the Fresh Expressions movement because the tall steeple church I served as pastor began three fresh expressions of church (one before I arrived). Our church began a fresh expression of church for people in recovery and another for the international community. The third fresh expression out of that church sought to engage the prostitute community.

For more than three years several of us had gone out one Friday night each month, talking and praying with anyone who would talk and pray with us, but focusing on the prostitutes. We didn't shame them. We didn't flog them with our leather-bound copies of the King James Version of Scripture. We just talked with them and asked them, "Are you safe? Is there anything we can pray for?" We would quietly slip them a card with three phone numbers on it—numbers to call in case they wanted to try and escape the lifestyle in which they were trapped.

Valerie Carter, the leader of our team and a pioneer, attended a Fresh Expressions Vision Day and God gave her a dream. "Why don't we start a fresh expression of church for the prostitutes?" she asked. So she led a handful of female team members to begin *Wendy's on Wednesday*—a fresh expression of church meeting on Wednesday afternoon in the dining room of the Wendy's near the area of town where we often met the prostitutes. In that Wendy's dining room ladies read Scripture together. Once they spent an hour talking about Psalm 139:14 and how they are "fearfully and wonderfully made." They would pray for each other and speak of God's goodness together. It was church in its infancy.

But, ultimately, Wendy's on Wednesday didn't "make it." After a year, participation was so spotty that often no one showed up. So Valerie Carter and the team thanked God for what they'd seen in the year and, instead of meeting on Wednesdays, started going to the streets *two* Friday nights per month. At this writing they are still praying about what the next step toward an ongoing community of faith there might look like.

All that to say that in the enterprising world of fresh expressions, it is certain that many ventures will not live up to our expectations.

Pioneers are going to have to understand that, and those of us in established churches are going to have to bless that. "Failure is an option" was once the motto for Domino's Pizza, indicating its willingness to try all manner of new things until it hit on the dish that would dazzle our taste buds. "Failure is an option" is not a bad motto for new forms of church.

This speaks to the powerful opportunity we have in established churches to bless the spiritual entrepreneurs among us, to endorse their holy risks and not insist on some sort of bottom line. We can encourage their experiments and vouch for them when others disparage their model. We can be patient until these pioneers truly know if what they are doing is working and, if they determine their efforts are not effective, we can encourage them and help them discern God's next step for them.

We need leaders of existing churches who are willing to create a missional atmosphere in the congregations they lead. *And* we need to bless and release those with the unique giftings and callings to create new wineskins.

Jerusalem and Antioch

Many of us see in the story of Jerusalem and Antioch an example of the mixed economy—an established church and a fresh expression. Chapters 11-15 of Acts tell the story of two congregations: (1) the established, inherited, resourced congregation attracting new Jewish believers in Jerusalem and (2) the creative, flexible congregation engaging Greeks in Antioch. In the story of these two churches is the complicated but beautiful story of inherited churches and fresh expressions of church.[3] In Steven Croft's foundational work on Fresh Expressions, *Mission-Shaped Questions*, is the following about Jerusalem and Antioch: "The relationship between these two churches plays out all the tensions between fresh expression and continuing church. The foundation of the Antioch church in 11:19–21 is a classic fresh expression."[4]

Jerusalem and today's inherited church

It takes little imagination to see Jerusalem as a model for today's inherited church. The church was founded by faithful believers and flourished by the power of God's Spirit, often at great sacrifice by its members. It valued its Jewish traditions and enjoyed the stability of substantial roots.

The Jerusalem congregation witnessed the conversion of multitudes of people, had a rich history, could be appropriately proud of its spiritual heroes, was very Jewish, and was grateful for the spread of the gospel beyond its context, and yet found such strength in tradition that it could be said to have been shackled by traditionalism.

We should be slow to condemn our ecclesiastical ancestors in Jerusalem. It is unfair to label them as stonewalling progress. Think about it: many of *our* traditions are young in comparison. Sunday school, for example, is only two hundred years old in America. Many of the gospel hymns over which many a worship war have been fought were written in the 1700s and 1800s. Even the Protestant Reformation is only five centuries old for us. The Jewish Law, however, had been around *fifteen hundred years* by the time the Jerusalem church was born.

We look back and might wonder why so many of the Christians in Jerusalem were so obstinate, so selfish, and so unbending. Yet we need to be a bit more understanding of our spiritual ancestors in that first-century Jerusalem church. After all, we have been obstinate, stubborn, and unbending over practices much younger than the Jewish Law was for them.

Beyond the constraints

In Acts 9–11 God is seen breaking out of the confines constructed by well-meaning but myopic people. The church in Antioch sprang up out of the ground bearing faint resemblance to its older sister in Jerusalem. Acts 11:20–21 tell us, "Men from Cyprus and Cyrene, went to Antioch and began to speak to Greeks also, telling them the good news about the Lord Jesus. The Lord's hand was with them, and a great number of people believed and turned to the Lord." New converts to the Way went to Antioch and crossed the ethnic boundary. No longer were Jews the target audience. A mission to the Gentiles was born and Antioch was its incubator.

The congregation in Antioch was more diverse ethnically than Jerusalem, and the blending of cultures resulted in a model of church that was, at best, surprising to the folks in Jerusalem. Because the new believers did not come primarily out of the Jewish faith, this new form of church was less bound by traditions. They read Scripture with new lenses. The Antioch church enjoyed the flexibility and vibrancy that come with upstarts.

Tension

Not surprisingly, there were some tensions between the two. (New offshoots of established organizations often cause people angst.) The people in Jerusalem and Antioch had different ideas about the importance of Jewish traditions, for example, and probably had different ideas about how involved the people in Jerusalem should be in Antioch's affairs. The people in Jerusalem were likely skeptical of such a loosely defined church which had an apparent disregard for sacred tradition.

The relationship was messy. The Jerusalem Christians wondered why their beloved brothers and sisters to the north believed they could violate the time-honored model of church which had served Jerusalem so well. The Antioch Christians wondered why their beloved brothers and sisters to the south didn't mind their own ecclesiastical business.

While Barnabas, being the encourager that he was, probably was sent to nurture those at Antioch, there was that brouhaha over circumcision. Read this pregnant passage from Acts 15.

Certain people came down from Judea to Antioch and were teaching the believers: "Unless you are circumcised, according to the custom taught by Moses, you cannot be saved." This brought Paul and Barnabas into sharp dispute and debate with them. So Paul and Barnabas were appointed, along with some other believers, to go up to Jerusalem to see the apostles and elders about this question. The church sent them on their way. (vv. 1-3)

From that terse passage we see a clash of cultures, raw emotion, convictions, and defiance. It would be interesting to know all the conversations behind such words as "sharp dispute and debate." And when the congregation at Antioch "sent them on their way," I imagine they gave Paul and Barnabas some choice phrases to share with the good folks in Jerusalem.

Yet they needed each other

Of course it wasn't all bad. The concern on the part of Jerusalem for the orthodoxy of Antioch was, no doubt, genuine. The Christians in Antioch received Paul and Barnabas well, probably because they sensed in these two men a sincere concern for the well-being of the new church. The Antiochians' response to the Jerusalemites appears to have been respectful, even somewhat deferential.

The church in Antioch expressed their connectivity to Jerusalem by taking up an offering after a preacher from Jerusalem encouraged them to contribute for the needs of an impending famine. Moreover, although they were offended by what was considered meddling by the Jerusalem church, they did not cut themselves off from Jerusalem. Instead, they sent Paul and Barnabas down to see if they could work things out.

Not to be missed is the fact that Antioch had advocates in the Jerusalem church, and the advocates' role in the Jerusalem church must not be undervalued. People respected by the established congregation spoke on behalf of the new thing. The Jerusalem congregation was moved by the reports of Paul and Barnabas and followed the leadership of Peter and James in blessing the flexibility of this new form of church up in Antioch that still seemed so strange to them. They were eventually wise enough to see how the negotiable, peripheral practices—important as they were to the Jewish Christians in Jerusalem—were unnecessarily impeding the new expression of faith in Antioch.

People in existing churches today often will struggle to appreciate the new and unpredictable churches. The more seasoned church members will worry about the orthodoxy, be puzzled by the methodology, and sometimes question the sanity, of those who begin new works. Existing churches who sponsor fresh expressions will sometimes have to fight the temptation to withdraw their support. In those times, it is stalwarts in the established church who will need to defend and justify the newfangled efforts of the fresh expressions of church. Like James, Paul, and Barnabas, these defenders of the new churches will have to go to bat for them. The role of the champions in existing churches in the launching of new churches is critical.

Jerusalem and Antioch needed each other. The stability and depth of Jerusalem, together with the rather cutting edge evangelistic ministry of Antioch, provided effective outreach to a world hearing of Jesus for the first time.

Chris Backert spoke of the mutually beneficial relationship of these two, very different, churches, and how the Spirit of God blessed these rather untidy circumstances.

> The Holy Spirit uses the fresh expression, and the work coming from it—to not only reach beyond where the church currently is (to reach people that would never darken the doors of the church at Jerusalem or those like it), but to pull the existing church into the future. This happens because a relationship exists between what is happening out on the edge of mission and what is happening in the center of the church.
>
> And it is for the betterment of both communities. The church at Jerusalem, its leaders, and its people (even the Pharisees who were present) are all changed through this . . . and of course . . . that impact is not limited to Jerusalem. Antioch is also changed as they are pulled more substantively into the roots of the church and God's work throughout time

and the scriptural and theological basis for doing what they are doing. They are also emboldened by this for further mission because it is affirmed that the Gentiles could receive the faith as gentiles (in other words—in their own context). And as a result they send out Paul again—this time with Silas—to reach even further into the unreached territory.[5]

A new approach required?

We could argue, for the sake of argument, whether the Jerusalem church even had the *capacity* to reach the Greeks. Even if they had the will, the desire, and the passion for people unlike them and without Jesus, *could* they have engaged them effectively? Perhaps we can agree that it would have been difficult. Perhaps, one could argue, it was best for a new kind of church to try such radical things, saving the existing church the pain of potential division and even implosion.

One could also argue that there are many congregations today who simply are incapable of crossing cultural barriers. Most congregations do have limits. We can reach people who are a *little bit* different from us, but the approaches required to engage those really far from us can only be attempted by agile, adaptable, new forms of church.

A Word of Hope for Today

The trends noted in the early chapters of this book are alarming. There is anxiety over declining participation and the absence of young adults and children in our churches.

But could all this cultural and spiritual upheaval end up being a catalyst for helpful new directions in church? Could the result of the shakeup be genuine spiritual renewal for our continent?

There was certainly anxiety in Jerusalem over the persecution that led to so many of their members scattering. Yet note the wonderful happenings that resulted.

Now those who had been scattered by the persecution that broke out when Stephen was killed traveled as far as Phoenicia,

Cyprus and Antioch, spreading the word only among Jews. Some of them, however, men from Cyprus and Cyrene, went to Antioch and began to speak to Greeks also, telling them the good news about the Lord Jesus. The Lord's hand was with them, and a great number of people believed and turned to the Lord. (Acts 11:19–21)

Could not a similar thing happen in our time? This is not to suggest that God is turning people's hearts against Him. But perhaps He is going to use the upheaval in our culture to dismantle our structures, to deprogram our assumptions, and to deflate our egos so that church will, perhaps in our anguish, be open to letting the wind of the Holy Spirit blow in and through us in new ways. We are already seeing beautiful new partnerships between denominations; we are now focusing on our common mission.

Furthermore, fresh expressions of church are seeing people come to faith in Jesus who likely never would even be open to attending church as we know it. These could be, by God's grace, the incipient days of true revitalization. From the ashes of Christendom could come the phoenix of a new and stronger church and the transformation of masses of people.[6] Just as Antioch became a missionary center, perhaps in the next several decades these new forms of church will emerge as the evangelistic seedbeds of North America.

As in the days of the earliest church, God is moving us (admittedly, sometimes at a pace and in directions we might not choose on our own) beyond our present limited categories and imaginations. There is reason for hope.

A Fresh Expressions Story

R CHURCH

Following is a story about a fresh expression of church. As you read it, note the various stages we are about to study.

1. Listening
2. Loving and Serving
3. Building Community
4. Exploring Discipleship
5. Church Taking Shape

The stages might sometimes seem to overlap, for the steps toward a fresh expression of church are often not sequential.

Matt Senger was a youth minister who sensed a clear call from God to plant a church in his own neighborhood. But this would not be your typical church plant. Matt began by listening to what people in his neighborhood were saying. He explained how he got started: "I just started hanging out with people from the neighborhood I already knew. I told them I felt like God wanted me to pull people together to talk about what is going on in the world."

The first thing they did was to love and serve their neighbors by hosting a lot of cookouts and neighborhood events. Matt, his wife, and another couple walked the neighborhood and prayed. The four of them met regularly for planning, discipleship, and fellowship.

Matt and friends never hid the fact that they were hoping to start a church, even if it was obvious it wouldn't be your normal, everyday church. For example, one flyer they distributed to publicize a fall cookout read, "We will start with prayer and the Harts will be sharing a short story of faith followed by a reading from the Bible. After that there will be plenty of food for everyone." Not every flyer was so overt. Nor did every event include a faith story and reading from the Bible. Once Matt just said, "Hey, we love you and love God and believe if He were here He'd want you to have a good time. Let's eat!" A sense of real community began to build.

Matt's strategy began to shift when he suggested to the original, core group, "Let's take these neighbors we've met at all these big events and make disciples out of them." They decided to have smaller gatherings—dinners in Matt's house—where they would read biblical texts and Matt would talk about them. While fifty to seventy-five still come to the larger gatherings, these dinner talks draw about twenty-five.

Now a regular group of folks are on their way to Jesus together. A few are reconnecting with church for the first time in a long time. Others have made decisions to follow Jesus and are in the process of expressing it. Several more are still considering that important step. Together they make up R Church. It is a new form, a fresh expression, of church.

Part Three

FRESH EXPRESSIONS (NEW FORMS) OF CHURCH

Chapter 15

A FASCINATING, ENCOURAGING STORY

Over the centuries, from the monastic movement to the Reformation to base communities to house churches and cell churches, many creative and novel forms have given new expression to the church. This relatively new Fresh Expressions movement is in an admirable line of creative ventures.

"We Are from Your Future"

Those of us outside of England have the advantage of learning from our courageous brothers and sisters there. England's trend away from church participation is generally thought to be some years beyond lands like the US.[1] (Thus Bob and Mary Hopkins, Anglican church planters working in England, spoke in the US in 2010 and said, "We are from your future.") So, if the spiritual demographics of other lands are going to soon follow those of England, we would do well to pay attention to what God is doing there to reverse the alarming tide.

American Thomas Brackett wrote that, when he asked his British brothers and sisters for advice, they answered,

> Start now—don't wait until you have all this figured out. Experiment joyfully and publicly with new forms of ministry

that match the cultures in which you find our ministries. Fail early and fail often until you learn what works. Learn to trust the young prophets in your midst and don't be afraid when the visions they share are out beyond your comfort zones. Be daring and be bold![2]

British Born

The Fresh Expressions movement was born in England. John Bowen traced the roots of Fresh Expressions back to the teachings of evangelical Anglican scholars of the mid-twentieth century, people like J. I. Packer, Michael Green, David Watson, David McInnes, and, in particular, John Stott.[3] The hearts and minds of several Anglican leaders of today were shaped by those evangelical scholars.

The movement itself began to emerge in the early 1990s, as Anglican leaders began to take note of a budding, rather nontraditional, church planting movement. In 2002 a study group was established for the purpose of analyzing these new forms of church.

The term "fresh expressions of church" first appeared in that study group's report, titled *Mission-Shaped Church*, in 2004.[4] The *Mission-Shaped Church* report did not invent fresh expressions of church; however, the researchers uncovered, recognized, reviewed, blessed, and fanned the flames of what God's Spirit had begun to do at the edges through these new forms of church. Bishop Graham Cray (the archbishop's missioner and former bishop of Maidstone) chaired the study group that produced the *Mission-Shaped Church* report, and eventually become the leader of the Fresh Expressions Initiative in England. (Steve Croft was the first team leader of Fresh Expressions UK.)

Those on the study team (including a Methodist leader[5]) that produced *Mission-Shaped Church* became increasingly aware of something happening around them—new forms of church were reaching people the inherited church was not reaching. Bishop Cray declared, "Some things that looked like little groups on the edge of our life are actually vital to our future."[6] A year after the publication of that watershed document, the network/movement/initiative called

Fresh Expressions was born. The movement among Anglicans has been facilitated by the establishment of a new pathway to ordination called "Pioneers," as well as recognition of lay pioneer ministry.[7]

British Methodists, then others, joined in the effort, and now multiple Christian groups in England are finding fresh expressions of church to be effective means of evangelizing and ministering to human needs. Bishop Graham Cray once noted that, from 2004 to 2010, the growth of the movement was rather slow and required perseverance. It was not until around 2010, he said, that expansion began to accelerate. Fresh Expressions has now grown into a multi-denominational, multinational movement.

Across the Pond

In 2009, leaders of the Baptist General Association of Virginia became interested in the Fresh Expressions movement as a potential means of evangelizing North America. A trip to England to see the movement firsthand convinced Virginia Baptist leaders that Fresh Expressions was worthy of their investment.

Thus the Baptist General Association of Virginia was the first US organization to resource Fresh Expressions and became the initial holders of the movement in North America. Virginia Baptists paid the salaries of the original facilitators of Fresh Expressions in the United States and offered administrative help for coordination of the work.

Other denominations soon joined the effort. Methodists, Anglicans, Presbyterians, Nazarenes, Brethren, and others now are integral to the movement. This is far, far beyond the boundaries of any one denomination.

Good News from England

The Fresh Expressions movement wasn't named until 2004, and in many ways didn't gain widespread traction for some time after that. Yet God had begun to raise up these new forms of church in England years earlier. After two decades or so, researchers in the

Church Army (an Anglican evangelistic, training, and research ministry) began to ask hard questions about the effectiveness of these new forms of church.

In October 2013, helpful data was released in a document titled, *Report on Strand 3b: An analysis of fresh expressions of Church and church plants begun in the period 1992–2012*.[8] This information, gathered over two decades, is encouraging.

Researchers found the impact of fresh expressions of church to be deep and wide. The number of people deciding to follow Jesus, and the percentage of British worshipers attending a fresh expression of church, are thrilling. According to the Church Army's report cited above, "Nothing else in the C of E [Church of England] has this level of missional impact."[9]

One of the tasks of those studying the effectiveness of fresh expressions of church was to narrow the parameters and arrive at a working definition. When the Church Army's upcoming study was publicized, researchers had to decide what they would count as fresh expressions of church. Hundreds of faith communities sent in their work as examples of fresh expressions, and a little more than half met the criteria. Researchers considered such criteria as the frequency of the gathering; whether participants see it as church; the level of engagement with unchurched people; their intentions regarding self-governance, self-support, and self-propagation; and whether the community exhibits the four marks of church: in, out, up, and of.[10]

Encouraging results

Here are some of the encouraging results noted in that document:

- "It is striking and notable that in 7 out of 10 cases the growth attributable to fresh expressions of Church attendance more than offsets (the ongoing decline in average worship attendance in the Church of England)." While we cannot yet declare a turnaround for the Church of England, there are genuinely hopeful signs.
- Of all Church of England congregations, about "one in seven to one in eight" now is a fresh expression of church. Furthermore,

on a typical Sunday about ten percent of the people in Anglican churches are in one of these fresh expressions of church.

- "For every one person sent (from existing congregations), at least another two and a half are now present. This is a 250% increase over time. There is nothing else in the Church of England that can do anything like this."
- 40% of those who are now part of fresh expressions of church were previously not at all part of any congregation.
- Fresh expressions of church have been effective in engaging young people. "On average at the fresh expressions of Church, 41% of the attendees are under 16. This is significantly higher than in inherited church and is a promising beginning."[11]
- While many of these new forms of church engage people within a particular sub-population, most include multiple generations.
- These fresh expressions are flourishing in a variety of settings, from the city to the farm, from the suburbs to low income neighborhoods.

The data is in: in England God is using fresh expressions of church to begin reversing the decline of church attendance and to reach people inherited congregations probably never will reach. Michael Moynagh, a leading Anglican researcher, reflected on the report and declared that, "in terms of outreach and evangelism these new expressions of church must surely be considered our best chance for a renewed impact of the Gospel in the West."[12]

Emergence of the female/volunteer/part-time minister

Among Fresh Expressions' important contributions to the expansion of the church is the expansion of the leadership pool. A slight majority, 52 percent, of fresh expressions in England are led by nonordained laypersons. Moreover, half the ordained leaders of fresh expressions of church also have responsibilities at other churches. The future of the Church of England (and the church in North America) will depend more and more on lay leaders.

This is not merely the expansion beyond ordained persons, it's the expansion beyond gender restrictions. There are as many women as men pioneering fresh expressions of church (52 percent female in those analyzed in the Church Army's 2013 report).[13]

Not large

The Church Army's research demonstrates that the most common approach, for those inherited churches who are trying to start a fresh expression of church, is to send a team of three to twelve people. Thus even small to medium churches can follow this model.

The average number of participants in a fresh expression of church in the UK is forty-four. Of course, that means there are lots under twenty and some more than one hundred. Yet this average (forty-four) is a reminder that fresh expressions of church rarely need buildings and staff. Most fresh expressions of church are so simple they do not require lots of people or money.

Many new communities of faith (like fresh expressions) "emphasize hospitality, and are therefore small. They are small not because of their limited appeal but because they are committed to maintaining their values of community, accountability, and service, and to being reproducible on an exponential scale."[14]

Making disciples

A little more than 40 percent of those who make up fresh expressions of church were genuinely unchurched (not at all connected to church) people. Not many of us can say that we ever did anything—including starting a new service or even planting a new church—that resulted in 40 percent of the new people coming from completely beyond the church.

Furthermore, the statistics about discipleship debunk the myth that fresh expressions of church are "church light." The overwhelming majority are intentional about helping people move to the next, and deeper, steps of faith.[15]

Fresh expressions of church at their best begin with the realization that *making disciples* is the heart of our mission. Graham Cray declared, "The ultimate test of any expression of church, whether a fresh expression or a more traditional one—is what quality of disciples are made there?"[16]

We will explore discipleship in fresh expressions of church later in the book.

Fresh Expressions US

Fresh Expressions US is an evangelically ecumenical initiative already helping shape the conversation about new churches for a new world. This is an emerging Christocentric movement in North America affirming Trinitarian theology and the ancient creeds of the church. Chris Backert, national director of Fresh Expressions US, said "Fresh Expressions is a movement that sees the empowering work of the Spirit in a new era of 'missional ecumenism'—a unity around the mission of God through the Resurrected Son and empowered by the Spirit." We are inclusive of all open-hearted orthodox Christians.

At Fresh Expressions US we are discovering what the Spirit is doing and telling the stories. We are encouraging both pioneers and established churches to join in what we believe is a genuine work of the Holy Spirit. We are providing training, coaching, and strategy to those pioneers and congregations.

Perhaps it will be helpful to clarify that the Fresh Expressions movement is not synonymous with what is often referred to as the Emergent Church. The two movements are fairly new to the scene and share many things in common. Fresh Expressions is indeed one of the emerging, burgeoning, missional church movements. Yet, organizationally and culturally, Emergent Church and Fresh Expressions are not the same. Among other distinctions is the intentional affirmation from the Fresh Expressions movement of the critical role established churches and their denominations play now and will play in the future.[17]

In What Way Ecumenical?

Fresh Expressions is certainly a multidenominational movement.
But is it ecumenical? And in what ways?

On the level of encouragement, inspiration, training, and best-practices learning, people from various branches of the Christian family tree are getting together. Of course, most fresh expressions of church are started by one local congregation or at least cooperating people from one denominational tradition. Thus the fresh expression takes on the DNA of the congregation or denomination behind it.[18] Yet there is a premium placed on interdenominational partnerships when at all possible, and those partnerships are resulting in a fresh sense of unity.

Beautiful relationships are emerging. While maintaining their distinctions, mission practitioners from various denominational traditions are sharing resources, learning from each other, networking, and actually praying for each other! Denominations, agencies, tribes who might have seemed unlikely ever to partner are now in beautifully cooperative relationship. While no one is asked to violate their particular traditions, affirmation of our common essentials, peer learning, and partnership where partnership is possible, have resulted in new alliances for kingdom purposes.

These alliances might come even more naturally in the future. Ecumenism was born, after all, on what our forefathers called the "foreign mission fields" in lands where missionaries were rare and where long-living missionaries were even more rare. Therefore, today, when there are fewer Christians in North America, those things that divide us might become less important. Candidly, desperation breeds cooperation.

A Program to Join?

People often ask if identifying with the Fresh Expressions movement is like affiliating with an organization. People ask, "Is this a program to join? Is there a fee? Do we have to sign on to an agreement of some sort? If we identify with Fresh Expressions, will there be controls over our new church?" The answer is "no" to all of the above questions. Fresh Expressions US is a loose network of pioneers and new communities of faith who believe God has led them to a new way of being church for a new world.

This is not an organization with members; it is a network of people and congregations linked merely by a common apostolic passion and calling. The Fresh Expressions US staff exists only to encourage, to equip, and to link people. We are grateful people with front row seats to a fascinating, encouraging story.

There are lots of new forms of church whose people have not yet even heard the term "fresh expressions," and we are not trying to force everything under our label. We simply want to be one of the tributaries feeding into a great stream—a movement of God's Spirit among people who don't give a hoot about who gets credit.

Chapter 16

APOSTLES AND PIONEERS: "DREAMERS WHO DO"

A Fresh Expressions pioneer is a person who has begun, or is attempting to begin, a fresh expression of church—either alone or (more than likely) as part of a team. "Not only do they dream up new strategies, they implement them—they are 'dreamers who do.'"[1] These are the words of Johnny Baker (quoting Gerald Arbuckle) in the book *The Pioneer Gift*. The Fresh Expressions movement depends on pioneers—dreamers who do—people with a passion for people far from God, innovative leanings, and the courage to do something without knowing exactly what that something will turn out to be.

Fresh Expressions UK, on their website, describe pioneers in these words.

> A pioneer minister is someone who has the necessary vision and gifts to be a **missionary entrepreneur**: with the capacity to form and lead fresh expressions and new forms of church appropriate to a particular culture. Pioneer ministers may be ordained or lay (not ordained) and different denominations and streams have ways of training and authorising pioneer ministers.[2]

Who *Are* These People?

They often are the last people the church's minister would expect to step forward. Like the lady my friend Mike Queen tells about in this story.

> One day it happened. A well-dressed young woman walked into my office. She was a member of the congregation and had something on her mind she wanted to talk about.
>
> "I park on Princess Street every Sunday," she said, "and I walk through the back lot and look up at that building over there," pointing in the direction of the jail. "I just think about the folks that are in there and here we are right next door. We worship and they can't. We ought to go to them."
>
> As a pastor you dream about the moment when somebody is going to catch the vision you've been nurturing and sharing for so long. The high heels, the manicured nails, and the fine car parked in the driveway gave no indication that this was that moment.
>
> I affirmed her compassion and desire to help and told her that we'd been trying for years to get such a ministry started, but to no avail. The look on my face must have given me away. If she was the last reliever left in the bullpen, it was time to call it a game.
>
> Abruptly, she stood up and said, "You don't think I can do this, do you?"
>
> I replied cautiously. "You're not the first person I would have thought of for jail ministry."
>
> With that, she leaned over my desk, looked me square in the face and said, "Mike Queen, I am a convicted felon and I know a hell of a lot more about what goes on in that building than you'll ever know. Now do I have your permission to start this ministry or not?"

That lady would be a good candidate to pioneer a fresh expression of church!

Ordinary Folks

Don't get the idea that these pioneers are super-Christians. One of the things about the Fresh Expressions movement to be celebrated is its unleashing of ordinary people to live extraordinary stories. A little more than half of the fresh expressions of church in England are led by laypeople. This comes from the Church Army's report in 2013: "52% are lay led and what is new is 40% are people without any official badge or training. They are equally likely to be led by women as men."[3] Moreover, even the typical ordained leader of a fresh expression is an everyday minister who loves Jesus and loves people and has no desire for superstar status in the Christian subculture.

Very few senior pastors lead fresh expressions of church. They have neither the time nor the connection (typically) with unchurched people. Some pioneers are on the ministerial staff of existing congregations with the assignment, or permission, to lead a fresh expression of church.

Not the First Time

Lay leadership was a key to church multiplication in the frontier days of the United States. Bivocational and often uneducated, these champions of the gospel preached and started churches wherever they could. There were lots of them, and they were deeply devoted to the cause of church planting. It has been suggested that the Methodists were on a long-lasting, significant upward numerical trajectory until they began feeling inferior to the Presbyterians and Episcopalians, and thus began to insist on seminary-trained clergy.[4]

They might not have known Latin, Hebrew, and Greek, but these lay preachers incarnated the gospel.

> Each day, they sought to reach farmers, cattle ranchers, and cowboys. To do so, they tailored their methodology to the sociology. And they did so without research firms and Excel reports of population trends. How? By living among the community rather than existing within a religious subculture.[5]

The story of the Methodist laypersons on horseback is encouraging as we look to the planting of new forms of twenty-first-century churches.

Of course we value formal theological and ministerial education. Yet we also recognize the power of pioneers with a deep sense of call and an ability to identify with people without Jesus. Evangelistic passion and the ability to identify with unbelievers seem to get educated out of a number of seminarians. Not all, of course, but enough to make space for pioneers with a heart for God, a heart for people, and the power of the Holy Spirit. While seminaries continue to train students for churches as we know them, God is raising up people to reach those who are not yet part of any church. These ordinary people take their place in a long line of noncredentialed pioneers, including the circuit riding preachers and the first apostles of Jesus.

Pioneers: Born or Made?

If someone were to ask you to describe a pioneer, what kind of words would you use?

Rugged?

Individualistic?

Rebel?

Edgy?

Those words certainly apply to many pioneers of fresh expressions. But certainly not all. Our stereotypes often fail us.

Karlie Allaway wrote the following in the book *The Pioneer Gift.*

Are you born a pioneer? I am not sure. Some natural talents help but often people identified as pioneers are people with a passion, which leads them to need to cut a new path. Their dedication drives looking for a new way to do things, alongside the will to develop the skills to do this. They put their natural talents in the service of whatever they are passionate about, which is why pioneers are a diverse group of people, approaching their challenges in different ways.

There can be a pioneer stereotype and we can sometimes limit ourselves in discussion around pioneering. This type of pioneering is an entrepreneurial loner, off doing their own thing at the frontier where the majority would not go. I always want to push back against this, mostly because, at my best, I am naturally relational and try to follow my passions in community. At heart I do not want to be a lone missionary, I want to be part of a missional community. I think we all hold a piece of the wisdom and I love to collaborate within that approach.[6]

Not easy

The life of pioneers is often lonely. When, in a gathering of ministers, pioneers try to explain what they are doing, they often are met with blank stares . . . or worse. The groups they lead and serve are often small. Their social lives may suffer because, if they are bivocational, many of their nonworking hours are spent on the new initiative.

What they do is hard. That's one reason pioneers find it helpful to work in teams. It is also why training is so helpful.

From the initial observations of the burgeoning movement, in *Mission-Shaped Ministry*, there was an Anglican call to formalize and recognize this unique gifting and calling. The Church of England thus put its weight behind the preparation and credentialing of pioneer ministers, and multiple opportunities are available there. Their Church Missionary Society provides degreed programs in *Pioneer Mission Leadership Training* as well as less formal, less intensive training for pioneers.

The Fresh Expressions movement in the US facilitates year-long cohorts, called *Pioneer Learning Communities*, in various parts of the US, and more opportunities for preparation are in development at the time of this writing. Moreover, I believe select seminaries will see what God is doing and will want to equip their students to facilitate those efforts. Those schools will become the missional centers, and other schools will want to get on board.

Apostolic gifting

A number of missional thinkers look to Ephesians 4:11, "So Christ himself gave the apostles, the prophets, the evangelists, the pastors and teachers . . ." and see there what is often called the "fivefold ministry," or known by the acronym APEST. The belief is that each of us will excel in one of those areas of ministry as apostles, prophets, evangelists, shepherds, or teachers.[7]

The following is a general (brief) description of this fivefold ministry:

- Apostle: Extending the kingdom through new churches, missionary movements.
- Prophet: Maintaining faithfulness to God among the people of God.
- Evangelist: Helping individuals to faith in Jesus.
- Shepherd: Nurturing people spiritually, emotionally, physically.
- Teacher: Teaching biblical wisdom and understanding.

Pioneers of fresh expressions are likely to be apostolic in their gifting. Of course, members of a core team might have various giftings, and that would make for a well-rounded team. Those who strike out on their own, however, are likely to be apostles.

Alan Hirsch has written extensively about APEST, and says the following about apostles:

> We believe that out of all the APEST ministries, the apostolic is the most generative and catalytic of them all, and because of this, it carries the most promise in helping to reverse the decline of the church. . . . Clearly the apostolic model in itself does not have all that is needed to get the job done. The ministry of all five APEST vocations is required to develop the kind of church that Jesus intended us to be. . . .
>
> At heart the apostle is a pioneer, and it is this pioneering, generative spirit that makes it unique in relation to the other ministries. . . . Apostolic ministry usually concentrates at the spearhead of all Christian movements where the gospel is

extended and received across cultural and spatial spheres. . . . Apostles maintain outward momentum as they oversee the contextual embedding of the gospel (the DNA of ecclesia) in the culture."[8]

Bivocational ministry

In a few fresh expressions of church, the ministers are full-time, drawing a full salary from the new form of church. Those, however, are in the minority. Some of those who earn a living are on the staff of an existing church and assigned to the fresh expression. Others actually receive a salary from the fresh expression of church they lead.

The overwhelming majority of pioneers, however, are either volunteers or earn only a partial salary. In some fresh expressions of church, people called to vocational ministry will choose to be bivocational (or maybe even trivocational). They will earn their primary livelihood through some other employment, and receive no more than a stipend from their work with the fresh expression.

Those in this bivocational category will benefit from an excellent resource—the book *BiVO*, by Hugh Halter. Halter is a bivocational church planter and has lots to say to those who are sensing a call to lead a fresh expression of church without earning a full-time salary from that church. One of the wonderful lessons Halter teaches is that secular work is sacred work, too. We shouldn't see our non-church work as *a means to ministry* but, rather, *a way of ministry*. Whether making widgets, selling real estate, pushing papers, or digging ditches, we are joining God in what He is doing in the world. *In addition to that*, we might get to join Him in starting a new form of church for people who are far from Him.

Balance and flexibility

In fresh expressions of church, team members will figure out how to balance their day job with the call to be involved in the new form of church. Some will even choose jobs with schedules that allow for maximum time to invest in the new form of church. There are lots of beautiful stories of pioneers who have sensed such a call to planting new forms of church that they have taken smaller salaries than they otherwise could have made, and adapted their leisure activities, just so they would have the flexibility to incarnate the gospel in new communities.

There is actually lots to be said for bivocational, or completely volunteer, ministry: "To be flexible, able to stop or turn on a dime. To be quick to adjust, unconstrained by the chains that hold most people down . . . If you are open to a little re-org of your life, you can experience greater freedom at both a personal and financial level."[9] In addition, there is the very real temptation to be driven by a paycheck instead of a divine calling. The apostle Paul acknowledged the lure to "peddle the word of God for profit" (2 Cor. 2:17). Bivocational ministry minimizes that temptation.

Ed Stetzer championed volunteer and bivocational ministry.

> For church planters who desire to engage in this kind of ministry, common sense and mission strategy dictate that these models be intentionally nonpaid from the beginning. . . . Missional/incarnational church planters do not need a prospectus, strategy plan, and time line; they need a job in the marketplace. . . . Most of those who planted relation-based churches without funding did well. However, those who wanted to plant relation-based churches while receiving funding did not; their funding ran out too soon, and people in the context wondered who was paying the salary in the first place. . . . If this approach leads to thousands of committed believers not entering vocational ministry, but instead entering the marketplace to plant churches in homes, businesses, community centers, etc., that is good news.[10]

The trend toward bivocational ministers has been picking up steam for several years. Now, with fresh expressions of church being an increasingly viable option for the beginning of new Christian work, the bivocational minister is more important than ever. Lots of leaders of fresh expressions of church are earning only a fraction of their total salary from their work with the fresh expression. Many are earning nothing. Of course the apostle Paul advocated for, and modeled, bivocational ministry.[11]

This won't be easy. Pioneering ministry is already hard enough, even when personal finances are not a concern. The stress of managing schedules and financial responsibilities will test the mettle of these new missionary church leaders. Yet there is reason to highlight and celebrate this promising approach to ministry. In the words of Hugh Halter, "The gospel came to us through a church of barely paid and non-paid saints, and we can once again recover the beautiful freedom that will bring the gospel to the next epoch of history."[12]

New Heroes

A new hero is emerging. We still admire the charismatic CEO-type, and many of us secretly wish we were more like that. But that is no longer the template; it is no longer the assumed picture of the effective church leader. There is a growing admiration of people who follow their unique callings, use their unique giftings, and even take their unique risks. A willingness to fail is now a celebrated quality. A propensity for experimentation is now applauded. Pioneers are the new heroes. Perhaps like never before, people are encouraged to follow their peculiar and God-given passions. Molds and assumptions about what success looks like are getting tossed aside.

Doors are opening for pioneers.

New Monasticism

I cannot leave this chapter about pioneers without a brief mention of what is called "new monasticism." Drawing from the deep, ancient monastic tradition, growing numbers of pioneers are finding a meaningful, effective, new form of church.

In the book, *The New Monasticism*, Ian Mobsby helps us understand this approach to ministry.

We remember that the original evangelization of Britain in the Romano-Celtic and Anglo-Saxon eras occurred through the missional endeavors of monks, nuns and friars, and not primarily through bishops, priests and parishes. Curiously, in the postmodern context we find ourselves drawing on the resources and models of pre-modern approaches to mission and evangelism.[13]

These new monastics are among the most avant-garde of the pioneers. They often move together into a neighborhood, living in their own houses but in close proximity. They live their lives very intentionally as a community, sharing worship, goods, and close friendship.

New monastic communities share leadership, lean on each other, and follow a common rhythm of life. They also practice intentional and beautiful hospitality to their neighbors and new friends. They engage the people around them through a wide variety of means: coffeehouses, advocacy, hostels, education, and magnanimous acts of Christian service, to name a few.

Often the areas they move into are unsafe, and almost always the people they live among are not being reached by existing churches.

Later in the book you will see the story of a new monastic community called Grace and Main.

Clearly, not all pioneers live as close to the edge as do these new monastics. Most, in fact, live their lives very much the same as before they were called by God to start a fresh expression of church.

Shawn and Tammy

There is no typical pioneer story. No firm, absolute model. No pioneer prototype. There are no rules. So I don't tell the following story to say this is what a pioneer looks like. I just think you'll enjoy meeting Shawn and Tammy.

Shawn Mickschl had sensed a call to ministry, was a seminary student at Asbury, and was pursuing a vocation in the local church. But his call was still rather vague. He told me, "I'd stand in worship, look toward those preaching and leading worship and think, 'I know I'm called, but I'm not sure what I'm called to. I just know it's not *that*.'" It's not that he doesn't honor pastors and the existing church. To the contrary, he is still involved in, and loves, his longstanding congregation. He loves pastors. He simply knew that service in an existing congregation was not that to which God's Spirit was leading him.

Then his church, Nicholasville (Kentucky) United Methodist, began to talk about planting a church. But they had a sense that they shouldn't go about it the traditional way. They came to Shawn, knowing that he and his wife, Tammy, already were intentionally, naturally, and with a missionary purpose, developing relationships in their neighborhood.

Shawn's and Tammy's call to be fresh expressions pioneers was born.

Shawn intentionally works as a restaurant waiter to develop relationships. It took him many months to be trusted enough for people to accept even invitations to his home for dinner. But he persevered, and people began to trust him. An invitation to a coworker to hang out after hours and talk about life from God's perspective turned into House Church After Dark, meeting at a craft beer pub, a new form of church for people who almost certainly would never have walked into Nicholasville UMC. They meet on Thursday nights after the restaurant closes. (This is just one of the fresh expressions of church that Shawn has started.)

Through Shawn, House Church After Dark has a tether to Nicholasville UMC. Shawn meets with their strategic leadership group every Wednesday. He processes issues with them and they support him. His reports and stories expand their vision.

Shawn's salary as a waiter is supplemented by some support from the Kentucky Annual Conference of the United Methodist Church and from Nicholasville UMC. He considers himself a layperson. He hit pause on the ordination track, and is now heading toward what his tradition calls a "licensed local pastor."

Shawn and Tammy Mickschl are pioneers.

Chapter 17

PRELIMINARIES

So how would one prepare to launch such a novel kind of church? There are no rigid rules, no inviolable plan, no sacrosanct methodology that church leaders and pioneers are bound to follow. There are, however, some proven principles that have consistently resulted in communities of faith among otherwise unreached people. We will talk about them in the following chapters.

First comes some groundwork.

And the groundwork depends on the approach. Many pioneers of fresh expressions go out on their own, perhaps with a small circle of friends, without the support of, or connection to, an existing congregation. Conversely, fresh expressions are often started by people in a particular congregation with the support and participation of the congregation. Those in the Fresh Expressions movement believe there are important advantages in a partnership of pioneers and existing congregations who support them, yet we certainly can point to lots of effective fresh expressions of church that have little or no backing from an existing congregation.

Keep those two basic approaches—(1) a pioneer or pioneers on their own or (2) pioneers in partnership with an existing congregation—in mind as you read this chapter and translate what you find here into your particular calling and approach.

Cultivating a Missional Culture

God can give the vision of a fresh expression to a congregation, and from that congregation call out the people who will launch it. Or, the divine vision can come to individuals within a congregation who, in turn, ask for their church's support. Either way, if you are in a leadership role in a church, the first step in starting a fresh expression of church will be to cultivate a missional culture. You will have to help your congregation turn their attention to the world. Fresh expressions of church can happen naturally when a church has a culture of creative engagement with people beyond their walls.

Remember, a missional church is . . .

a church that is shaped by participating in God's mission, which is to set things right in a broken, sinful world, to redeem it, and to restore it to what God has always intended for the world. Missional churches see themselves not so much sending, as being sent. A missional congregation lets God's mission permeate everything that the congregation does— from worship to witness to training members for discipleship. It bridges the gap between outreach and congregational life, since, in its life together the church is to embody God's mission.[1]

Or, in the words of Alan Roxburgh and Fred Romanuk,

A missional church is a community of God's people who live into the imagination that they are, by their very nature, God's missionary people living as a demonstration of what God plans to do in and for all of creation in Jesus Christ.[2]

A missional church is driven by its mission; not by the pastor, not by its governance model, not by its obsession with the absence of conflict, and not by the budget. A missional church is mission-driven. That means, for example, that budget discussions are not merely debates about how much we spend for missions versus how much that church spends for recreation or worship or children's ministries. Rather, the entire budget is seen as funding a mission.

An identity of "sent-ness"—a clear sense of being on mission—colors *everything*. So whether the discussions are surrounding the budget, the church calendar, or staffing plans, the question is, "How do they enable us to *be on mission*?"

Pastors and lay leaders can cultivate a missional culture, and thus lay the groundwork for thinking about fresh expressions of church, by helping the people inside the church understand all of the different types of people the church isn't reaching. They can help people inside the church understand God's passionate and holistic mission to the world by encouraging creative, strategic thinking about how to engage those far from God and the church.

Often it is a matter of turning a congregation's attention to the original vision that launched their church or denomination. Remembering the evangelistic passions, courage, and creativity that drove their founders is a wonderful motivation for church members thinking of innovative approaches.

This missional culture, by the way, begins with church leaders and the examples they set. If the church leaders are not engaging people beyond the church walls, it is unlikely that many people in the church will either. In most cases, the example set, as well as the enthusiastic blessing and backing of the senior pastor, will be important.

Finding Those Who Might Join in the Adventure

Those called to begin fresh expressions of church will want to pray for others who might provide partnership and support along the way. Of course, lots of fresh expressions have been started by lone pioneers without the assistance of a team. There is value, however, in having the support, camaraderie, and fellowship of others who share the pioneer's passion for people whom Jesus so desperately loves.

As you tell of your vision, your sense of call, notice the responses. Some will look at you as if you have two heads, others will change the subject, and others' insincere expressions of interest will be really obvious. A few, however, will want to know more. As you speak, they will lean in. They will express their sense that, maybe, they are supposed to do something like that. They might even say their heart has been stirred recently, as if God Himself is calling them to step out in faith and try something new.

These potential team members can be invited into conversations, perhaps over a meal or a cup of coffee. These prospective partners in ministry are likely from within one congregation, but sometimes individuals from various congregations come together with a common sense of mission to plant one of these new forms of church.

Luke Edwards is the pioneer of a fresh expression of church in Boone, North Carolina (see his story earlier in the book). He explained that, when looking for people from his local church to join him in the adventure, he looks for people who are street smart, who are at home with unchurched people, and who actually have friends who are not believers. He explained that it's okay if they have some rough edges, have a past, and don't have everything together.

That's not to say that everyone has to have a dramatic story in order to join in starting a fresh expression of church. The task does require, however, flexibility in the face of uncertainty and a love for all kinds of people (including people who are not yet Christians). It is important that those beginning a fresh expression of church not recoil at salty language and other improprieties.

You should mostly steer clear of those who are just looking for something exciting, or the next cool ministry; they are not likely to stick with you. An adventurous spirit is good, but you are looking for people who have a missionary-like call; not just a desire to be edgy.

Besides potential members of the core team, are there people who would be willing to support the core team in prayer? And is the pastor or other mentor willing to coach and encourage the new team? Both pray-ers and mentors are really helpful.

On the fringe of the core

Minh Ha Nguyen, a pioneer of a fresh expression of church among internationals, talked about the missional value of church members on the "fringe of the core." He said people at the core of a church want to maintain what they have, while people at the fringe are not close enough to the center of things to have sufficient insight or influence. But there is a ring (if you can picture concentric circles) of people at the fringe of the core. They are close enough to know what is going on, and are respected by people at the core, but not so invested in the status quo. Minh Ha suggested that it is at the fringe of the core where we will find people who are interested in beginning fresh expressions.[3]

In the Fresh Expressions booklet *Listening for Mission*, the following questions are recommended as you dream together with your newly formed core team:

- *What draws you to explore beginning a fresh expression?*
- *What group or community do you think we are called to work with?*
- *What do you think God is doing already in this community?*
- *Where are the needs and pains and points of darkness and difficulty?*
- *What gifts and resources do we bring?*
- *Who might your partners be?* (Explore partnerships with service organizations. Could you join them in what they are doing and establish yourself in the new community? Is your church interested in supporting this venture? Would sister churches in your area partner with you?)
- *What will make you shout "Hallelujah!" in one year's time and in five years?*
- *How do we find out more about the community we think we may be called to serve?*[4]

Not too many

There shouldn't be too many church people on the team that starts the fresh expression of church, or else those who are not-yet-Christians might feel intimidated, and/or the effort might not feel contextual. Our British friends say to begin with a team of three to twelve.

The team to start a fresh expression of church should consist of people of prayer, with a vision for reaching people far from God. It would be helpful to have strategic thinkers, inspirers, organizers, relationship-builders, vision-casters, and encouragers. Primarily, though, you simply need those who love God and love people.

Becoming a team

At this stage, a handful of people are about to embark on the adventure of their lives—a quest to meet new people, to listen intently and serve humbly, to engage people in spiritual conversations, and to trust God as perhaps never before. So that your group will become a team, you will want to openly share your individual stories—your calls, your hopes, your fears, and your experiences with church (good and bad) that have shaped you.[5]

It is likely that this vision has begun in the heart of an individual—someone to whom the Spirit of God has spoken. That person might be the leader of this venture, or that person might recognize the leadership gifts of another person and humbly encourage the group to follow the one with the gifts. No matter who emerges as the leader, it is important that, from the very beginning, team leadership be built into the new church.

Your home church

Keep the lines of communication open with your home church if, indeed, you are going out with their blessing and resources. They need to share this journey with you. Many of those who step out to start a fresh expression of church continue worshiping with their home church, and that might be helpful for you.

The People to Whom You Are Called

Have you noticed how segmented our society is becoming? David Houle noted this complex reality.

> Accelerating connectivity allows us to find others like us anywhere around; we create and identify with "tribes" of like-minded people. We can find places and groups that we can develop affinity with rather than be alienated from. Our identities are aggregations of our choices. . . . We no longer measure

ourselves against the mass models; instead, we group ourselves around our interests and activities. The concept of conformity has lost its grip on us. We are all individuals who may choose to be like others, but being like others is no longer as socially imperative as it was just a few decades ago.[6]

Houle continued,

We deal now with an aggregation of small, targeted micromarkets. . . . The word "fragmentation" has been used a lot in the last twenty years, but it is an old reference point, as it speaks to the fragmentation of the marketplace, which assumes a mass market. Think instead of this transition from mass to micro as a historical process that will continue and accelerate.[7]

The Fresh Expressions movement has recognized "networks of common interests"[8] from the beginning, and most of these new forms of church begin among a particular subculture. That subculture could be based on affinity, geography, or vocation. Fresh expressions are attentive to a particular population group—i.e., a group of people who share a similar interest, hobby, need, community, or vocation. Fresh expressions of church can seek to engage people in a particular neighborhood, as well as people who have interests and activities that tie them together and identify them.

We often speak of affinity groups, which Linda Bergquist and Allan Karr have defined.

Affinity is a "sympathy marked by community of interest, an attraction to or liking for something." This kind of connection can be based on language, subculture, first or second generation ethnicity, socioeconomics, lifestyle, interest, workplace, preferred worship style, a common antagonist, or any number of things around which people naturally relate.[9]

The strategic advantage to focusing on an affinity group is widely recognized. For example, Ed Stetzer and Warren Bird wrote,

We believe the rapid reproduction of churches needs to happen among hundreds of niche population groups—from

SUV-driving young families in fast-growing suburbs to urban
hipster environmentalists to unchurched rural country music
lovers. . . . To truly reach our world, churches need to multiply
among every thin slice of society: suburban, urban, rural,
cowboy, artistic, senior adult, collegiate—and on the list goes.
These groups each have their own language, culture, values,
and perspectives. If a biblical church effectively reaches any of
the varied members of the human race, we're in favor of it.[10]

Discerning the affinity group

If you are thinking of starting a fresh expression of church, first
think *who*, not *what*. In other words, an initial step in beginning a
fresh expression is to decide who (which affinity group) it is God
is calling us to reach. *Then*, after listening to people and serving
them, we consider what discipleship and church might look like
in that context.

So how does one discern the subculture, or slice of the population, to which you are called? Begin with your interests: What do
you do well? With what subgroups do you identify? Who are the
people among whom you feel at home?

And what about those who might have come alongside you to
start your team? Are they members of a population segment who
need a church? Do they sense a call to engage any population in
particular?

It is helpful if at least one of you—either you or someone in your
core team—is an insider. In other words, if people want to start a
fresh expression in the arts community, at least one person in the
group should actually be a member of that community. If the goal is
to be church for military veterans, a veteran should almost certainly
be part of the initial group of gatherers. If the fresh expression is
simply intended to reach people in a certain neighborhood, at least
someone from the core team should live in that neighborhood. In
some cases, numbers of people actually move into neighborhoods
they are trying to serve.

It will be beneficial, also, to find a person of peace of which
Jesus spoke in Luke 10—someone in that target community who is

drawn to the mission and message, and can open doors and make introductions.[11]

Church builders and bodybuilders

I recently attended a large denominational gathering and stayed at the hotel adjacent to the conference center where the denominational group was meeting. Also there that week were crowds of bodybuilders who had come for a convention and competition. We were all in the same hotel, and the difference between those who had come for the church gathering and those who had come for the bodybuilding event was noticeable and, often, comical.

I thought, "I can't imagine many of the churches represented here making a dent in this subculture of body-sculpting. Look at how different we are! But what if a couple of these impressively sculpted people were Christian pioneers? What if, as insiders, they were to begin something in their individual city among this unique affinity group?"

The pioneering team could ask members of the bodybuilding subculture how the pioneering team could serve. They might meet in a fitness center, right? It might begin, at least, with a focus on holistic care for our bodies, including the spiritual element of that. Maybe the first Bible teaching would be about our bodies as temples of God's Spirit.

A fresh expression of church could begin there, in the subculture of bodybuilders. These muscle-bound people already have a tie that binds them together. We wouldn't be demanding they come to our church buildings where we don't understand their passion for body-sculpting, and where, frankly, their passion might be disparaged. We could take the church Jesus loves closer to where the people Jesus loves actually are.

Praying

This is a prayer-based movement. So please pray. Pray that God will send out laborers into His harvest. Pray for a vision from God—for a sense of who it is among whom you are to begin a new form of church. Pray for persons of peace—people who will open doors and provide an ongoing presence among the community to be served.

And wait. Wait until the Spirit says it's time to move. At His ascension, Jesus told His friends to wait in Jerusalem for the Holy Spirit. *Then* they would be witnesses (Acts 1).

When God's Spirit *does* prompt us to step out, however, it is vital that we courageously obey. There are, almost certainly, more of us dawdling when God says move than there are those of us moving out prematurely. The needs of our world demand from us a courageous obedience.

Chapter 18

HOW THIS GENERALLY UNFOLDS (PART 1)

There is no manual. No one can anticipate or prescribe exactly what others should do in their particular contexts. God's Spirit blows where He will and how He will. Nevertheless, data collected over the last couple of decades, primarily in England, and observations in the US as well, suggest recurring themes, reappearing patterns, and observable advantages to a general progression by which these new forms of church come into being.

Getting Started

Someone once said, "A vision without a plan is an illusion." Once the direction of the fresh expression has emerged, it will be helpful to make sure there is the right amount of organization. The goal is just enough structure to provide a way forward without squelching Spirit-led adaptability.

Direction

Things might (and most likely will) develop in ways no one can anticipate. It might even get messy! It would be unwise to be rigidly tied to a preconceived design.[1]

We don't want to plan down to the rigid details, for to do that would be to assume far too much understanding of a context we will not yet have entered. However, having a sense of direction will prevent the team from chasing every captivating idea that arises.

So, begin thinking early on about sustainability—asking such questions as how long the initial core team can be counted on for participation and what kind of emotional and spiritual support there will be for them. It will also be helpful to anticipate how decisions about the fresh expression of church will be made. Asking how the new form of church will identify with the wider church, including a potential denomination, will be important as well.[2]

It is critical to remember that this planning is not merely a strategic exercise. The planning phase is a time of *spiritual discernment*—a deliberate attempt to know, as best finite humans can, the vision God has for you and the place He has for you in His mission to the world. This is far too big for any of us to figure out on our own.

After some time, you might want to decide on a name. Not all fresh expressions of church have a formal name. Many find it helpful, however, eventually, to be identified by a name of some sort, even when those names emerge months or even years into the venture.

You might talk about leadership. How will you determine qualifications for leaders? How will you invite leaders in? Will there be a formal leadership council or will people with the calling and gift of leadership meet informally to prayerfully make decisions?

As church takes shape, you might want to discern together your values—those things you hold dear that will shape your future.

Many of these decisions will have to be revisited after the fresh expression of church takes shape, and an obsession with the plan could have a restricting effect. A sense of *direction*, however, will help keep you out of the ditches.

Considering finances

The amount of money needed could vary tremendously, depending on the kind of new church being considered. For many fresh expressions of church, the only money needed is for coffee! Fresh expressions tend to be fairly inexpensive.

So, if this is going to be a cell group in someone's home that's one thing. If it's going to require costs such as rent, upgrades, and other ongoing costs for a facility, however, it's quite another. Leaders might need to consider up front the potential operational costs, sustainability, possible grants, and other funding streams.

Leaders will also need to consider whether or not they will receive some financial remuneration for ministry in this fresh expression of church. The growing consensus among missiologists, by the way, is that bivocational ministry will be at the leading edge of missional movements in the future. The next generation of great leaders in missional communities like fresh expressions probably will earn their primary living from secular vocations.

The Process

The following process, roughly in this order (though there is often overlap), has helped guide the development of fresh expressions of church all over the world. Read these stages not with any sense of obligatory conformity, but rather with the encouragement that comes from knowing that God has used this process multiple times. You might, under the prompting of God's Spirit, veer from this pattern. It is helpful, however, to know the pattern and to understand when you are intentionally or unintentionally deviating from it.

Warning: Those of us who are driven to achieve have to remember that this approach is often longer, more amorphous, and more organic than that with which we might be most comfortable. This is not nearly as clean and simple as securing a facility, sending a core team and a preacher from an existing church, blanketing the area with marketing, and holding the big, inaugural worship service.

Much like the patience required of Jesus' disciples in the Upper Room (Acts 1-2), patience in the beginning of a fresh expression of church is imperative. A basic element of the Fresh Expressions movement is that we should not launch out prematurely. Launching out too quickly, and implementing strategies we formulated in our heads before actually getting to know the community, can short-circuit the proven process by which fresh expressions of church come into being.

With the method proposed here (and confirmed multiple times) we have to be willing to learn new things, to set aside some assumptions, and to shape our approach based on our new awareness, not on presuppositions.

underpinned by prayer, ongoing listening, and
relationship with the wider church

Listening

A fresh expression of church begins not with proclaiming but with listening, and our first listening is to God's Spirit. It is imperative that, through spiritual disciplines such as prayer, Bible study, and perhaps fasting, we listen as best we can to hear the voice of the Creator. Discernment of God's will is a key to fresh expressions of church. God inspired the apostle Paul to write, "Do not be foolish, but understand what the Lord's will is" (Eph. 5:17).

Having heard from God, we then turn to hear from those among whom we are called to serve. Remember the prayer attributed to St. Francis reads, *O Divine Master, Grant that I may not so much seek . . . to be understood, as to understand.* That is certainly applicable here. We listen to the community—to the people among whom we believe God might be leading us to plant a fresh expression of church—before we start trying to communicate anything. And we remember that God was at work there before we arrived.

Some of us have too many meetings to go to . . . or books to read . . . or classes to teach . . . to actually sit and talk to people. Our definition of productivity might not include a leisurely coffee (sans smart phone) in a place where people just hang out. Giving our world the gift of our time seems awfully difficult.

Yet, casual conversations with people on the street, in coffee shops, and even in other churches, are invaluable. Asking questions of influencers, community leaders, and business or agency owners can be really helpful. If you are trying to reach a certain community, study the census reports, demographic data, and history. But we cannot truly learn a community by staring at a laptop. We're going to have to actually move among the people . . . and listen.

Cathy Ross noted that "pioneers are good at hospitality." Lots of learning takes place, she writes, around tables. "Pioneers," she said, "like to loiter and listen, enjoy food and drink."[3]

Listening is such a novel idea for most of us. The following, from Paul Sparks and Tim Soerens, is warranted despite its length.

> Can you walk or wheel yourself through your neighborhood on a regular basis as a prayer practice, inviting the Holy Spirit to guide you into relationships with a posture of openness? Have you met the local business owners within your walkable neighborhood? Who are they, how are they doing their business, and what kinds of support do they need? What about the schools? What nonprofits are present, and what do they see? . . . In a very real sense, this is about your presence in the parish. Most of your presence in the neighborhood is incredibly ordinary, but that doesn't mean it shouldn't be intentional. For example, you decide to drink coffee at the local café instead of driving miles away. You play pickup basketball with neighbors at the park around the corner instead of playing in a church league. You and a few neighbors decide to share a meal every Wednesday, or you pick a time to meet each other at the playground where the kids can play together.[4]

Of course these words from Sparks and Soerens are most applicable if you are considering a new church in a particular neighborhood. But what if you are called to a people group that is not geographically based, such as artists or people in a certain profession? The same principles apply: Before we act, we listen. In the hallways, in chat rooms, in the blogosphere, after rehearsals, before meetings, and so on . . . we listen.

Instead of assuming what people need or what they think or where they are spiritually, we simply must ask people important questions—questions about their social lives, their common needs, struggles, values, and spirituality. Then we have to listen, really listen, before we start something. It is imperative that we not decide what will work before we listen; our strategy should emerge naturally out of what we hear. We have to become, in the words of Mark Lau Branson and Nicholas Warnes, "reflective participants in the context."[5] And, as Hirsch and Catchim counseled us, "Think like a beginner; not an expert."[6]

Halter and Smay reminded us that we will have to lighten up a bit if we are going to have an in with people who are not-yet-believers. We will have to learn to "be with people regardless of their angle of life without casting any judgment their way," to help people "feel comfortable enough to be themselves, feel loved, and dignified as human beings."

Halter and Smay suggested "whimsy," and explained further,

> It's not making an issue out of anything that's not the main issue. That simply means we don't flinch at sin or bad language or nasty T-shirts or crude music or a not-yet-believer who over-indulged. Whimsy . . . (is) the essence of missional posture that helps gain someone's heart so that someday, their behavior may also change.[7]

Remember, Jesus' opponents blasted Him for liking sinners and actually eating with them! And, frankly, if that sounds impossible to you, then you probably aren't the one to help start a fresh expression of church. Everyone is not called to this.

Another reason to listen first is to remember and practice a spirit of humility. These are the words of Max Warren:

> Our first task in approaching another people, another culture, another religion, is to take off our shoes, for the place we are

approaching is holy. Else we may find ourselves treading on people's dreams. More serious still, we may forget that God was here before our arrival.[8]

Loving and Serving

Having listened for some time, the next step is to serve people.

Of course not all fresh expressions of church follow this pattern. Some of these fresh expressions begin almost spontaneously, without a lot of thought, as people simply live out their faith among people who respect them. And worship is sometimes the first identifiable step in the launching of a fresh expression of church, more like a typical church plant.

Generally speaking, however, the pattern that has seen the most effective impact is that which does not begin with a worship service. Michael Moynagh wrote of the advantages of "service first" over "worship first."[9] Beginning with a worship service has not proven to be very effective in engaging those who have no history with church, see no value for them in the church, or have negative emotions associated with church.

The most effective fresh expressions of church begin where followers of Jesus are genuinely interested in serving the neighborhood or the specific microculture of people they want to reach. That service might be as simple as volunteering for a key group or activity—volunteering for projects facilitated by other organizations. Those other organizations do not have to be faith-based. There are several advantages to joining in with secular groups, one advantage being the chance to build relationships outside the Christian bubble.

Service could mean meeting physical needs if the people among whom we feel called to work are under-resourced. It might be that the core team and their friends clean up a park or schoolyard on Saturdays, or maybe they host educational events for the so-called target audience. A number of fresh expressions have begun with community cookouts in which the service provided is simply helping people get acquainted.

We cannot know how best to serve people until we spend ample time truly *listening* to them. Sometimes we assume we know what people need and later find that we made wrong assumptions. Listening before acting enables us to serve people in meaningful ways.[10]

Presence/insiders

If one is thinking of a fresh expression of church in a neighborhood, a physical presence there is imperative. A number of fresh expressions have grown out of the decision of a group of like-minded Christians to actually move into a community. There are some beautiful stories of people who have joined other believers in planting themselves in the neighborhoods they are trying to engage.

Of course that is a big-decision—to pack up and move to a new place. And we should not assume all well-intentioned investments in neighborhoods are well-received. Occasionally the longstanding residents of a community resent what they see as a bunch of do-gooders wanting to take over.

Not everyone wanting to plant a new form of church has to relocate to the neighborhood, but neither can the group be made up of complete outsiders. There must be at least one insider—one resident of the neighborhood. This insider principle holds true in just about any new form of church. Whether affinity group or physical neighborhood, it is not helpful to parachute in from the outside with a bunch of answers to questions no one on the inside is asking.

Take the gaming community, as an example. Gamers are part of a distinct subculture—people who love video games and/or modern board games. They get together often, either in person or online. They play together, share important elements of their lives together, and make up a unique culture-within-the-culture.

A typical congregation would have a difficult time engaging people in the gaming subculture. In northern Virginia, however, there are two gamers who love Jesus and who understand the gospel as well as God's mission to the world. They are insiders. They are passionate about the church and about the gaming community. They are extending grace to gamers and wondering if perhaps a fresh expression of church will result.

Gamers are but one example. Think of bikers, wounded warriors, those who work in the hospitality industry, or surfers. Think of people who live in a particular neighborhood or work in a particular industry. A fresh expression of church engages subcultures like those and just about any other you can imagine.

Closely related to the idea of the insider is the strategic necessity of a person of peace. The idea of a person of peace comes from Luke 10. The person of peace is that one in the neighborhood, the affinity group, or the subculture who is drawn to the mission and message, and can open doors and make introductions. He or she is the gatekeeper, the introducer, the validator.

Persons of peace will be interested in what you're up to. They will be sympathetic if not initially supportive. They will be curious about your life and somewhat transparent about their own. They will give evidence that God is up to something in their hearts and heads. They will then be your informants, introducers, and instructors.

Neil Cole wrote about persons of peace.

1. They are persons of receptivity.
2. They are people of relational connections.
3. They are people of reputation.[11]

In talking about Luke 10 and the persons of peace, Bob and Mary Hopkins wrote,

> Jesus did not send his disciples out with a mission strategy of attracting people onto their territory on their terms. He sent his disciples out to look for people who responded to them—who welcomed them—and then to stay with their hosts on their terms.[12]

Also about the person of peace the Hopkinses wrote, "You don't need to think that you have to force the gospel on the other 90% who don't respond to you. . . . This actually frees us all up not to fear or be stressed about evangelism but to have confidence that God will put the right people in our path."[13]

God opens doors through the person of peace.

More to come

So far we have covered two of the typical stages in this process: (1) Listening and (2) Loving and Serving. The remaining stages are awaiting us in the following chapter.

Chapter 19

HOW THIS GENERALLY UNFOLDS (PART 2)

As a quick reminder, we are talking about the process by which these new forms of church emerge. Remember that there is not a single way to do this; there is no inviolable technique. There certainly are no rules as to how these new forms of church come into being.

Broadly speaking, however, fresh expressions of church follow a pattern. It is a flexible pattern, to be sure, yet it is a pattern that is observable now after more than two decades of the movement, beginning in England.

underpinned by prayer, ongoing listening, and
relationship with the wider church

The first two general stages are Listening and Loving and Serving. The following are the remaining stages.

Building Community

Community is simply a collection of people who enjoy each other, look at the world through somewhat similar eyes, have at least an informal willingness to care for each other at some level, and have a relationship deeper than acquaintance. There is something that feels intentional about their interactions.

Community in the Fresh Expressions sense begins with the group of people, probably three to twelve, who serve as the core team for the fresh expression of church. The roles of these initial ensembles vary, but the simple task is to get things going. Earlier we considered how to assemble this group, but for now let's just state that a handful of pioneer-types are going to step out courageously to embark on a great adventure.

In time that initial handful will grow. As the core team members listen to people and serve them, as they chat with neighbors over meals and coffee, as they invest themselves among a new group of people . . . a sense of community emerges. Relationships develop around meaningful activities. The initial team begins to expand.

Perhaps the people they are meeting will naturally connect with them and their band of missional believers. Perhaps the members of the initial fresh expression team will verbalize an invitation for new friends to start gathering regularly with their existing circle. Maybe they will invite people to join them in their service to the community. Organically, naturally, their community will grow as newcomers feel a part of things.

This is how Kelly Bean described the emergence of community in her situation.

> After three years of learning from our Aurora neighbors and building community through barbecues in motel parking lots, birthday parties at local parks, gardening, conversations on the 358 metro bus, etc., we felt it was time to create a space together where our lives could intersect more intentionally on a daily basis . . . and so, the Aurora Commons came to be.[1]

Among the questions that have to be answered are these: When, and how, do we go public with the mission of this little group of people who are listening, loving, and serving? Do we say from the very beginning we are starting a church? Do we avoid that topic and simply build relationships, unveiling our plan only when people are connected?

That plays out differently, depending on the context. Some pioneers might be more explicit in their approach, others more subtle. Whatever the case, a good pioneer of fresh expressions will neither lie to nor overwhelm people. He or she will be open about the community's Christian identity but also will neither smother new people nor baffle them with the language of Zion.

At some point it will be clear that this initial handful of people are followers of Jesus. The good news about that is that a group of Jesus-followers doing life together, following a shared sense of mission and actually getting along, is a more compelling testimony to people who are not yet believers than an individual talking of how Jesus changed his or her life. Sparks, Soerens, and Friesen put it like this: "The gospel becomes so much more tangible and compelling when the local church is actually a part of the community, connected to the struggles of the people."[2]

As this happens, the early stages of a fresh expression of church emerge. It is thrilling to watch God bring togetherness out of what began as casual conversations. Yet we have to be careful not to rush the process so that we can say we have begun a church. At this point we are simply nurturing a community. Church will emerge in due time.

Exploring Discipleship

As conversations about spiritual issues arise naturally, discipleship—walking with people into a deeper and more meaningful relationship with Jesus—has begun. In the early stages this discipleship could be really informal, as in impromptu discussions. With time, planned discussion groups might emerge. Mentoring, intentional conversations, and relationship-based learning are almost always key means of making disciples.

Of course, discipleship is more than the dishing out of information. As followers of Jesus live faithful lives in close proximity to not-yet-believers, discipleship happens—a kind of social discipleship occurs. *Relationships . . . organic . . . doing life together . . . exploration . . .* those are the descriptors of discipleship in the twenty-first century.

Sometimes those looking in from the outside comment that fresh expressions of church seem weak on discipleship. Often that comment comes from the assumption that discipleship consists of the sharing of information, and most often the model is a lecture-style setting like Sunday school. Discipleship, however, is broader than that.

Bob Hopkins, a Fresh Expressions pioneer from England, noted that the Greek word translated "disciple," *mathetes*, means *learner*, and goes on to discuss three different means of learning, each of which is important. (Hopkins quickly acknowledges he picked this up from Ted Ward, professor of education at Michigan State University.)

In the book *Messy Church*, Hopkins talked about these three means of learning: formal, socialization, and nonformal (apprenticeship).

Formal learning is what most of us in the Western context think of first—the dispensing of information through a class, a course, or even a sermon. Hopkins suggests Jesus' Sermon on the Mount and other teachings would fit this model of learning/discipleship.

Socialization learning is the natural, unstructured, instinctive kind of learning that happens in relationships. Hopkins wrote, "Put us with others and we learn from them and the interactions between us and them." He goes on to note that Jesus invited twelve to "follow me" and thus invited them into this second model of learning.

Nonformal learning is best understood as apprenticeships. This happens when a master takes someone to mentor, to coach, and to pass on a skill. Hopkins sees this kind of learning taking place as Jesus gave His disciples instructions and then gave them feedback.

So what does this have to do with fresh expressions of church?

It is true that many fresh expressions of church will not emphasize the first method—classes and courses—at least not in the beginning. Yet fresh expressions of church are great at socialization learning and nonformal learning. And those models are wonderfully effective in the formation of Christian disciples. Once more we hear from Bob Hopkins.

Here again it is significant that the Gospels show us so much of Jesus working with the disciples in non-formal learning settings as he sought to bring his radically re-interpreted vision of what the Kingdom of God meant, nothing less than "repentance," *metanoia*, a change of thinking, values, worldview.[3]

This is a stage in the journey toward a fresh expression of church that often requires a great deal of patience. "Discipleship is a lot slower than I realized," said one pioneer of a fresh expression of church. We should be deliberate, but we should not try to force people to move more quickly than they are willing or able. Think back to how patient Jesus was with those He called to be His disciples.

Church Taking Shape

The intent of pioneers is not just to do good. The intent is that a community of Christ-followers, with the potential to transform their world, come into being. Of course, if the work of the pioneers does not ultimately result in a church, they still have served God and people. They will have lived and served well, can celebrate that, and seek to discern God's next steps for them. However, the clear aim is the establishment of a fresh expression of church.

As people move closer toward following Jesus, they will naturally want to associate with others on the same journey. They might or might not understand how church typically works, but there will be a desire for support and mutual learning. Church in some form—church that fits both the setting and the biblical principles of church—will emerge. In some sort of rhythm, members of this emerging group will get together and do things that foster their spiritual growth. There might be a small handful of people, or there might be many more.

It is, of course, true that those new to the idea of fresh expressions might struggle to define the group as "church," for it probably is unlike their presuppositions about church. Nevertheless, the intent is that there will be, in God's timing and by His Spirit, a group of people bearing the marks of church—genuine church.

At what point does the *community* become *church*? In the fresh expressions model it is somewhat difficult to discern—a little bit like asking, "At what point did that man become bald?" According to the more traditional model, we knew it was church when a group had a building, a paid pastor, was constituted, and was recognized by its denomination. These new forms of church, however, are not as easily recognizable.

In the Fresh Expressions movement, a common means of determining church is whether the group of Christ-followers exhibit the following elements: *up* (they worship), *in* (they engage in fellowship and discipleship), *out* (they invest themselves in ministry, mission, and service), and *of* (they see themselves as part of the global family of churches).

Churches might look very different from our notions of church, but if they bear the biblical marks of church they are churches indeed.[4]

Do It Again

Even in some of the early conversations it will be helpful if you talk about the call to join God in His mission to the world. We want those we engage with the gospel to see themselves as participants in God's ongoing story. Thus we can build into the personality of the group a sense of responsibility for the well-being of their friends, community, and world. Then it will be natural someday for a conversation to arise about some in the group branching off and starting a new fresh expression of church. If people have been brought along in the process, they won't know any other way.

In their book, *Vital Churches*, Ed Stetzer and Warren Bird wrote about the "Tribbles," furry little creatures on an episode of *Star Trek* that multiplied rapidly because they were born pregnant![5] That is what we're talking about when we say, "Do it again." We're talking about fresh expressions of church who are "born pregnant"—who see themselves from the beginning as people who one day will begin multiple new forms of church.

Chapter 20

WORSHIP

A fresh expression of church typically begins with *service*, not *a* service. Of course it is not church in the full sense of the word, though, without an *upward* element—the direction of our tribute, in some form, directed toward our Father and Creator.

What indigenous worship looks like in these fresh expressions of church is an interesting topic. Contemporary worship is one thing; worship with no band or choir, no sermon, and no announcements (all of which might be absent in a fresh expression of church) seems almost unchristian!

Because of the central and often controversial nature of worship, we will devote an entire chapter to the topic.

At What Point to Begin?

People sometimes ask, "At what point in the development of a fresh expression of church should we begin worship?" There is no definitive answer on this. Some begin fairly quickly to worship together; others take much, much longer before a worship element is introduced.

We do want to make sure we are not guilty of a "bait-and-switch." It might be unfair and counterproductive to ask people to join you in an effort to clean up the city . . . then out-of-the-blue spring the "church thing" on them. So, one man, in the initial stages of a fresh expression that he began in his home, invited folks to an Easter egg hunt and said to those gathered, "We are followers of Jesus and Easter is a big deal to us so we wanted to celebrate with you. Welcome to our place!" He didn't overwhelm them with Christian lingo, but neither did he hide his identity.

Those whose fresh expressions of church begin as an effort to clean up a neighborhood might say, "We believe God cares for His creation and that He charges us to keep it healthy." Those beginning a fresh expression in the running community might, in the first conversation, quote Olympian Eric Lidell from *Chariots of Fire*: "When we run we feel God's pleasure."

All along there can be subtle but clear elements of spirituality, of God-centeredness. At some point in the development of the community, however, there will probably be an intentional move toward clear acknowledgement and appreciation for who God is. There will be some introduction to what it means to follow Jesus in the particular context.

Your intuition, input from the group, and your attentiveness to the promptings of God's Spirit will help you discern when the time is right.

So When We Begin, What Does It Look Like?

Lots of people wonder what worship and preaching might look like when a fresh expression of church makes the transition to some sort of worship experience. Remember: we are not talking about attracting people who are on the positive periphery of church; we are talking about engaging unchurched people. Since our task here is to figure out new forms of church for people who are unlikely ever to come to our existing churches, it is best to think first about biblical principles of worship, not specific practices, so that what emerges fits naturally in the varying contexts and is meaningful for people new to the faith.

On the one hand, the Bible offers few specifics when it comes to the shape of Christian worship. Certainly, if one searches, one can find general descriptions of early worship services. Yet biblical prescriptions for corporate worship are not as common as one might think or hope. (One might even observe that the New Testament emphasizes the corporate worship experience far less than does the average church today.)

On the other hand, worshiping God together has, for two thousand years, been that which—more than any other act of the congregation—has bound us together, inspired us, comforted us, challenged us, and identified us. The centrality of worship should not be jettisoned.

Perhaps, then, what should be open for discussion is the form, the rituals, and the practices of worship.

We can take a lesson from the growing Christian movement in the Global South. One of the keys to that explosion has been the contextualization of worship. Christian movements emphasizing indigenous worship have far out-paced their more Western-looking counterparts in terms of participation and vibrancy.

We already have considered in this book the importance of indigeneity, and the area of worship is no exception to that principle. If our concern is to be biblical in our worship, and to reflect the best of the local context, a helpful model is that of dynamic equivalence. Dynamic equivalence (traced to Bible translator Eugene Nida) helps us figure out how to be both biblical and contextual. Dynamic equivalence is about translating the sense or meaning of biblical texts into words, symbols, or practices that carry the same sense or meaning for a contemporary context. Dynamic equivalence is summed up in the words of David Bosch: "What we are really called to do, in a nutshell, is 'to be faithful to the old text in a new situation.'"[1]

Charles Kraft helped us here. His proposal was that we determine the biblical forms, functions, and meanings in New Testament worship and then find the dynamic equivalents in today's culture. The book of Acts and the Pastoral Epistles are offered by Kraft as the sources which one might consult in the search for the biblical model.[2]

Is there truly a biblical model for worship? Williams Dillon observed,

> Outside of the Lord's Supper there is no stated order or form of service in Scripture. However, there are certain limitations and suggestions given which are designed to keep local church services "decent and in order" and from becoming one-sided in any phase of scriptural teaching.[3]

Dillon found such "limitations and suggestions" in 1 Corinthians 14.[4]

It seems appropriate, then, to follow our best understanding of the model (characteristics) of a biblical worship service and then determine their dynamic equivalents. Such is the biblical model for worship.

Core elements of biblical, contextualized worship

If it is possible to summarize this concept of biblical, contextualized worship, we can say it includes, but is not limited to, these elements:

- It is accessible and understandable to the common worshiper.
- It is real; it is authentic.
- It is missional, both in the sense that there is something really attractive to lots of people when they see followers of Jesus truly worship and in the sense that worship prepares us for engaging the world.
- It is relational (relationships trump style).
- It is transformational.
- It is creative, without creativity becoming an idol.
- It is God-centered; not us-centered.
- It is "chaordic"[5] It is somewhat *chaotic*, in that everything is not orchestrated and cannot be fully anticipated. Yet there is *order*; there is (1) flexibility within the parameters of what we understand to be biblical standards and (2) at least a reflection on the worship experiences of the historical, global church.

Up, in, out, and of

Another way to summarize the core of worship in a fresh expression of church is to remember the "up, in, out, and of" regarding church itself. This fourfold description of the nature of church is a good reminder of the nature of worship as well. Worship, of course, has to do with the *up*ward expression of our awe and the vertical encounter with God's Spirit. Worship is, at its heart, the intentional acknowledgement of the majesty of God and the penetrating experience of His grace.

Worship directs us *in*ward in that there is a relational element to worship. Certainly one can worship God alone, yet in the faith community corporate worship is key. One may worship God privately, but not in isolation.

Furthermore, an acknowledgement of, and encounter with, God's magnificence thrusts us, necessarily, *out* into the world. He is, by nature, on mission, and to encounter Him genuinely is to be compelled to join Him on mission.

Finally, worship at its best finds similarities to worship within the global Christian family. Thus, there is an *of* element to worship. We are at our best when we learn from, and appreciate our solidarity with, the larger family of faith.[6]

Practical Matters

No matter the style of worship, or if the worship even fits in any category of style, here are elements that are emerging as helpful in fresh expressions of church. This list grows out of the real world of fresh expressions.

1. *Let people tell their stories.* Some of us used to call these "testimonies." The stories, offered when the church is gathered, are genuine, personal, often raw, accounts of what God is doing.

2. *Use simple music*. Simple music means being free to have no soloists, no band, and no choral group. And it is certainly acceptable if you consider not singing as a group.

Halter and Smay wrote,

> Yes, singing together is still a meaningful experience for a large section of the existing church population, but you'll find that as your church reaches deeper and deeper into the culture, this experience will be perceived as weird for some and nice for others, but surely not the most important reason they gather in a church service.[7]

I sat with a man one day who sensed a call to start a new form of church. He was already thinking about what the worship would look like. He told me of his plan to pull together a worship team, with the complete complement of musicians that typically lead churches in what we call contemporary worship. All this would be in addition to the other responsibilities that come with beginning a fresh expression of church. He had no intentions of quitting his day job, so I asked him if he had thought of all the time it would require to pull together the musicians, rehearse them, come up with a worship set, find fill-ins for the last-minute cancellations, and so on.

He hadn't.

"So what if you were to plan for a much simpler worship?" I asked him. "What if," I asked, "you were to just see who shows up? If someone says, 'Hey, I know how to play the guitar if you guys want to sing,' then maybe you could let them do that." And, I boldly suggested, "who says you have to have a 'music set' anyway?"

He was relieved. "I really can do it like that?" he asked. Yes, you can.

It goes without saying that well-planned worship, including beautiful music, has been and still is deeply meaningful for many of us. Nevertheless, lots of new churches worship God "in spirit and in truth" without paid worship leaders, without acoustic guitars, without choirs, without big worship budgets, and without an overly scripted event.

This simple music is perhaps offered by those who have come new into the community. This is a risk, particularly if excellence is a value for you, but its authenticity makes up for what you lose in excellence.

3. Use teaching themes/topics that are relevant to the context. If
you were going to begin a fresh expression of church among professional fishermen, would you not choose in the beginning to talk
about the fish stories in the Bible, and about God's love for the
common person? And if you were going to begin a fresh expression
of church among people with an environmental bent, would you
not often consider the texts surrounding creation, its beauty, and its
care? Like Paul meeting the Athenians "where they were," tailoring
the thematic emphases to the subculture we are working with is
good missionary strategy.

4. Don't assume people know basic Bible stories. We preachers
are tempted to take shortcuts, such as, "You know the story of
Daniel . . ." Nope, many don't know that story or the others. Don't
assume biblical literacy.

5. Share leadership of worship. Responsibilities for leading worship
and doing the biblical teaching are being shared, or rotated, in many
fresh expressions of church.[8] Shared leadership is modeled, and the
new form of church is not built on the personality of the founder.

6. Consider worshiping in public spaces. Darrell Guder wrote, "The
walls and windows of churches need to become transparent."[9]
Worship in public places, baptize where lots can see—both are
wonderful means of witness. District Church in Washington, DC,
recently celebrated its baptisms on the sidewalk in a tank. Find ways
to let outsiders look in, to see what you're doing.

7. Explain to new people what is going on. Simple instructions to
guests would go a long way toward making people feel included.
Don't assume that because you understand the meaning behind a
practice, and know what is coming next, a guest will understand
(or should). Church is not a secret society, with secret handshakes
and symbols known only to the initiated. This is *church*, and clear
instructions are a matter of Christian hospitality.

8. Be creative. There is no predetermined model for worship in a fresh expression of church. The worship might be as simple as reading Psalms, or might involve someone new to the group sharing their musical gifts.

Here is an interesting idea about worship in a new form of church.

> Picture a church where you walk in the door and there are eleven groups of coffee tables with eight chairs in a half circle around them. . . . After the preaching, three simple yet searching open-ended questions are presented on the screen. Coffee, tea, and cakes have mysteriously arrived onto your table during the post-preaching song, and you're eager to talk about some of the thought-provoking, convicting, and encouraging things you've heard. As you talk with the people you quickly realize that everybody else is as human as you are. . . . There needs to be a group leader to prevent absolute chaos and steer the group while not hogging it. The key is to let nonbelievers in your midst talk . . .[10]

Of course your room might have neither coffee tables nor screens. And you might not have the kind of sermon that is implied here. But you get the idea. Maximize participation. Remember that people learn in different ways, so offer the most varied styles of teaching possible. Listen to people. Don't give up control, but also don't over-orchestrate.

9. Make it participatory. Most fresh expressions of church engage a particular subculture. So what would participatory worship in your subculture look like? Let's say your fresh expression of church originated in the hearts of people who share a common concern for those who are under-resourced. What would it look like, in the new form of church, if the first thing you do when you gather would be to involve everyone in a group activity whereby you invest in people starting microbusinesses, using Kiva[11] or some other such tool? Or, let's say your fresh expression of church is in the arts community.

Perhaps some joint art project with a theme to match the theme of the worship would be possible.

10. Check in often. Begin simply, and check in often with the new members of the circle to see if what you are doing is meaningful. It is important that we be careful not to revert to styles that are comfortable for the already-believers; this is about people who are new to faith. So check in with the recent Christ-followers. It is not theirs to dictate the direction of worship, but it is ours to ask if what we are doing is connecting.

Before we leave this very practical conversation, let's remember that in worship, as in all the aspects of fresh expressions life, the issue is *incarnation*, not *relevance*. The goal is not to be relevant, but to incarnate the gospel in subcultures among people who need Jesus.

Where and how often?

For corporate worship, the gatherings most often take place in venues other than church buildings. The 2014 Church Army report, cited elsewhere, revealed that 56 percent of the fresh expressions in the Church of England met somewhere besides the facilities of existing churches. It is my experience that the percentage is higher in the United States—with a larger majority gathering in non-church buildings.

Assumptions about the required frequency of public gatherings have been challenged by fresh expressions of church. Not all fresh expressions of church gather for worship or study every week; some meet every other week and some even gather monthly. Sunday is the most common day for fresh expressions of church (at least in the UK), although meetings take place on other days as well.

Preaching and Communion

When the topic of worship comes up, in the context of a fresh expression, traditional church leaders often raise questions about preaching. Many ask whether anyone in these fresh expressions of church stands and delivers a sermon, and the more skeptical ones ask whether the Bible is actually taught. Likewise, people ask about the celebration of Communion (and Communion can indeed be challenging).

Many of us have known no other kind of worship than that in which someone stands and talks for half the worship service. And many of us have such an exalted view of Communion (Holy Eucharist, the Lord's Supper) that we struggle to envision an appropriate celebration of that sacrament (called "ordinance" in some traditions) in this new form of church.

Because these two practices—preaching and Communion—are so central to our understanding of worship, we focus on them in the next chapter for a deeper discussion.

Chapter 21

PREACHING AND COMMUNION

As our Fresh Expression US team presents on fresh expressions of church, some of the most frequent questions are about preaching and Communion. Thus those two issues are worthy of particular attention.

Preaching

One of the most important, and particularly difficult, decisions a pioneer of fresh expressions will make is how the teaching will be communicated. The Bible certainly prioritizes the proclamation of biblical truths, but in Scripture we find multiple models of proclamation. And the monologue-sermon has probably never been more in question than it is today.[1]

On Sunday mornings across North America large numbers of people sit quietly while experts on the Scriptures and the living of life stand for half an hour or so and orate. The topic is chosen by the speaker, and questions or comments are not normally expected or particularly welcomed. That approach has served the church well for a long time and remains to this day a significant element of the discipleship of many. Yet that model is being challenged. With countless religious experts a mere YouTube search away, many contend that the monologue-sermon is not the best way to engage people with no church background.

Not many will contend that great preaching, in and of itself, will grow great churches anymore. Pulpiteers used to be able to draw great crowds with their oratorical flair; but that was a different day.

True, there are numbers of large churches driven by the personality of their pastors, but that is different from preachers attracting and impressing large crowds with their rhetorical devices. In fact, one could (and some do) argue that we should place less emphasis on the sermon today.

> The era of the monologue sermon that can have an impact is coming to an abrupt and sad end. . . . We're not signaling the end of the spoken word to communicate, but preachers will need to have a long hard look at how they speak if they expect to be heard. Except for the preaching of outstanding communicators (and they have to be very good), sermons have little or no impact. And let's not forget that preaching as we know it is only a tool and a somewhat overused one at that, one that comes more from Christendom's love of the philosophical art of rhetoric than it does from the Bible. Furthermore, it addicts the congregation to the communicator. . . . We invented the sermon (actually we borrowed the technique from the Greek and Roman philosophers), and then it reinvented us. We have become totally reliant on it![2]

Missiologist J. C. Hoekendijk asked the question of international missionaries in 1964: "Shall we in fact still preach?"[3] His question was an attempt to help Western missionaries to non-Western lands think seriously about "traditional forms and procedures." He warned of "being hypnotized by familiarity."

Hugh Halter posited,

> The reality of adult learning is that the average adult listening to us only retains about five to ten percent of the content we've worked so hard to prepare, and by the time they feed the

kids at McDonalds an hour after church, they've pretty much forgotten most of what we said. And yet, week after week, we make mammon of our time, thinking that the sermon is the center of disciple-making. But it's not even close! Adults learn primarily through sensory experience, not cognitive downloads, and the acceptance of this fact should unhinge us from this weekly grind that bears so little fruit.[4]

With so many voices downplaying the importance of preaching, what shall pioneers of fresh expressions do?

Nothing ever will take the place of people who are well-prepared and have honed the spiritual gift of teaching. Yet those teachers will always be in search of the most contextualized and effective means of communicating.

Neither the places where many fresh expressions are meeting, nor the people most fresh expressions are engaging, tend to lend themselves to one person standing up talking while everyone sits there quietly. Interaction, dialogue, personal discovery, and flexibility are elements we should consider as we decide on the medium we will choose by which to share biblical truth. The synagogue's blend of teaching and discussion, with the teacher seated, is a helpful model.

A Lesson from Tanzania

A missiologist spoke of evangelization among the Baraguyu of Tanzania. His observations inform also those of us interested in crossing cultures within our own country to establish new forms of church.

> Such things as . . . three-point homiletical sermons . . . hinder initial response to the gospel. Meeting in the shade of a tree, using Maasai proverbs in "mini-sermons," spending much time around the cooking fire prior to going to sleep . . . all help in the communication of the gospel.[5]

So, whether in Africa or in Anytown, USA, in the beginning, simple conversations about parables, Proverbs, or Bible stories might help. Often, in fresh expressions of church, someone will read from Scripture, make some opening comments, ask a series of discussion questions, and then wrap up with a brief application. This is a basic and nonthreatening approach to communicating biblical truths.

Your setting should determine your method of proclamation in the same way that the Tanzanian setting shaped the above method (shade of a tree, Maasai proverbs, minisermons, and conversation around the fire). Of course, we have to be careful here not to let our desire to be relevant and creative rob our fresh expressions of the rich biblical content necessary for good discipleship. ("Faith comes from hearing the message, and the message is heard through the word about Christ," Romans 10:17.) We should not ignore the learning styles popularized by such pervasive realities as Google and Twitter, but neither should we sacrifice solid content for the sake of coolness.

We are all still learning about effective methodologies in this new world, so try new methods. Follow Jesus' model of incarnation and explore various approaches to see how best you can communicate divine truth.

Communion

Celebration of the sacraments ("ordinances")—including, at the least, baptism and the Holy Eucharist (also known as Communion, or the Lord's Supper) is essential for church. The sacraments are both beautiful and indispensable, whether we are talking about the most traditional of churches or the newest form of church.

Yet, it is at this point that some of the most difficult conversations take place regarding fresh expressions of church. On the one extreme, one might argue, are those who restrict the celebration of the sacraments so stringently that the spirit of the sacraments get lost in the letter. On the other extreme, one might also argue, are those who handle these sacred events so loosely that the meaning of the sacraments gets lost in the quest for coolness.

The missional context of fresh expressions of church demands a reasonable, prayerful approach that treats seriously both the sacrosanct significance and the evangelistic attraction of the sacraments. Thus Damian Feeney asked, "Can fresh expressions find an appropriate and creative balance between creative innovation and the ecclesial rootedness of the Eucharist?"[6] That is the question.

Some of those concerned about surrendering the means and meanings of sacraments look with an understandably skeptical eye at fresh expressions of church. They wonder, for example, if it is appropriate for noncredentialed persons to offer primary leadership of a church or celebrate the sacraments. These are questions that deserve serious ponderings.

Of particular interest here is Holy Eucharist. Important and recurring questions like the following arise from the more liturgical wing of the church: Are unbaptized people allowed to participate in Communion? Can the bread and wine be blessed by nonordained persons? Does the Eucharist not lose its meaning if it is handled loosely?

Church leaders from denominations in the sacramental tradition often struggle with what could be perceived as an unfitting informality, even a sacrilegious nonchalance, regarding Communion. Yet, no less than Anglican Bishop Steven Croft, first leader of the Fresh Expressions movement in the UK, suggested "a lively doctrine of exceptions."

> I content myself, though not easily, that God is well used to people doing things in the wrong order, and it underlines for me the need in sacramental fresh expressions to have a "lively doctrine of exceptions." It is not a question of letting go of appropriate norms in the stewarding of these mysteries, or of any permanent re-ordering, but believing that these gifts are so essential to authentic Christian life, and our duty to offer them so crucial to our own identity and faithfulness, that agreed exceptions on the way are worth the risk.[7]

I recently asked the pioneer of a fresh expression associated with a Methodist congregation about the celebration of Communion in his new faith community. He spoke of the flexibility expressed within the *United Methodist Book of Worship*. That resource sets forth the encounter of the resurrected Jesus with the two men on the road to Emmaus as a basic pattern for worship. This pioneer believes the worship he leads, though very unconventional by most measurements, conforms to that Emmaus model.

So we talked about Communion specifically. We agreed that the celebration of Communion is an attractive means of introducing people to Jesus, of giving people an experience of grace that is unique to Communion. My pioneering friend then noted that the United Methodist Church grants some flexibility in the celebration of Communion among those who are not yet followers of Jesus. He pointed me to the following from the *United Methodist Book of Worship*, page 15.

> Invitation to partake of Holy Communion offers an evangelical opportunity to bring people into a fuller living relationship with the body of Christ. As means of God's unmerited grace, Holy Baptism and Holy Communion are to be seen not as barriers but as pathways. Pastors and congregations must strive for a balance of welcome that is open and gracious and teaching that is clear and faithful to the fullness of discipleship.
>
> Nonbaptized people who respond in faith to the invitation in our liturgy will be welcomed to the Table. They should receive teaching about Holy Baptism as the sacrament of entrance into the community of faith—needed only once by each individual—and Holy Communion as the sacrament of sustenance for the journey of faith and growth in holiness—needed and received frequently. "Unbaptized persons who receive communion should be counseled and nurtured toward baptism as soon as possible."[8]

This is, I suggest, a beautiful example of not forfeiting the spirit of Communion, but employing "a lively doctrine of exceptions" for missional purposes.

Baptism in the ICU

In May 2008, right about midnight on a Sunday night, our home phone rang. It was Denise's best friend. Denise had terminal cancer and had taken a rapid turn for the worse. She was in the Neuro Intensive Care Unit at a Richmond hospital.

Denise was not a member of our church, but a few weeks earlier her friend, who was one of our church members, explained that Denise and her husband wanted me to visit. I did. Denise was very vulnerable and transparent. She explained that she had inoperable, incurable cancer and wanted to talk about important life issues. She explained that, along the way, she had made some bad choices and had suffered the consequences.

Denise also explained that as a young person she had made the decision to follow Jesus. She'd been sincere about that but, in time, she wandered from that and had made some really bad decisions. She regretted the decisions but also regretted that she never had gone public with her faith, though she believed in Jesus. As I spoke with her it seemed to me that her faith was real. I'm not in charge of judging anyone's heart, but I was (and still am) convinced that Denise's faith, for this world and the next, was in Jesus and not her own goodness. She wanted to give a public indication of her faith and so I told her of our upcoming annual baptism service in the James River. Denise was thrilled at the idea of being baptized in the river as a sign of her spiritual commitment and began looking forward to it.

But suddenly Denise was deathly ill. The midnight phone call was asking if I'd come to the hospital. Denise wanted to be baptized that night.

When I arrived, the room was full. Close friends were there. Her family was there. Her former husband and his wife were there. Even two nurses saw what was about to happen and came in to add their support.

I spoke with Denise and, indeed, she wanted to be baptized then and there. I looked across the room and saw a sink and some Styrofoam cups. I filled a cup with water, then I grabbed a towel. I explained what I was going to do and said, "Before I baptize Denise, why don't we sing?" So I began . . . *Amazing Grace how sweet the sound, that saved a wretch like me . . .*

Everybody joined in. Lots of folks know the words to "Amazing Grace." It was beautiful. At night in an intensive care unit, where the only sounds are the occasional beeping of IVs and the subtle puffing of ventilators, the notes of "Amazing Grace" echoed movingly.

. . . *I once was lost, but now I'm found . . .*

Denise was too weak to sing more than a few words at the time. But she'd sing a phrase or two. Then catch her breath. Then sing again.

. . . *was blind, but now I see.*

We sang the whole thing. Including the part about being there ten thousand years.

And then I baptized her. I poured the water gently over her forehead. Common water from a Styrofoam cup became a sacred symbol of unconditional, undeserved, unlimited, unrelenting love.

Shortly after I baptized her, Denise drifted off to sleep.

At about 4:30 the next day Denise awakened . . . in the presence of God.

Why sing "Amazing Grace"? Because Denise seemed to be slipping away fast and I wanted Denise to know that God delights in her. Denise had some regrets, some "what was I thinking?" from her past. But I wanted Denise to know that the Father whom she soon would meet face-to-face absolutely adores her. I wanted her to know that, because her faith was in Jesus, not her own goodness, she didn't have to be afraid of what would follow her last breath on earth.

Here's the point: communicating grace often requires a careful coloring outside the proverbial lines. The method of her baptism was outside of my belief about the mode of baptism. As a Baptist, immersion is central to our identity and doctrine. Yet, it seemed more than obvious that, in that situation and in the name of grace, my beliefs about the mode of baptism were relatively unimportant.

Could we apply that principle, perhaps, to the celebration of the Eucharist? Could we, for missional purposes in particular contexts, allow for some flexibility?

We have biblical precedent for the prayerful relaxing of our sense of appropriateness. After all, "The reason why Christianity grew beyond being simply a sect of Second Temple Judaism was that these traditions [i.e., circumcision, laws of clean and unclean] were now seen to be restricting and preventing the grace of God in its full expression."[9]

Creative Solutions

It is argued by many that, until Communion can be administered by common (nonordained) Christians, and until Communion can be experienced by people who are still on the way to faith in Jesus, the sacraments will be obstacles to the effective establishment of fresh expressions of church. Many, in fact, believe that relaxing the requirements for both celebrants and participants could be wonderfully effective. To be invited to remember, mourn, and celebrate the death of Jesus can be viewed as a mystical honor, many say, and could be a powerful experience for the not-yet-believer. And wouldn't it be wonderful, many believe, if we didn't have to wait on people with particular credentials to celebrate the sacraments?

Key traditions of several denominations rightfully hold high the sacred nature of the sacraments, and, for many, relaxing the requirements would be profane. There is much to be said for the power of tradition to minimize deviation from, and maximize passion for, the sacraments. After all, standards are necessary for any movement or organization.

Yet the unique challenges of post-Christendom beg at least for the revisiting of some of our customs. Could creative solutions be found—new approaches that both honor our heritage and engage not-yet-believers?

We again turn to Anglican leader Steven Croft.

The Church must ever be attending to its stewardship of these mysteries and we all need to recover our love for the sacraments and our belief in them as places of divine encounter. I'm going to be arguing therefore for a fresh approach, and that we need to consider "chilling out" with regard to the rules and regulations with which we steward them, so that they may be the blessing they truly are. . . . I suggest that reflection about an agreed doctrine of exceptions is one of the hard questions that we, and especially church leaders, must address. . . . Perhaps the guardians of the faith, as bishops are sometimes called, are in danger of overprotecting the Lord. Like the disciples with the children we become stumbling blocks to an encounter with Jesus. . . . There is a need for deregulation in evangelistic circumstances, for a proper and agreed doctrine of exceptions . . .[10]

Croft reportedly said one of the symbols of his ministry in this field is a can of WD-40 "to help loosen up traditional procedures to make possible more of these fresh expressions."[11] It makes one wonder if perhaps the future will see some loosening up of some of our traditions for the sake of mission.

Naturally, the idea of "loosening up" smacks of lowering the bar, of surrendering standards, of violating the meaning of some of the most sacred of Christian acts. It could appear that we are calling for a sacrifice of the sacraments on the altar of freshness. However, that is not the intention of anyone I know. The intention of pioneers is to reimagine means by which the sanctity of our important Christian acts can be maintained while recognizing the missionary nature of these new forms of church.

Many still wonder how, where, and if fresh expressions of church fit within the polity of some traditions. The plea here is simply that, for the sake of God's mission, we continue this conversation toward the end that the preaching of the word and the celebration of Communion (as well as other sacraments, of course) honor our Lord and enrich our faith without being obstacles to the introduction of people to the kingdom.

Chapter 22

ANSWERING THE QUESTIONS (PART 1)

Any movement titled "Fresh Expressions" is bound to provoke questions. After all, there is a cat litter called Fresh Expressions and a line of candles called Fresh Expressions. It's not surprising that people would be asking so many questions about fresh expressions of *church*.

The questions are not only a matter of curiosity; some of the questions reflect a deep concern about the movement's validity. The caution on the part of many to embrace this movement is understandable. The hesitancies merit a thoughtful response.

This movement is so young we will have to wait years for the full answer to some of the questions, such as questions about longevity, sustainability, and the like. But it is not too early to answer the most common queries, even if the answers are not yet complete.[1]

What's to keep them from going rogue?

This was the very first question asked publicly of me about fresh expressions of church: "What's to keep them from going rogue?" This is a legitimate question reflecting a sincere concern for orthodoxy. It is not unreasonable that people might be nervous about what could happen if leaders who are not theologically trained, and not fully credentialed, are left to themselves to lead new believers.

While the apprehension is understandable, I believe we can be confident in the direction these fresh expressions of church are going. One reason for calm is the mixed economy. If the fresh expression of church is tethered to a mature congregation, we would expect there to be healthy mentoring, resourcing, and encouragement. It is a very good thing to have the leader of a fresh expression in regular dialogue with a seasoned minister.

A more important answer to the concern about potential unorthodoxy is the work of the Spirit and the power of Holy Scripture.

Joshua Hearne helps lead a new monastic community called "Grace and Main." (See his story later in the book.) Once I asked Joshua, "So what keeps Grace and Main from going theologically rogue?" "The Spirit," Joshua immediately answered. "Beyond that," he continued, "we gather daily in our homes to read Scripture together, to listen to the Spirit together. We take Scripture very seriously. We also believe the best guard of orthodoxy is orthopraxy. Practicing the teaching of the text keeps us faithful to the meaning of the text."

Joshua continued, "I am seminary trained, but I am not as good a guard of orthodoxy as a community of people seeking the face of Christ together. We also partner with local congregations whose pastors meet often with us, suggesting books to us and remaining in conversation with us."

He noted, halfway in jest, "No one asks established congregations what is to keep them from going rogue." Yet he added, "Our answer is the same one they would give if they were asked. The answer is: 'Commitment to following the guidance of the Spirit and mutual interpretation of Scripture in the community.'"

As it was in the beginning of the church, is now again—people with no formal theological training are relying on the illumination of God's Spirit for people on a journey toward Jesus. Ultimately we have to, and can, trust the Spirit to do as He did in the book of Acts with a new movement.

Will they last?

Perhaps the second most common question asked publicly has to do with the sustainability, the lasting power, of these new forms of church. And this is one of those questions which history will have to answer.

Presumably we all would prefer that a particular church (new or otherwise) last a long time. Longevity, however, is not itself a measure of success. And every organism, including all churches as we know them, have life cycles.

We should not judge the effectiveness of a fresh expression primarily by how long it is around. The promise of durability might have to be sacrificed for the sake of flexibility and adaptability. While we would love to see our fresh expression of church last a century, our attempts to engage particular segments of a rapidly changing culture might make for shorter life spans.

If we could gaze into a crystal ball we would see, more than likely, that some of these new churches will be short-lived. Early evidence from research done by the Church Army of the Anglican Church, though, indicates that fresh expressions of church have powerful durability.

In other words, regarding their life spans they will resemble all other forms of church. Some will have long histories; others will not.

What if participants in our fresh expressions relocate?

Davison and Milbank (in the book, *For the Parish*) note that when an active member of a parish moves to another city, he or she is likely to look for a congregation in their new locale. But, the authors ask, what about those involved in a fresh expression of church? Each fresh expression is unique, the argument goes, so it is not likely that people will find another one like it in their new locale, and it is also not likely that people will plug into anything after relocating.

This is not a new risk. John Drane wrote of the churches in the New Testament, "There was never any guarantee that the church in one place would be the same as the church in a different setting. Indeed, this ability to contextualize itself within such diverse cultures is perhaps the one thing that, above all others, explains the attraction of the Christian gospel."[2]

Though the issue is not a new one, the concern is legitimate. It is indeed important that people find a new family of faith after moving to a new place. We can make sure everyone in our specific fresh expression of church understands our connection to the larger church and how important it is to involve one's self in local expressions of that church wherever we are.

Is this a fad?

Of course, there have been lots of fads in the church world, and some people appropriately wonder if Fresh Expressions of church is just another passing fancy. I sometimes hear from people (particularly people whose congregations have been closely tied to their denominations), "We've seen initiatives like this come and go. Soon this will fade and another will take its place as the newest fail-proof method of winning the world for Jesus."

Frankly, only history can answer this question.[3] At this point, no one can predict the future of fresh expressions beyond this first generation. And, as with an individual fresh expression of church, the impact and effectiveness of the movement is not to be measured solely by the length of its life.

Furthermore, if this lasts only a few decades, yet results in transformed lives and a rethinking of methodology, then that would be a blessing. If our children can be inspired by, and build on, our efforts and thus be part of a spiritual renewal, then this movement will have served a holy purpose.

Indications are, however, that this movement has significant traction. Results of the Church Army's research into the impact of the Fresh Expressions movement in England are more than encouraging. The data are unquestionably promising. Something is up. God is moving in people's hearts and there is an unmistakable depth and breadth to what is happening. Much like the Pentecostal movement of the twentieth century, God is refreshing His people and, in many ways, diversifying us by bringing inherited churches alongside these new forms of church.

The danger of signing on to what could turn out to be a faddish program is not nearly as great as the danger of turning one's nose up at, and one's back on, a potential reshaping of the church and a renewing of its sense of mission. To be guilty of following a fad is, at worst, a distraction. To miss out on a movement possibly as significant as the Protestant Reformation, on the other hand, would be tragic.[4]

Are inherited churches truly valued?

Admittedly, in some circles, our older, inherited churches are dismissed as irrelevant and passé. That is unfortunate. Churches with steeples, committees, and hymns are still effectual. I cannot imagine a time when churches like that, who take seriously their mission, will be obsolete. The church you've known and loved for a long time offers continuity, a place where people with varying backgrounds and preferences learn to do life together, and a connection to the universal church.

The future of each local congregation is, of course, not assured. Yet there will long be a place for churches of all kinds who honor the Lord of the church and the people for whom He died. Moreover, the pastors and priests of those congregations will long have the platform that gives them a central spiritual role in their communities, in ways that leaders of fresh expressions will not.

Smart pioneers of fresh expressions recognize the value of inherited churches, the debt they owe them, and all they can learn from the leaders of those churches. Philip Roderick, spiritual leader of a fresh expression of church called Contemplative Fire, put it this way: "The treasury of engaged belief, gleaned and garnered over the centuries, is the spiritual lineage upon which we draw."[5]

Those of us who are investing ourselves in fresh expressions of church would do well to remember these words from the book of Romans:

If . . . you, though a wild olive shoot, have been grafted in
among the others and now share in the nourishing sap from
the olive root, do not consider yourself to be superior to those
other branches. If you do, consider this: You do not support
the root, but the root supports you. (Rom. 11:17–18)

We know this text is talking about Jews and Gentiles, but it
is also a good reminder to us not to smugly dismiss the inherited
churches and to remember that both the steeple churches and the
fresh expressions of church depend fully on the Lord of the church.

Of course we must not, for the sake of playing nice, ignore
the obstacles which traditionalism presents. While we affirm our
heritage, we do not naïvely deny the potentially stifling effects of a
tradition-laden mentality. It is one thing to respect and draw from
our tradition; it is quite another to be chained to it.

And while we're on the topic, I appeal to leaders of inherited
churches for your blessing on fresh expressions of church. Your
support, mentoring, and championing—in short, your blessing—of
fresh expressions of church would go a long way toward both the
effectiveness of fresh expressions and their appreciation of you and
what you do.

What do we do with the children?

One of the most common questions churched people ask about these
new forms of church is, "What do we do with the children?" The
answer to that question varies from fresh expression to fresh expression. In some cases, participants share responsibilities for teaching
children in separate rooms from the adults (much like traditional
churches). In others, the children are right in the middle of things,
participating in whatever worship looks like in particular contexts.

These new forms of church give us an opportunity to ask:
Should children really be sequestered? Is separating them from older
generations really the best way to disciple them? One could argue
for age-appropriate teaching methods, and even for giving young
parents a break. But one also could argue that multigenerational

church experiences shape lives—young and old alike. In many cultures and religious experiences, the adults would not think of segregating the children from the adults.

The give-and-take required of multigenerational experiences could minimize the often-lamented selfishness of churchgoers of all ages. If discipleship is as much caught as taught, then having the children in the room can positively shape their perceptions of Jesus and His church. Neil Cole wrote,

> When we moved to the city and started organic churches, our kids began to learn in a more experiential fashion. They saw lives transformed. They listened to people share their horrid stories of abusive lifestyles and then watched them live for Jesus. . . . My son learned something about love, kindness, and hospitality that he could never learn with a flannel graphs story of a Good Samaritan. . . .
>
> The reason that kids are not an interruption for us is simple: there is nothing to interrupt! Oh, don't get me wrong; we do have a learning time discussing God's word, but it is not a monologue by a gifted teacher that demands silence and respect. Instead, it is a community learning time that involves the entire family, including the children, so there is no such thing as interrupting it. If you think of church as family rather than a weekly religious event, you begin to see differently the whole idea of what it should be. Children do not interrupt family because children *are* family. . . .
>
> There are moments (although not too many) in our church context where a mom or dad will pick up a small child and go outside for a couple of minutes. Occasionally, I may even take someone else's child out to read a storybook while mom and dad stay and participate in the group learning. We allow kids to go out back and shoot baskets if they want to. Often children draw pictures while we discuss the Scriptures. They are kids and they act like kids; we would expect nothing else. . . . I personally believe that the familial interactions in church are a more potent way to change lives than listening to a sermon once a week.[6]

With a little preparation, the children can participate in ways that enrich adults and disciple children. They can draw pictures of the worship theme and offer prayers. If there is singing, one of the songs can be a children's song. Or if a topic is PG-13, then an alternative activity for the young ones can be provided.

There is a lot to be said for the targeted, interactive, often high-tech learning experiences that established congregations can offer specifically for children. And there is a lot to be said for the family-like experience of many generations learning from each other in new forms of church.

Are fresh expressions of church merely a convenient home for antiestablishment Christians?

Since we trumpet fresh expressions of church as a means of engaging people who need Jesus, it is fair to ask whether the goal is being reached. Some have wondered if fresh expressions are little more than a soft spot to land for people who don't like the demands of inherited churches.

To many, there is indeed something attractive about the fact that a fresh expression of church is not the hierarchical, corporate, institution that so many typically associate with church. However, fresh expressions of church are not a nouveau Christian hippy movement. This is not Christian antiestablishmentarianism.

It is important that we remember what is a fresh expression of church.

A fresh expression is a form of church for our changing culture established primarily for the benefit of people who are not yet members of any church.

Of particular import here is that phrase, "primarily for the benefit of people who are not yet members of any church." Certainly we will be glad if people who once were part of a congregation find their way back to the family through a fresh expression of church. If people who have been hurt by churches, who have become disenchanted, or who for whatever reason have drifted from the church find their way home, then fresh expressions of church will have served a marvelous purpose. There are millions of people who find present forms of church unhelpful to their spiritual journeys, and need a meaningful, Christ-centered community in which to fully live their faith. If they can find what they need in a fresh expression of church, then praise be to the Father.

Yet, the fact remains and must be understood: this is not first of all about reclaiming absentee church people and it certainly is not about siphoning off people from inherited churches.

Fresh expressions of church find their deepest purposes among those who are not yet followers of Jesus and those who are drawn to Him and seeking to follow Him. This is not about recycling disciples and transferring them from an inherited church to our cooler church. This is about making disciples who then join God in His mission of grace, reconciliation, and justice to the world.

Chapter 23

ANSWERING THE
QUESTIONS (PART 2)

N ew is not necessarily better than old; fresh is not necessarily superior to established; and effervescence is not a substitute for substance."[1] Those words from British academician Martyn Percy offer a window into the questions (sometimes criticisms) of the Fresh Expressions movement.

Here we continue the attempt to answer these challenging inquiries:

How much "form" can we eliminate without losing "content"?

This question is particularly important for liturgical traditions, but all of us should ask if it's possible to stray so far from our heritage that our methods lose their meanings. In the celebration of Communion, for example, how far from the bread and the wine can we go before the actual message is lost? Can Mountain Dew and Cheetos, for example, carry the weight of Jesus' words about the body and blood? Is "How Far Is Heaven?" by Los Lonely Boys ultimately adequate to speak of eternal realities? With every innovation, we must ask whether we are making the content of the biblical message more plain . . . or whether, in fact, we are sacrificing content for the sake of creativity and relevance.

Are we just perpetuating the consumeristic culture of the American church shopper?

It could seem to some that "taking the church Jesus loves closer to where the people Jesus loves actually are" implies a lowering, perhaps even an abandoning, of standards. Thus it might appear that fresh expressions of church are distancing themselves from Jesus' words, "Take up your cross and follow Me."

Leaders of the Fresh Expressions movement are aware of this risk, and are asking themselves questions like, "Have we just become too good at identifying people's needs and producing a version of the gospel that apparently meets the need, but fails to transform it?"[2]

The intent of this Fresh Expressions movement is certainly not to perpetuate or kowtow to the consumeristic approach to church life. The intent, rather, is to acknowledge the chasm between church as we know it and the multitudes of people "separate from Christ . . . without hope and without God in the world" (Eph. 2:12), and to decide it will be *us*, not *them*, who should take the initiative.

It's one thing to cater to the sometimes selfish expectations of church shoppers. It's quite another to minimize the obstacles for people to overcome to move from non-faith to faith in Jesus. It is the latter which motivates pioneers of fresh expressions.

Mature disciples, not marginal spectators, is the goal. Scripture won't let us be satisfied with infant Christ-followers, or infant congregations, who never grow beyond their infancy.[3] We must be careful lest someone say of our fresh expression something like Robin Gamble said: "I've been in café-church that was all café and no church."[4]

What if people want more?

Some have asked what happens if people involve themselves with a fresh expression of church but, with time, want more—a fuller, more program-driven, experience? So, let's say a family is involved in a fresh expression of twenty people who happen to be linked by a passion for the arts. They meet weekly in a small theatre. Their spiritual leader is not an ordained minister. Their organization and gatherings are really simple. So, where does their daughter get married if she wants a church wedding? What if the family needs counseling? What about interaction with the larger Christian community?

What about those traditions that people want to maintain, but for which a fresh expression of church doesn't fit? What if people want more than is available in a typical fresh expression of church?

It is not uncommon for people participating in fresh expressions of church to connect with the Christian world beyond them in practical ways. They are supplementing their fresh expressions experience. Some are joining with other small Christian communities to rent larger church facilities and doing things like "hymn festivals."[5] Some are going to Christian counselors when a seminary-trained pastor is not available. People are going to seminars and often listening to sermons on iTunes. "People's Seminaries" are springing up, which put a theological education within reach of ordinary persons. Some parents are looking to more traditional churches for confirmation classes for their children. Like home schoolers often get together with other home schoolers in their area for social and athletic events, people in smaller expressions of church are often getting together for things that a small group cannot provide . . . "points of convergence and connection where scattered saints can periodically gather and share in meaningful and corporate worship."[6] In other words, they can take advantage of the unique ministries that established and well-resourced churches offer while maintaining their primary affiliation with the more intimate model of church.

In the Fresh Expressions UK booklet *How Can We Be Sustainable?*, for example, we read the following:

> Fresh expressions will manage the flow of their members to another Christian community, where appropriate, so that individuals have a sustained church involvement. If individuals need to change church as their spirituality evolves or

circumstances change, they will be helped to do so. Sometimes sustainability will be more about flow than durability.[7]

I've spoken to multiple pioneers of fresh expressions who regularly encourage people who have come to faith and matured in the faith to explore other options of church so that they may be best nurtured in their Christian life. I'm sure there are leaders of fresh expressions of church who want to hold tightly onto members of their circle, just as many pastors of inherited churches want to do. But that is not the typical modus operandi of these fresh expressions pioneers. Those who pioneer fresh expressions of church tend not to be ego-driven.

However, and this is important, a fresh expression of church is not *intended* to be a channel through which people flow into "real" churches. A fresh expression of church is not the minor league, the prep league for big church. A fresh expression of church is neither a cheap imitation of, nor a trendy replacement for, any other form of church.

A fresh expression of church is a church, a community of faith, a family of people following Jesus or on their way toward following Jesus in covenant relationship and exhibiting all the elements of church.

What about the future role of clergy?

I brought up the topic of Fresh Expressions not long ago in a large room of ministers from multiple denominations. Their concerns were significant: "What will the role of clergy be in these new forms of church? Will the new leaders be adequately equipped theologically?" And, "If all our churches die, where will our pensions come from?" (Yes, someone asked that.)

It is understandable that vocational ministers might wonder about their place in the future church. But there will always be plenty of churches needing credentialed ministers, and for as long as any of us can imagine, there will be church as we know it.

Are fresh expressions of church too homogeneous?

This is arguably the most important question about fresh expressions of church, so we will spend some time on this topic. The emphasis on starting new forms of church within niche populations raises suspicions of ecclesiastical segregation. Critics of fresh expressions suggest we are merely creating special interest groups, forming "homogeneous units," blessing the segmentation of the family of God, and feeding the selfish preferences of people.[8] In fact, Donald McGavran and his Homogeneous Unit Principle of Church Growth are getting a lot of new attention, and not all of it is positive.

Donald McGavran opened Pandora's box when he wrote, "Men like to become Christians without crossing racial, linguistic or class barriers."[9] He was speaking of homogeneous units—subcultures of similar people. McGavran asked, "In this vast mosaic, how does the Christian Faith spread from piece to piece? Does it invite members of all pieces to leave their own people and become parts of the people of God? Or does the Church form inside each piece?"[10]

McGavran had a clear answer to his question. He postulated that people "like to join churches whose members look, talk, and act like themselves," and he posited that "nothing in the Bible . . . requires that *in becoming a Christian* a believer must cross linguistic, racial, and class barriers."[11] Note the italics in McGavran's statement. He would go on to explain that with spiritual maturity such barriers matter less and less. Initially, however, when one is considering the faith, he or she is drawn to people like himself or herself. Furthermore, one is able to communicate the gospel most effectively within his or her cultural unit.

Simplistically put, McGavran said, "Birds of a feather flock together. Like it or not. Accept it and plant churches for particular segments of the population. Don't make people cross barriers in order to be part of a church." It is important to note that Donald McGavran was a missionary to India in the mid-1900s and was thinking of the international scene. His homogeneous unit principle, however, has been adopted by church planters everywhere.

McGavran's practical methodology makes great sense. Pragmatism, however, is not the end-all of our efforts. McGavran's theory has drawn substantial disapproval. René Padilla put it like this.

> It is a fact that hardly needs verification that the growth of the church takes place in specific social and cultural contexts and that people generally *prefer* to become Christians without having to cross the barriers between one context and another . . . The real issue is whether church planting should be carried out so as to enable people to become Christians without crossing barriers and whether this principle is in fact "essential for the spread of the Gospel" as well as biblically and theologically defensible.[12]

Padilla went on to cite the growth of New Testament congregations across social barriers. "Conversion," Padilla wrote, "was never a merely religious experience; it was also a means of becoming a member of a community in which people find their identity in Christ rather than in race, social status, or sex."[13] Padilla found the homogeneous unit principle biblically and theologically indefensible.

Numbers of people today also criticize the rather homogeneous approach of the Fresh Expressions movement because of the reasons cited by Padilla. Because of the emphasis that *Mission-Shaped Church* placed, and that the Fresh Expressions movement continues to place, on churches within networks, several have cried foul. It certainly is an understandable protest; it is a protest worthy of our attention. It is not a protest, however, that should derail this movement and its emphasis on starting churches among subcultures.

Does the incarnation give us a clue here?

God the Son was for all the world, yet was incarnate in a particular place, among a particular people, taking on a particular ethnicity. The incarnation of the Son within a specific culture argues for churches within particular networks and niches of society. While Jesus loved all, He became flesh among an unmistakably distinct people. This does not provide us with a mandate, but it does provide us with a model for our incarnation of the gospel via new forms of church of, with, and for individual subcultures.

Were New Testament churches homogenous?

Michael Moynagh has helped us see that the house churches mentioned in the New Testament were likely rather homogeneous. They were located in particular neighborhoods that, almost certainly, consisted of people from particular strata and stratum within the population. Groupings among the congregations were based practically on groupings occurring naturally among the people. That was not by some bigoted design on the part of church leaders, but simply a reflection of the physical segmentation of their cities.

The fact that they gathered frequently as one—with the house churches combining regularly for worship—demonstrates that they were at least working at breaking down the walls of prejudice and ethno-centrism.[14]

Inclusive, One Subculture at a Time

Most strategies regarding fresh expressions of church involve engaging certain segments of the population—subcultures, if you will. However, that does not in any way imply a segregation by class or race. Today's networks are often ethnically, economically, and educationally diverse. Subcultures are often eclectic. Frankly, most subcultures of our nation are more inclusive than are our churches! In most populations and affinity groups, there is greater ethnic and socioeconomic diversity than in most congregations you know.

There are countless examples of cultural niches that are not at all grouped by the hue of people's skins, the accent of their tongues, or their rung on the social ladder. Many of those microcultures span political, educational, and even physical boundaries.

Of course, one's primary social circle is likely to be fairly homogeneous. But, remember, we are not talking primarily about social circles here; we are talking about affinity groups—circles of people formed around hobbies, interests, life-situations, vocations, neighborhoods, physical needs, online gatherings, and so on. These affinity groups are probably much more likely than one's immediate social circle to be richly diverse.

We truly are joining God in the expansion of His kingdom, the growing of His family. So we have to strike a balance between what works (like attracts like) and the heavenly vision from Revelation 7:9, "I looked and there before me was a great multitude that no one could count, from every nation, tribe, people and language, standing before the throne and before the Lamb."

If we are planting a fresh expression among the arts community, for example, then we must include everybody in that community, regardless of race, gender, salary, and so on. We must make sure we are intentionally inclusive, even within those groups. So it's something of a targeted inclusion.

I know of no one in the Fresh Expressions movement whose intent it is to separate and isolate segments of the Christian family. To dismiss this approach because of an opposition to the Homogeneous Unit Principle would be imprudent and an overreaction.

Where People Do Life

Putting the church Jesus loves closer to where the people Jesus loves actually are means planting new forms of church *where people do life.*[15] When people feel at home with a circle of people they are simply more likely to take the often uncomfortable first step toward belonging.

If our goal is the introduction of the gospel among people truly far from God, then the risk of overly homogeneous groups is a risk worth taking. Specific efforts to break down barriers must accompany our discipleship efforts, without a doubt. Yet we should not disavow the proven strategy of minimizing the obstacles people have to cross in order to come to faith in Jesus.

God inspired the apostle Paul to write, "I have become all things to all people so that by all possible means I might save some"

(1 Corinthians 9:22). David Bosch thus noted, "Paul insists that no unnecessary stumbling blocks be put in the way of prospective converts or of 'weak' believers."[16]

For the purpose of incarnating the gospel, it is helpful to engage focused segments of the population. In addition, for the purpose of living out the gospel we should ensure that, either within the new church itself, or through intentional partnerships and relationships beyond the new community, we are intentionally developing a diversity of connections.

AT THE INTERSECTION
OF GRACE AND MAIN

If you drive to Danville, Virginia, and want to find the intentional community called Grace and Main, logic would tell you to look for the intersection of Grace Street and Main Street. You'd not find it that way, for there is no such street intersection. However, where Grace—the unconditional, undeserved, unlimited, unrelenting love of God—meets Main Street . . . now *that* is where you'll find Grace and Main, a new form, a fresh expression, of church.

Joshua and Jessica Hearne are leaders of Grace and Main Fellowship. Joshua is also the executive director of Third Chance Ministries, a ministry of Grace and Main.

Joshua, a graduate of Duke Divinity School, used to be on staff as associate pastor for discipleship ministries at an established, inherited church. Then he stumbled upon Matt Bailey, an ER nurse at the local hospital, and a Bible study in Matt's home where five people gathered and were trying to learn how to serve the least of these. That encounter between Joshua and Matt was the spark that eventually turned into Grace and Main, a self-described nontraditional Christian community committed to worship, community, and service in downtown Danville, Virginia.

They have no building, nor would they take one if someone were to give it to them. Speaking of those among whom they live and whom they serve, Joshua insists, "Like our beloved, we are placeless." They gather and worship in homes of the leaders of their faith community—moving around to a different home each Sunday evening to satisfy their diverse needs. The leaders are made up of people who have moved into the area and those who are long-time residents of the area, some of whom are formerly addicted and homeless. Nearly all of the leaders, including Joshua and his family, live in the neighborhoods among marginalized and disenfranchised—areas of high poverty and profound need.

Their worship is simple. Children are right in the middle of things. Without any accompaniment, they might sing a hymn and a song that someone in the group wants to teach everyone. The "preaching" happens like this: someone reads the Scripture for the evening aloud, and the one in charge of the service takes three to five minutes to say, "This is what I hear in the text." Then that leader asks, "What do *you* hear?" Open discussion follows.

Space won't allow an adequate description of the ministries in which Grace and Main is engaged. Such things as their "roving feasts," their "tool library," and their advocacy for victims of slumlords would require an entire chapter.

The wonderfully unique thing about Grace and Main is that they are committed to the practice of hospitality. That means opening their guest bedrooms, their dinner tables, their showers, and their bathrooms to homeless and near homeless, poor, addicted, and hungry people.

Joshua acknowledges the risks associated with what they are doing but said, "We are finding that the things the world has taught us to be afraid of are not as scary as the world says. We don't often let strangers in, but we live our lives in honest relationship every day with people in our neighborhood so the people we invite in are our friends and loved ones."

They would like to cultivate small communities in areas of profound need in the shadow of partner congregations. "We're not looking to create a big, traditional congregation, but something people devote their life and time to," Joshua told me.

In Fresh Expressions terms, they want to "Do it again."

People have found great joy at Grace and Main. Josh, who raises his own support, said, "I cannot imagine another way to live and minister."[1]

Part Four

A WAY FORWARD

Chapter 24

EXISTING CHURCHES ARE NOT OBSOLETE

The presence and power of the Holy Spirit are not related to the date of a church's founding, the style of its worship, the median age of its members, or the denominational designation (or lack thereof) on the marquee. Where the church is, there the Spirit of the Lord is. We certainly can "quench" the Spirit (1 Thessalonians 5:19), and some seem to have done just that; but let's not write off any of the temples in which the Spirit dwells (1 Corinthians 3:16).

Churches are also home to God's people. That's no insignificant truth. As church planter Payton Jones admitted,

> My idea for church reform was once placing a time bomb underneath every empty church building and blowing up superstructures sky high so we'd have to start all over. Like construction workers say, "A new build is easier than a rebuild." There's only one problem with that. People. There are people in your churches for whom Christ bled, and we've got to take them with us.[1]

A Future for Old Churches?

Is there truly an ongoing place for the local church with the steeple, the 11:00 Sunday morning worship service, and all those committees? Absolutely, there is. That congregation has been making a difference in the lives of its people, and in its community, for a long time. It has an identity that is inimitable, a footprint that is undeniable, and an influence that is irreplaceable. That congregation still is at the heart of God's mission to the world.

One of the mistakes of the missional church movement has been, on the part of some, the premature dismissal of churches as we know them. In the introduction to the second edition of *The Shaping of Things to Come*, for example, Alan Hirsch and Michael Frost said they wanted a "re-do" from the first edition. They wanted to "soften the polemical edge of the early section that appears to dismiss all traditional approaches as inherently non-missional; and . . . be less pessimistic about inviting the leaders of established churches to incorporate missional principles into their churches."[2]

Hirsch and Frost wrote, humbly, "We acknowledge that we were rather too quick in dismissing existing traditional churches and their leaders from being able to re-missionalize what they were doing. . . . we are rather more optimistic about missional revitalization within the established church."[3]

It is wrong to dismiss, disparage, or disengage from existing churches. It is naive to assume a particular form of church has preferred status with God. It is, in fact, arrogant to assume the latest expression of church is the only one God's Spirit is blessing.

There is a worthy debate, of course, about whether denominations should pour increasingly limited resources into churches that have little hope for survival. Good arguments can be made for the prioritization of hope-filled efforts to start new communities of faith. Yet, to write off church as we know it for the sake of something more cool is careless, egotistical, and myopic.

Resisting Renewal Is Not the Answer Either

Of course, it is equally careless, egotistical, and myopic to believe the answer for church renewal lies in a stubborn resistance to new approaches. Doing what we've always done, but trying to do it better, is increasingly inadequate.

Some of our best thinkers are calling for a revolution, not mere evolution, of church. More and more voices seem to be advising against fads and tweaks. Trendy worship style adjustments and crafty marketing techniques are almost universally dismissed as insufficient.

While reasonable voices are not calling for the abolition or abandonment of existing churches, there are lots of people calling for radically new approaches and fundamentally new structures. Such seems to be the consensus among those prayerfully hoping for a renewed impact of the church on our culture. We could be on the cusp of a Reformation as radical as that prompted by Luther's 95 Theses. To borrow a phrase from Leonardo Boff, we are experiencing an "ecclesiogenisis."[4]

Conversion of Inherited Churches

So, the answer to "Is there an ongoing role in the mission of God for churches as we know them?" is an unequivocal "Yes." However, churches as we know them constantly have to be in prayerful dialogue about how best to engage such a rapidly changing culture. It's time for the conversion of inherited churches.

It has been noted that the story in Acts 10, about Peter, the sheet, and a Gentile named Cornelius, is as much about the conversion of Peter as it is about the conversion of Cornelius.[5] This story of the reshaping of Peter's perspective on outsiders reminds us that this conversation about fresh expressions of church is also a conversation about the conversion of existing congregations. This conversion will involve structures, priorities, more helpful metrics, and even, in some cases, a new passion for people who are far from God.

Michael Moynagh made a great point by noting that in the 1980s people in Britain wrote off the cinema; they preferred videos and TV. But instead of giving up, cinema owners "spruced up the buildings, installed more (and smaller) cinemas to give people a wider choice of films and times, made the seating more comfortable, and sold better popcorn. It worked. Attendance rose." He added, "Like cinemas, if slowly, the church too is adapting to social changes."[6]

Adaptations, if skillfully and prayerfully implemented, could breathe new life into presently atrophying churches. While we consider fresh expressions of church, we must always be looking for fresh energy, and effective fresh initiatives, from existing churches.

As Long as We Recognize that Christendom Is Gone

Re-dreaming existing churches is a vital piece of this missional puzzle, and increasing our opportunities to meet people where they are can be nothing but positive. Enhancements to our present congregations are marvelous . . . as long as we recognize that Christendom is gone.

Near Front Royal, Virginia, sits Christendom College. That college's name might be the only remnant of Christendom left in the Western world.

Christendom is the term often used to describe the church-dominated European society rooted in Constantine's conversion to Christianity and the place of privilege churches enjoyed for so many centuries. Christendom reflects a tight, if unofficial, relationship between society and the Christian religion. Such things as the former "blue laws" (businesses were prohibited by law from opening on Sunday morning) reflected a governmental preference for Christianity. The informal alliance between society and Christianity was reflected in such cultural realities as the tacit expectation that a town's good citizens would be members of a church.

It has taken longer in the US for Christendom to disappear than in Europe, but there are only faint traces of Christendom left even in the US. Because so many of our social circles include only Christians, many of us seem oblivious to the cultural/spiritual tsunami that has taken place. It's time to recognize that we can no longer operate as if we lived and did ministry in a Christian-dominated world.

Your church, unless you live in one of the remaining corners of semi-Christendom, no longer holds a place of privilege. You are part of a fringe group now. Pastors are no longer placed on pedestals. "Deacon" and "Elder" are no longer titles that impress people outside the church. And communities' deference to the wishes of the local church no longer exists.

Perhaps the only thing sadder than the decline of Christianity's impact on our continent is the fact that so many church people do not recognize it; many are operating as if we live in the Europe of the Middle Ages. The "renewing of your mind," called for in Romans 12:2, now involves a more accurate view of the world in which we are "doing church." Many of us are still planning services and building buildings in order to attract people who are, for the most part, no longer alive.

Courageous Ministers Serve Existing Churches

Although Christendom is past history for North America, entrepreneurial ministers should not assume a church plant or a fresh expression of church are your only options for meaningful ministry. Meaningful, life-transforming ministry is possible in a congregation perhaps twice your age. The work of helping deeply entrenched people consider new ways of being church is a daunting task. Yet, if all our courageous ministers who love people outside the church dismiss existing churches, we will lose the impact of all those churches with deep roots, strong histories, and beautiful stories. God certainly will call many of you to new expressions of church, but it would be wrong to believe God will no longer call missional pastors to existing congregations.

Tucked away near the end of Gordon McDonald's book *Who Stole My Church?* is an acknowledgment that lots of local church shepherds fantasize about abandoning their tradition-bound flocks for the joyous adventure of planting a new congregation. And yet, while church planting is an honorable and important vocation, it is not a calling for every missional minister. Maybe, McDonald suggests, if people would invest themselves in existing churches, they might just "see a miracle—a hundred-year-old church that acts with the spirit of an enthusiastic teenager."[7]

We celebrate the divine calls to fresh expressions of church and, of course, that is the thrust of this book. Yet many of us will live out a daring adventure in ministry in existing, traditional (by Fresh Expressions standards) congregations. And many of us will, in those settings, encourage the congregations to bring alongside them fresh expressions, new forms, of church. Unique skills are required to facilitate the ongoing renewal of inherited congregations and to encourage the birth of new forms of church in conjunction with that inherited family of faith. Yet, that can be a wonderfully rewarding, missional life. That is, in fact, something worth giving one's life to.

A Quick Word about Denominations

The Fresh Expressions movement affirms the role of established denominations and sees in them the potential to encourage and resource pioneers and new forms of church. The affirmation of, and relationships with, denominations is one of the strengths of Fresh Expressions. From Methodists to Presbyterians to Baptists to Nazarenes to Anglicans and beyond—people from various traditions are at the table inspiring and learning from each other. Without denying the emphases and particular practices, policies, and doctrines of each group, the common call to mission is celebrated.

No one is offering well-documented optimism for denominations as we know them. Yet, there is a great value in connection with like-hearted and like-minded Christians, so it would appear that considering the new roles for denominations would be more prudent than writing them off.

Some denominations already have seen a place for them in the facilitation of networks. A re-orientation toward networking will require some rapid adaptation, for the window will not be open long. And it will require tough prioritization, for the inevitable pull will be toward churches that have paid their dues of loyalty and now are desperate for help. Yet, the facilitation of such things as best-practices conversations, and the kind of relationships that keep effective ministers from burnout, are vital contributions of denominations.

Besides encouraging networks, denominations also can bless the consideration of fresh options. There are lots of church leaders who will be emboldened by the encouragement, permission, and recognition from admired denominational leaders for new ways of thinking about church.

Michael Moynagh rightly observed:

> The challenge for denominational leaders, therefore, lies not in writing a strategic plan, valuable though this can be. It is to encourage imaginative conversations about witnessing communities, in which honest exchanges can breed new ideas and generate energy to carry these ideas forward. If this is to happen in the myriad conversations of a denomination, leaders must use their agenda-setting influence to excite individuals and get them talking.[8]

Chapter 25

CREATING A MISSIONAL CULTURE, HOWEVER, IS CRITICAL (AND HARD)

If you are considering helping an existing congregation change—namely, to make the shift toward a more missional mindset—you are headed into a genuine adventure. Many choose not to tackle what you are about to tackle. Many have thrown up their hands in acquiescence, assumed the congregations they lead will forever be stuck in maintenance mode and/or in an attractional mode and/or in a perpetual state of decline, and thus will not embark on the kind of journey you are considering. They have chosen to remain in their churches and serve faithfully, but they have also, sadly, given up the dream of changing their world and reaching people far from God.

Others, deeply frustrated by what they see as the intractable bureaucracy of existing churches, have chosen other paths. They have either left their positions in existing churches to plant a church, bypassed existing churches altogether in order to go straight to church planting, or simply chosen some non-profit work.

Some of you, however, are making the terribly important decision to help your congregation transition toward a missional identity. That is a courageous choice with the potential for deep rewards. The spiritual return on your investment—both in terms of transformed lives and the deep sense of purpose that you and the church can experience—could be spectacular.

So, you should feel a deep sense of satisfaction at even considering this. You also ought to know that this won't be easy.

A new order means people will have to give up some things they love about the old order, and that will not come without pain—theirs and yours. This will be viewed by many as loss, and loss is not experienced casually.

Halter and Smay remind us of Newton's Law of Inertia, and comment that "the church as it currently exists will continue on its present trajectory, for better or worse, until we begin to intentionally act upon it with new paradigms."[1] Yet they also remind us of another of Newton's laws, often simplified as, "for every action there is an equal and opposite reaction," and they warn against the inevitable resistance that will follow any attempt to make changes in a church.[2]

Let's Be Honest: Is This about *You*?

Those of us who lead churches have to ask ourselves an honest question: "Is this about *us*?" Did you, possibly, pick up this book so that you might find a way for your congregation to think you are a great leader with wonderful new ideas? Is it possible that you are thinking of being a more missional church with the hopes that it might result in being recruited by a larger congregation? Do you simply want to be the leader of a cutting-edge church? If so, then repentance is in order.

You probably know that the word "repent" comes from the Greek word *metanoia*, meaning, a new way of thinking. This doesn't make you a bad person; it simply makes you a person who should adjust his or her thinking so as to gain a kingdom perspective.

This conversation about engaging people who need the Lord is not about our desire for a challenge or our personal reputations. It is not about our congregations' bottom lines. It is about the advancement of God's kingdom. It is about the fact that people without Jesus are "without hope and without God in the world" (Eph. 2:12). It is about how woefully inadequate it is for us to merely talk about tweaking our present approach.

Create a Missional Environment; Don't Set BHAGs

Alan Roxburgh astutely warns against the BHAGs, the Big, Hairy, Audacious Goals—a concept popularized by Jim Collins in his book *Good to Great*. I confess that, like lots of pastors at the time, I read *Good to Great* and felt inspired to drum up some BHAGs of my own for the church I was then serving and leading as pastor. In fairness to the concept, it is indeed fitting for a church to, in the words of William Carey, the Father of Modern Missions, "attempt great things for God and expect great things from God." God-sized dreams—doing our best to follow the promptings of God's Spirit into visions of efforts that will fail unless God shows up—are worthy of our pursuit.

There are some drawbacks to the BHAGs, however. For one, they often are the overreaching, personal goals of a solitary person who desperately wants to inspire the congregation and, perhaps, leave a legacy. Second, the BHAGs often are dreams of doing the things we are already doing, only doing them better. In that case, a major portion of the North American population are still beyond our reach. Furthermore, many congregations are so jaded after hearing big dreams from a string of pastors who have quickly moved on to a bigger-and-better project or a bigger-and-better church, the BHAGs simply elicit yawns.

Roxburgh has a point. So why don't we (1) help the congregation discern God's vision for the church and (2) follow the promptings of God's Spirit beyond mere tweaks of our present models to "experiments around the edge"?[3] In other words, what if your church were to figure out how to be more effective in discipling people who are open to church as we know it *and* courageously hazard beyond our known models?

Organic Change

Sometimes pastors announce the words of Jeremiah 29:11 to their new congregation, "I know the plans I have for you." We often forget that it is *God* who knows the plans for the people, not *us*. We often mistake ourselves for God.

Moreover, if the senior leader or leaders are really good, and introduce a really good idea, if the leaders are really persuasive, and if the congregation is really compliant . . . the congregation might just embrace the idea enthusiastically. But, with time, enthusiasm often wanes and, with the passing of not so much time, there often is little remaining of the really good idea.

If, on the other hand, the people of the church have discerned on their own what they believe to be a divine prompting, they are far more likely to take the idea and run with it. The impact of the shift is likely to be far deeper and more enduring. As Roxburgh observed,

> Leadership has a choice; it can either be in control of plans, programs, and outcomes or it can work at creating the environment that will release the missional imagination that is among the people of God. . . . The job of leadership is to create the environment in which that can happen, which requires them to learn new skills.[4]

So, determining and announcing a congregation's future is beyond the role of spiritual leadership. Yet, neither the leaders of the church nor the mission of the church can be held hostage to the recalcitrance, apathy, or fear of resistant people. There is a balance. We must not use people to fulfill our goals, yet we must not abdicate our responsibility for spiritual leadership. And sometimes the answer is helping the people discern God's promptings and then moving forward with those who will move forward.[5]

Not All Churches Can Make the Shift

Some of you serve churches that are simply unable to completely make the shift to fully missional. Nevertheless, you can still gently nudge them toward a more outward orientation. Every church does not have to wholly embrace the missional model in order to be a good church. Lots of good pastors are patiently turning the gaze of their congregations outward with the full awareness that their congregations will never completely fit the missional paradigm. The kind of transition required for some congregations to become fully missional (more than just adding mission projects, but living as a missionary people) would be terribly disruptive and the result could be a shell of what was there before.

If you are a pastor with an unequivocal calling to lead a truly missional church, you will have to make hard decisions. Can you lead a non-missional church without violating your call and your values? Some of you will only fulfill your calling in an existing church that is truly *becoming* missional or in a new form of church which has a clear missional identity.

Too Little, Too Late?

David Houle proclaimed, "Transformation is the only way. Reform is too little, too late."[6] He was talking about the field of education, but you've got to wonder if, perhaps, his prophetic words are also true of the church. Some would answer with an unequivocal "Yes! Only transformation is sufficient! Reform is, indeed, too little, too late!" And perhaps history will prove them right.

However, it seems awfully presumptuous to declare all churches as we know them in need of a complete teardown and reassembling. It seems far more prudent, and realistic, to work toward the reformation of those churches that are reformable, the transformation of those that are transformable, and the launching of new forms of church alongside them all.

Chapter 26

YOU AND YOUR CHURCH CAN DO THIS

Perhaps you are a leader, maybe the pastor, of people who are poised and ready to launch a fresh expression of church. It might be that those in your congregation have already sensed the call to start a new form of church and are simply awaiting instructions or praying for the "Go" from the Holy Spirit. Many others of you are in a leadership role, maybe as pastor, of churches that are still considering, or maybe even just beginning to consider, a fresh expression of church. Wherever you are in your preparation, this final chapter is intended especially for you. You and your congregation *can* launch a fresh expression of church.

Stark Realities and Inadequate Metrics

It's not a bad thing to celebrate when a long-time follower of Jesus decides to join your church, and it's not a bad thing to be disappointed when a member of your congregation joins another. Using such decisions as ultimate measurements of success, however, and competing with other churches for new members from among the shrinking pool of already-Christians, is a poor imitation of a missional church.

Of course, I have always been grateful for the Christians who come to join the churches I have served as pastor. People who move from another city where they were deeply involved in their churches and who felt led by God to join our church—I have always thanked God for them! We have needed them! We have needed people to join us to help fulfill our part in God's mission. The point is simply that we cannot be content only to celebrate sheep shuffling from pen to pen.

That is why fresh expressions of church are so important. Fresh expressions help engage the truly unchurched, who make up a growing percentage of the North American population.

If you have a heart for people who seem to have been written off by so many churches, and you recognize the ultimate futility of competing with other congregations over where already-Christians will give their offerings, then perhaps God is calling you and people in your congregation to begin a fresh expression of church.

Be Ready to Answer the Questions

Because this will be such a new concept to so many in your congregation, it should be helpful to anticipate some of the questions they likely will ask. While we cannot anticipate them all here, the following three questions are often asked of me when I speak at churches about fresh expressions.

"Is this going to grow our church?" We can understand why people would ask this question. Many churches are not as strong numerically as they once were. People lament the fact that their building is no longer abuzz with activity and echoing with the laughter of children. They love their church and want it to be vibrant.

The answer to this sincere question, "Will a fresh expression of church result in growth for the long-standing congregation that begins a fresh expression?" is "Possibly." In the church I served which started three fresh expressions we saw some numerical growth attributable directly to those new forms of church. Note that we saw *some* numerical growth, not an influx.

There were people who came into our congregation in three ways. (1) Some who were transformed by God in the new forms of church eventually wanted a fuller experience, usually having to do with the children's and youth programs, so they joined our long-standing congregation; (2) some in the greater community were drawn to our church because of our reputation for creative and meaningful involvement outside our original walls; and (3) I simply believe God blessed us with new people and greater resources so that we could continue to faithfully join Him on mission. After all, Hugh Halter and Matt Smay declared, "It's a known statistic that the churches that give away, that take risks, that send out, and that sacrificially push their people out, create vacuums that God fills with even more."[1] Alan Hirsch similarly observed, "It seems that when the church engages at the fringes, it almost always brings life to the center."[2]

Starting a fresh expression of church, then, *might* result in growth for an existing congregation. Yet there is certainly no guarantee. And, what's more important, the numerical expansion of an existing congregation is not the point.

The Fresh Expressions movement is about the Great Commandment and the Great Commission. A fresh expression of church is a selfless, missional, loving effort to incarnate the love of Jesus in the world.

It is helpful to remember that this is not about *us*. Steven Croft offered this helpful reminder to churches that are tempted to think too much about themselves:

> Church defined by the *missio Dei* never finds its true centre by turning in on itself. For example, when preoccupation with its own survival takes centre stage then church is deemed to have ceased to live in harmony with its very life-force, to have lost sight of its *raison d'etre* and inevitable dysfunction and atrophy set in.[3]

Will this siphon off our members? Church planters have not always been welcomed to their new neighborhoods by the pastors of churches already there. Despite the common claims of the church planters ("We are going after non-Christians; not your church members"), pastors have been highly suspicious. After all, every pastor knows that when a cooler, hipper church moves in, some of his or her members are at least going to check it out. And, despite the sincerity of the church planter, the truth is that lots of traditional church plants have grown at the expense of older congregations.

Fresh expressions of church, however, are different. These new forms of church are so different from existing forms of church that churchgoers are likely to feel uncomfortable there. I know of very few fresh expressions that would be appealing to people who have a history of significant church involvement.

True, some formerly churched people have found a home in fresh expressions of church. And while reengaging de-churched people is not the primary thrust or motivating goal of the Fresh Expressions movement, if the Spirit draws people back to the Christian community through these new forms of church, that would be cause for celebration. Yet people who find a home in fresh expressions of church are, almost always, unchurched or legitimately de-churched people, not just disgruntled church members or members on the margins looking for something more appealing.

This truth led Reggie McNeal to declare the following, which is applicable to fresh expressions of church:

> The rise of these missional communities will be the green edge of the Christian movement in the decades ahead. . . . My hope is that existing churches will see their way clear to expand the bandwidth of what they recognize as church to include these missional communities. Most congregations could sponsor dozens of these without ever harming their "bottom line" in terms of attendance and participation. These missional communities could, however, leverage an existing church's influence as salt and light across their community.[4]

Is this going to drain our church's resources? A rather typical strategy for starting a church is to have a mother congregation send out dozens of its best and brightest, purchase land, fund a church planter and make initial payments on a building. In both human and financial resources, it can be costly.

To begin a fresh expression of church tends not to demand as much from a congregation as a typical church-start demands. For one thing, there is rarely land to buy or a building to build. For another thing, there is often not a salary involved. Furthermore, a church doesn't have to send out large numbers of its best teachers and leaders. The core team for a fresh expression of church, at least in the UK, is three to twelve people. Moreover, those three-to-twelve often remain active in the Sunday morning programs and worship of their home congregation.

Pace Yourself and Look behind You from Time to Time

Answering all those questions is sometimes exasperating for missional leaders. We get frustrated when others don't quickly espouse our initiatives. Patience does not come easily for those with a passion for people beyond the reach of the church.

Lance King is the pastor of a church that began in 1773. He is leading them carefully into new models of church and understands the need both for change and for patience. He once explained, "We are making revolutionary change at an evolutionary pace." The shift to a missional paradigm, or even steps *toward* a missional paradigm, may require the patience of Job. It will also require that you pause, from time to time, to see if you are actually leading anyone.

Several years ago, while I was a pastor in Kentucky, we were making lots of changes and introducing new ideas. It was, in many ways, one of the most effective seasons of my ministry. One day Tom, a wise member of the church, dropped by my office and asked me if I'd ever been to a greyhound racetrack. I had not, so he explained things to me.

In order to spur the dogs to run, a mechanical rabbit is placed in front of them on a long pole that extends from an inside rail. When the gun sounds, that mechanical rabbit takes off and stays out in front of the dogs throughout the race as an enticement, a goal, if you will. The dogs chase that rabbit all the way to the finish line. If the rabbit ever gets too far out in front, however, the dogs will quit running; they will decide the goal is simply not achievable. The objective of those who operate the dog track is to keep the rabbit just enough in front so that the dogs will want to catch it, but not so far out in front that they quit.

I got Tom's subtle message. I was in danger of getting out too far in front of the congregation.

Missional leaders have to be careful not to get too far ahead of the churches we serve and lead. Those of us who see the world through apostolic lenses have been known to look back and notice that no one is following.

Get Buy-In

Jim Kitchins offers a helpful word of caution.

> Any proposal that is perceived as such a departure from the tradition will bear a greater burden of proof before the church decides that the proposal is, in fact, "of God." Those who propose the change will need to show how it is consistent with the deeper layers of the Christian tradition, even though on the surface it may appear radically different.[5]

Does everyone in the church have to embrace the idea that a fresh expression of church is "of God"? Probably not, because, for one thing, you are not likely to be significantly obligating the church financially. To start a fresh expression simply requires the passion of the few and the permission of the many.

If your choice is to lead the church to become more missional in its total approach, however, that is a much bigger transition. Now you're talking about a culture shift, a fundamental difference—something much more substantial even than the launching of a new form of church. A fresh expression of church could be a step toward, and a stimulus for, a missional mindset. But the process by which an existing church, with all its culture, tradition, comforts, and preferences, could become truly missional—that is a monumental shift that would require patience, tenacity, and the best leadership skills you can muster. For that you will need widespread (though not unanimous) buy-in from the congregation.

Speak to the Future

In the end, not everyone will get what you are talking about. They will find it hard to believe that the church does not simply need better music, better preaching, better programs, and so on. They will find it hard to believe that so many people are no longer reachable through traditional evangelistic methods. Frankly, many will find it hard to be passionate about people who are very different from themselves.

You cannot be discouraged or dissuaded by that. Speak to those who will listen. Appeal to those who have a heart for people outside the faith. Encourage those to whom God is already speaking about a new ministry. Target those who have an apostolic bent. Don't bash the resistant ones, but don't be deterred by them either.

This insightful story is in *Church Turned Inside Out.*

> It is said that Beethoven, who was a wildly successful musician in his own day, began at one point in his career writing pieces that were so unlike his previous works that his friends were astonished and asked, "Ludwig, what's happened to you? We don't understand you anymore!" According to the story, Beethoven, with a studied sweep of the hand, replied, "I have said all I have to say to my contemporaries; now I am speaking to the future."[6]

Let's not assume we are the only ones in tune with God's Spirit or the only ones with an accurate picture of the future. Arrogance has no place in this mixed economy of churches. It is absolutely true, however, that many will not understand or embrace this vision for new forms of churches. Your role is not to convince the inconvincible, but to join God in calling out those who were divinely wired for this very purpose. Your role is to speak to the future.

Deep Waters

Psalm 107:23–24 (KJV) reads, "They that . . . do business in great waters; These see the works of the LORD, and his wonders in the deep." This idea of new forms of church is, for most of us, the equivalent of a bunch of landlubbers launching out into deep waters. It's terrifying . . . and rightfully so.

In the deep waters God does miracles through ordinary people like us. You simply need to know before you set out for the deep, blue sea that it will not always be smooth sailing.[7]

Danger Lurks in the Deep Waters

Discerning the subculture God is leading us to engage, pulling together a team, figuring out the initial steps, and the things that go into the beginnings of a fresh expression of church are challenging. What you begin might not work. Thinking about having spiritual conversations is, for many of us, rather daunting.

Moreover, subcultures are multiplying rapidly in North America, leaving us all feeling like outsiders to countless circles of society. We experience culture shock at the shopping mall. We drive a couple of miles and don't understand the clothes, the language, or the worldview of those who live there!

And that's not all! Sometimes missional leaders experience resistance from within our Christian family. People will question the motives and the sanity of pastors who call their churches to such uncommon ventures as we are talking about here. In some cases, congregational conflict will arise and center on the pastor who, it will likely be said, should pay more attention to the needs of the sheep already within the fold. People in tradition-laden churches might take pot shots at inherited churches that start new forms of church, as well as the new forms of church. Missional pastors sometimes endure snide remarks from fellow members of the ministerial fraternity. Pioneers of fresh expressions can be the brunt of ridicule from conformists who cannot see beyond their provincial understanding of church.

These and other dangers lurk in the deep.

Launch Out Anyway

Hear again Psalm 107:23-24 (kjv): "They that . . . do business in great waters; These see the works of the Lord, and his wonders in the deep." This powerful text should ignite within us a passion for people and possibilities which lie beyond what can be seen, or even imagined, by people sitting in beach chairs (or pews) on the shore line.

They who remain safely on land, warmly huddled in the bait shop or the restaurant or on the pier, never experience the wonders of sailing the sea. If we're going to witness the wonders and works of the Lord, we're going to have to sail out to the deep waters!

God is inviting His people out to the deep—to earth's last frontier—out where the wonders are.

The fact that you read to the end of this book indicates at least the incipient longing to sail beyond the confines of the harbor. So sail on! Do business in great waters. You just might witness a miracle.

NOTES

Foreword

1. *Mission-Shaped Church: Church Planting and Fresh Expressions of Church in a Changing Context* (London: Church House Publishing, 2004).
2. At the time of writing the UK partnership consists of the Church of England, the Methodist Church, the United Reformed Church, the Congregational Federation, the Church of Scotland, and the Salvation Army. See freshexpressions.org.uk.
3. For example, in South Africa the partnership involves Anglicans, Dutch Reformed, United Reformed, Methodists, and the Association of Vineyard Churches. In Germany, Lutherans and Roman Catholics train together.

Chapter 1

1. We all thank God for the expansion of the Church in Africa, South America, and Asia. But even there the news is not all rosy. "Shorter and Onyancha (1997) found that 40 per cent of people attended church weekly in rural Kenya, but only 12 per cent did so in the modernizing capital of Nairobi (with 20 per cent attending less frequently)" (In Michael Moynagh, *Church for Every Context: An Introduction to Theology and Practice* [London: SCM Press, 2012], 75). If Kenya is not the exception, then the future might be somewhat uncertain even for the church outside the West. And if the Christian faith were to suffer outside the West as it is in the homelands of the Modern Missionary Movement, then "God help us" would not be a flippant prayer.
2. Robert Putnam, *Bowling Alone: The Collapse and Revival of American Community* (New York: Simon & Schuster, 2000), 16, 67.
3. Ibid., 42.
4. Ibid., 261.
5. Paul Taylor, *The Next America* (New York: Public Affairs, 2014), 131.

6. Archbishop's Council on Mission and Public Affairs, *Mission-Shaped Church: Church Planting and Fresh Expressions in a Changing Context* (New York: Seabury Books, 2004), 23–24.

7. "Christendom" is a term describing a culture in which the Christian faith is a central influencer. The term goes back to the granting of favored status to the Christian faith by the Roman Emperor Constantine in the fourth century. From that point, and for centuries in the West, Christianity, and thus the church, was at the heart of political, social, and educational systems. "Post-Christendom" simply means that the Christian faith and the church no longer occupy that place of prominence in the culture. "In the words of Stuart Murray, post-Christendom culture is 'a culture in which central features of the Christian story are unknown and churches are alien institutions whose rhythms do not normally impinge on most members of society.'" Leonard Sweet, editor, *The Church of the Perfect Storm* (Nashville: Abingdon Press, 2008), 14–22.

8. Jim Kitchins, *Postmodern Parish* (Washington, DC: Rowman & Littlefield Publishers, 2003), 27.

9. Sweet, *The Church of the Perfect Storm*, 14–22.

10. On the back cover of Darrell Guder, *Missional Church: A Vision for the Sending of the Church in North America* (Grand Rapids: Eerdmans, 1998).

Chapter 2

1. Linda Bergquist and Allan Karr, *Church Turned Inside Out* (San Francisco: Jossey-Bass, 2010), xiii.

2. How would we evangelize a people on the other side of the world who had once known a strong Christian influence in their culture but no longer do, who speak a different language than we do, who have a different worldview than we do?

3. Alan Hirsch and Dave Ferguson, *On the Verge: A Journey into the Apostolic Future of the Church* (Grand Rapids: Zondervan, 2011), 28. See also Ed Stetzer, *Planting Missional Churches* (Nashville: B&H Academic, 2006), 166.

4. Hirsch and Ferguson, *On the Verge,* 72.

5. Paul Taylor, *The Next America* (New York: PublicAffairs, 2014), 133.

6. David Fitch, in Mark Lau Branson and Nicholas Warnes, eds., *Starting Missional Churches* (Downers Grove: IVP, 2014), 9.

7. Ed Stetzer and Warren Bird, *Viral Churches* (San Francisco: Jossey-Bass, 2010), 116–17.

8. In Terry Austin, *Acceptance, Forgiveness and Love: Building a Church Without Fences* (Keller, TX: Austin Brothers Publishing), 1.

Chapter 3

1. Hugh Halter and Matt Smay, *The Tangible Kingdom* (San Francisco: Jossey-Bass, 2008), 34.

2. Stetzer and Bird, *Viral Churches*, 200.

3. "Since the traditional paths to employment have closed, since the college degree they are now in debt to pay off is not being honored in the traditional job space, they are increasingly viewing entrepreneurship as their future. We are going to see a higher percentage of entrepreneurship and levels of independent contractors in this generation starting at an earlier age than ever before" (David Houle, *Entering the Shift Age* [Naperville: Sourcebooks, 2012], 149).

4. In Alan Hirsch and Tim Catchim, *The Permanent Revolution: Apostolic Imagination and Practice for the 21st Century* (San Francisco: Jossey-Bass, 2012), 120.

5. Ibid., 121.

6. Ibid., 124.

7. Gordon MacDonald, *Who Stole My Church?* (Nashville: Thomas Nelson, 2007), 224.

8. Halter and Smay, *The Tangible Kingdom*, 1.

Chapter 4

1. Reggie McNeal, *Missional Renaissance: Changing the Scorecard for the Church* (San Francisco: Jossey-Bass, 2009), 50.

2. John Cusick, in Mike Hayes, *Googling God: The Religious Landscape of People in their 20s and 30s* (New York: Paulist Press, 2007), 162–63.

3. Neil Cole, *Organic Church* (San Francisco: Jossey-Bass, 2005), xxvi, 24.

4. Michael Moynagh put it like this: "we need a strategy to revitalize existing churches and, at the same time, to plant thousands of new churches. (Stuart Murray) explains, 'Churches have been leaking hundreds of members each week for many years. Planting more of these churches is not a mission strategy worth pursuing. But planting new kinds of

churches may be a key to effective missions and a catalyst for the renewal of existing churches'" (Moynagh, *Being Church, Doing Life: Creating Gospel Communities Where Life Happens* [Oxford, England: Monarch Books, 2014], 11).

5. "In the county I live in, 70 percent of the population is completely unchurched, meaning they have little or no connection or interest in Christianity. We have already reached most of the people who are open to the "come and see" approach. Therefore, the E/A (Evangelistic/Attractional) church (the majority of all churches) is effectively reaching only 30 percent of my local neighborhood, and I live in Georgia!" (Stetzer, *Planting Missional Churches*, 166).

6. Neil Cole, *Church 3.0* (San Francisco: Jossey-Bass, 2010), 49.

7. Tex Sample, *The Spectacle of Worship in a Wired World* (Nashville: Abingdon Press, 1998), 105.

8. Taylor, *The Next America*, 137.

9. David Houle, *Entering the Shift Age* (Naperville: Sourcebooks, 2012), 79.

10. Ibid., 125.

11. Ibid., 181.

12. Ibid., 182.

Chapter 5

1. See "Reaching Britain with the New Economy Church," http://www.christiantoday.com/article/reaching.britain.with.the.mixed.economy.of.church/27938.htm.

2. Steven Croft, *Mission-Shaped Questions* (New York: Seabury Books, 2008), 155.

3. See, for example, the Church Army paper, *Why Modality and Sodality thinking is vital to understand future church* (http://churcharmy.org.uk/Publisher/File.aspx?ID=138339).

4. https://www.youtube.com/watch?v=ZoZAb_1ss7k

5. Johnny Baker, *The Pioneer Gift* (London: Canterbury Press, 2014), 12.

6. In Graham Cray, Ian Mobsby, and Aaron Kennedy, eds., *Fresh Expressions of Church and the Kingdom of God* (London, UK: Canterbury Press, 2012), 75.

7. Paul Sparks, Tim Soerens, and Dwight J. Friesen, *The New Parish: How Neighborhood Churches Are Transforming Mission, Discipleship and Community* (Downers Grove, IL: InterVarsity Press, 2014), 77.

Chapter 6

1. In Bergquist and Karr, *Church Turned Inside Out*, 75–76; see also *Mission-Shaped Church*, 102.
2. Francis DuBose, *God Who Sends: A Fresh Quest for Biblical Mission* (Nashville: Broadman Press, 1983), 149.
3. David Bosch affirmed: "Mission was, in the early stages, more than a mere function; it was a fundamental expression of the life of the church. The beginnings of a missionary theology are therefore also the beginnings of Christian theology as such" (Bosch, *Transforming Mission: Paradigm Shifts in Theology of Mission* [Maryknoll, NY: Orbis Books, 2011], 15).
4. We seem to still have a ways to go, however, in some circles of academia: "This gap between theological reorientation and actual practice is still reflected in much of North American theological education. The doctrine of the church, ecclesiology, can and still is taught with little or no reference to the church's missionary vocation. Mission, or missiology, is a somewhat marginalized discipline. . . . There is little curricular evidence that 'mission is the mother of theology.'" See David Bosch, *Transforming Mission*, 16; Darrell Guder, ed., *Missional Church: A Vision for the Sending of the Church in North America* (Grand Rapids: Erdmans, 1998), 7.

Chapter 7

1. Without forgetting the prominent place of the Trinity, it is helpful to remember these words from Alan Hirsch: "Christology determines missiology, and missiology determines ecclesiology, which in turn returns back to Christology in a continuous cycle of renewal. It is absolutely vital that the church gets the order right. . . . It is Christ who determines our purpose and mission in the world (discipleship), and then it is our mission that must drive our search for modes of being-in-the-world." Alan Hirsch and Michael Frost, *The Shaping of Things to Come: Innovation and Mission for the 21st-Century Church* (Grand Rapids: Baker, 2010), 30–31.
2. In the Bible we read, "Hear, O Israel: The LORD our God, the LORD is one" (Deut. 6:4).
3. Millard Erickson, *Christian Theology* (Grand Rapids: Baker Book House, 1985), 321.
4. Lesslie Newbigin, *The Open Secret: An Introduction to the Theology of Mission* (Grand Rapids: William B. Eerdmans, 1995), 27.

5. J. R. Woodward, *Creating a Missional Culture* (Downers Grove: IVP, 2012), 27.
6. Phyllis Tickle, in *Fresh Expressions of Church and the Kingdom of God*, ed. Graham Cray, Aaron Kennedy, and Ian Mobsby (London, UK: Canterbury Press, 2012), 64.
7. Craig Van Gelder and Dwight J. Zscheile, *The Missional Church in Perspective: Mapping Trends and Shaping the Conversation* (Grand Rapids: Baker Academic, 2011), 27.
8. See Croft, *Mission-Shaped Questions*, 17.
9. Darrell Guder wrote that recent theological thought has highlighted "the implications of the Trinity for ecclesiology." Guder continued: "It has recognized that the *perichoresis*, or interpenetration, among the persons of the Trinity reveals that 'the nature of God is communion.' From this point of view, the church is learning that it is called to be a 'finite echo or bodying forth of the divine personal dynamics,' 'a temporal echo of the eternal community that God is'" (Guder, *Missional Church*, 81–82).
10. Ibid., 4.
11. *Mission-Shaped Church*, 85.
12. Bosch, *Transforming Mission*, 399.
13. Moynagh, *Church for Every Context*, 125.
14. Croft, *Mission-Shaped Questions*, 23–24.

Chapter 8

1. Van Gelder and Zscheile, *The Missional Church in Perspective*, 115.
2. Moynagh, *Church for Every Context*, 99.
3. In the words of N. T. Wright, "Jesus's bodily resurrection marks a watershed. If you accept the bodily resurrection of Jesus all the streams flow in one direction, and if you don't they flow in the other direction" (Wright, *Surprised by Hope: Rethinking Heaven, the Resurrection, and the Mission of the Church* [New York: HarperCollins, 2008], 191).
4. Alan Roxburgh, *Missional: Joining God in the Neighborhood* (Grand Rapids: Baker, 2011), 38–39.
5. Orlando E. Costas, *The Church and Its Mission: A Shattering Critique from the Third World* (Wheaton: Tyndale House Publishers, 1974), 162.
6. William Smalley, *Reading in Missionary Anthropology* (Pasadena: William Carey Library, 1974), 150.

7. Moynagh, *Church for Every Context*, 133.
8. Darrell Guder, in Hirsch and Catchim, *The Permanent Revolution*, xv.
9. Costas, *The Church and Its Mission*, 171.
10. Graham Cray, Ian Mobsby, and Aaron Kennedy, eds., *New Monasticism as Fresh Expression of Church* (London: Canterbury Press, 2010), 7.
11. Croft, *Mission-Shaped Questions*, 23.
12. World Missionary Council, *The World Mission of the Church*, quoted in R. Pierce Beaver, *The Missionary Between the Times* (Garden City, NY: Doubleday & Company, 1968), 135–36.
13. Hirsch and Frost, *The Shaping of Things to Come*, 106, 109.
14. Quoted in Gelder and Zscheile, *Missional Church in Perspective*, 30–31.

Chapter 9

1. Bosch, *Transforming Mission*, 11.
2. This statement was adopted by the Lambeth Conference in 1988. Also helpful is the Wheaton 1983 Statement: "Evil is not only in the human heart but also in social structures. . . . The mission of the church includes both the proclamation of the Gospel and its demonstration. We must therefore evangelize, respond to immediate human needs, and press for social transformation" (quoted in Bosch, *Transforming Mission*, 417). Also, "God's missionary purposes are cosmic in scope, concerned with the restoration of all things, the establishment of shalom, the renewal of creation and the coming of the Kingdom as well as the redemption of fallen humanity and the building of the Church" (see *Mission-Shaped Church*, 85).
3. Newbigin, *The Open Secret: An Introduction to the Theology of Mission* (Grand Rapids: Wm.B. Erdmans, 1995), 50.
4. I would contend that the ultimate source even of structural sin is the sinfulness of the human heart. Here I use "source" referring to the source at a practical level.
5. Philip Yancey, *Soul Survivor* (Colorado Springs: Waterbrook Press, 2003), 36.
6. Peyton Jones, *Church Zero: Raising 1st Century Churches out of the Ashes of the 21st Century Church* (Colorado Springs: David C. Cook, 2013), 39.
7. At a Fresh Expressions Vision Day, October 4, 2015.
8. Newbigin, *The Open Secret*, 121.

Chapter 10

1. Bob and Mary Hopkins, *Evangelism Strategies* (UK: Alderway Books, 2012), 28–29.

2. Leonard Sweet, ed., *The Church of the Perfect Storm* (Nashville: Abingdon Press, 2008), 14–22.

3. "In the traditional understanding, mission's goal was to save souls and build the church. . . . Through reflection on the *missio Dei*, the goal is now seen more broadly. . . . The 'classical' approach says that God is in mission in the midst of creation primarily through the atonement. . . . An emerging 'balanced' position seeks to retain the focus on creation while also emphasizing the church's role" (Moynagh, *Church for Every Context*, 128–29).

   "There can be no doubt that the interpretation of salvation that has emerged in recent missionary thinking and practice has introduced elements into the definition of salvation without which it would be dangerous narrow and anemic. . . . Hatred, injustice, oppression, war, and other forms of violence are manifestations of *evil*, concern for humaneness, for the conquering of famine, illness, and meaninglessness is part of the *salvation* for which we hope and labor" (Bosch, *Transforming Mission*, 407).

4. Those who focus myopically and singularly on the redemption of unfair social structures hone in on the writings of such prophets as Amos while ignoring the grand sweep of Scripture, particularly the New Testament. "There can be no doubt that social justice was at the very heart of the prophetic tradition of the OT. Since most of Israel's kings at least professed to believe in Yahweh, prophets like Amos and Jeremiah could, in the name of God, challenge them insofar as they had tolerated or perpetuated injustice in their kingdoms. The sociopolitical context in which the early church began to engage in mission was, however, fundamentally different. Christianity was a *religio illicita* in the Roman Empire. It was, at best, tolerated; at worst, it was persecuted. No Christian could address the authorities on the basis of a shared faith. . . . The innate justice dimension of the Christian faith has often been overlooked, mainly because it was—in the prevailing circumstances—couched in terms which differed substantially from those we encounter in the OT" (Bosch, *Transforming Mission*, 410–11).

5. Hopkins, *Evangelism Strategies*, 25.
6. N. T. Wright, *Justification: God's Plan & Paul's Vision* (Downers Grove: IVP, 2009), 10, 24.
7. Bosch, *Transforming Mission*, 403. Bosch also wrote, "In at least 18 cases the evangelists use it with reference to Jesus' healing of the sick. Thus there is, in Jesus' ministry, no tension between saving from sin and saving from spiritual ailment, between the spiritual and the social. . . . Does this mean that God's reign is political? Certainly, though not necessarily in the modern sense of the word . . . the manifestation of God's reign in Jesus is eminently political. To declare lepers, tax collectors, sinners and the poor to be 'children of God's kingdom' is a decidedly political statement" (see Bosch, *Transforming Mission*, 34–35).
8. Ibid., 403.
9. Ibid., 408.
10. Wright, *Surprised by Hope*, 200, 202.
11. Ibid., 205.
12. Bosch, *Transforming Mission*, 410.

Chapter 11

1. Newbigin, *The Open Secret*, 67.
2. John R. W. Stott, *Basic Christianity* (London: Inter-Varsity Press, 1958, 1971), 26.
3. John Hick, *God Has Many Names* (Philadelphia: Westminster Press, 1982), 6.
4. Newbigin, *The Open Secret*, 79.
5. Philip Gulley and James Mulholland, *If Grace Is True: Why God Will Save Every Person* (New York: HarperSanFrancisco, 2003), 125.
6. C. S. Lewis, *Mere Christianity* (New York: HarperSanFrancisco, 1952), 52.
7. "One can also be a pessimistic agnostic toward the unevangelized, acknowledging that special revelation is necessary for salvation but choosing to go no further than Scripture (which admittedly does not seem to offer much hope to those who have not heard). This leaves the difficult questions of salvation in the hands of God, who is righteous and merciful." (John Hick, Dennis L. Okholm, and Timothy R. Phillips, *More Than One Way?: Four Views on Salvation in a Pluralistic World* (Grand Rapids: Zondervan Pub. House, 1995), 20.
8. Newbigin, *The Open Secret*, 67.

9. Bosch, *Transforming Mission*, 151.

10. Frost and Hirsch, *The Shaping of Things to Come*, 144–45.

Chapter 12

1. Address at the National Gathering, Fresh Expressions US, March 27–28, 2014.

2. Newbigin, *The Open Secret*, 61.

3. Roxburgh, *Missional*, 116–18.

4. Ibid., 113.

5. Roland Allen, *The Spontaneous Expansion of the Church* (Grand Rapids: William B. Eerdmans, 1973).

6. Croft, *Mission-Shaped Questions*, 58.

7. Leonard Sweet, *Aqua Church* (Colorado Springs: David C. Cook, 2008), 339.

8. See Dallas Willard, *The Divine Conspiracy* (New York: Harper, 1998), 244.

9. Hopkins, *Evangelism Strategies*, 62.

10. In Marshall Shelley, ed., *Changing Lives Through Preaching and Worship* (Nashville: Moorings, 1995), 150.

Chapter 13

1. Millard J. Erickson, *Christian Theology* (Grand Rapids: Baker Book House, 1983), 1030.

2. Neil Cole, quoted in Stetzer and Bird, *Viral Churches*, 119.

3. See Simon Sutcliffe, *The Pioneer Gift*, ed. Johnny Baker and Cathy Ross (London: Canterbury Press, 2014), 173.

4. R. L. Omanson, "The Church," in *The Evangelical Dictionary of Theology* (Grand Rapids: Baker Book House, 1984), 233.

5. See Erickson, *Christian Theology*, 1032–34.

6. Williams, *Mission-Shaped Church*, v.

7. Moynagh, *Church for Context*, 106–7; see also 109.

8. See, for example, Moynagh, *Church for Every Context*, 107–8.

9. That focus on dogma, of course, grew out of the Reformers' profound differences with many Roman Catholic teachings, and thus reflect the almost exclusively doctrinal obsession of the Protestant Reformers. This helps explain why missiology was a subtopic, and often an afterthought, in the development of Protestant theology. It also explains why the modern missionary movement was three centuries in coming.

10. Theologians beginning with the Reformers speak sometimes of the invisible church and the visible church, with the invisible church being those known by God to have been redeemed through faith in His Son. The visible church is those who make up a particular group of people called a church. By that reasoning, seekers, not-yet-believers, and young children of the adult believers, are not yet part of the true, mystical, invisible church though they are very much at home, and part of, the visible church—the body of believers in a particular community of faith. There are New Testament texts that note the presence of those who are not faithful followers of Jesus and thus not, presumably, members of the church.

11. "It is particularly the case that something may be appropriately named a fresh expression of church without that being taken to imply that it has as yet all the essential qualities of markers of a mature Christian community" (Croft, *Mission-Shaped Questions*, 10).

12. Moynagh, *Church for Every Context*, 115.

13. Preface to *Mission-Shaped Church* in Croft, *Mission-Shaped Questions*, 190.

14. Max De Pree, *Leadership Is an Art* (New York: Dell Publishing, 1989), 141.

15. Cray, Mobsby, and Kennedy, eds., *Fresh Expressions of Church and the Kingdom of God*, 17–18. "The kingdom is the rule of Christ over the whole creation. The Church is the community that has submitted to that rule and seeks to live under it, in the midst of a world that locates ultimate authority elsewhere. . . . Both are 'now and not yet'. The Church on earth is an imperfect community of people, still in the process of becoming like Christ. The kingdom is the presence of the new age, which has not yet displaced the old age" (Cray, *Fresh Expressions and the Kingdom of God*, 14).

16. Emil Brunner, *The Word and the World* (London: Student Christian Movement Press, 1931), 108.

17. Bosch, *Transforming Mission*, 379.

18. http://www.ccel.org/ccel/wesley/journal.vi.iii.v.html.

19. R. L. Omanson, "The Church," in *The Evangelical Dictionary of Theology* (Grand Rapids: Baker Book House, 1984), 233.

20. "Christians through the ages have maintained community, formation, mission and worship as the nonnegotiable aspects of what it means to be the church" (Sparks, Soerens, and Friesen, *The New Parish*, 85).

21. Phil Potter, in an interview in Lambeth Palace, London, January 15, 2015. Here is another way of looking at this: "It is therefore important to distinguish between genuine fresh expressions of church and what might be termed 'refreshed expressions.' The latter is a more appropriate term for outreach events and new communities that flow from the life of the mainstream parish and what may be remodeled or rebranded in order to appeal to a wider constituency of parishoners" (Damian Feeney, *Fresh Expressions and the Kingdom of God*, 130).

22. The following, by Darrell Guder, helps us grasp more fully the historic understandings of church: "The process of naming and defining the 'marks of the church' at Nicea in the fourth century was another example of missional connectedness at work. . . . The church that is faithful to the gospel tradition, the Nicene Creed proclaimed, will always be experienced as 'one, holy, catholic, and apostolic.' The Reformation responded to the crisis of the sixteenth century by supplementing these classic marks with its definition of the 'true church' in terms of its basic functions: wherever the Word is properly preached, the sacraments rightly administered, and (the Reformed tradition) Christian discipline practiced" (Guder, *Missional Church*, 254–55).

Chapter 14

1. In talking about Luke 10 and the "persons of peace," Bob and Mary Hopkins wrote, "Jesus did not send his disciples out with a mission strategy of attracting people onto their territory on their terms. He sent his disciples out to look for people who responded to them—who welcomed them—and then to stay with their hosts on *their* terms. . . . By encouraging his disciples to stay in people's homes, on their terms, submitting to and even adopting their culture, Jesus showed that what he cared about was not people leaving their culture to find something 'better for them' but to respond to God within their culture and discover him alongside and at work in their lives . . . By staying 'in their home'—in the cultural territory of those who respond to us—we do things their way not our way. . . . This is crucial if we want to see our evangelism lead . . . to a church that is not the sort of church we like but the sort of church that's truly *their* church. God at work in their culture, with their social patterns, on their turf" (Bob and Mary Hopkins, *Evangelism Strategies* [ACPI Books, 2011], 73–74).

2. Jack Deere, *Surprised by the Power of the Holy Spirit* (Grand Rapids: Zondervan, 1993).

3. See Cray, Mobsby, and Kennedy, *Fresh Expressions and the Kingdom of God*, 75; Also Bosch, *Transforming Mission*, 44ff; Michael Moynagh, "Do We Need a Mixed Economy," in *Evaluating Fresh Expressions*, ed. Louise Nelstrop and Martyn Percy (London: Canterbury Press, 2008), 180–84; Alan J. Roxburgh and M. Scott Boren, *Introducing the Missional Church* (Grand Rapids: Baker Books, 2009), 16–17.

4. Croft, *Mission-Shaped Questions*, 144.

5. Florida Methodist Pioneer Retreat, February 26, 2015, First Methodist in Winter Park, FL.

6. See Roxburgh, *Missional*, 110–19.

Chapter 15

1. "Many commentators believe that the United States is on the same trajectory as Europe, where the church has been declining for decades, but one or two generations behind" (Moynagh, *Being Church, Doing Life*, 61). It appears that in England the concern for a disappearing Christendom and the call for a return to Christian roots was in the 20s and 30s, following WWI (see Roxburgh, *Missional*, 34). In the United States that seems to have been in the 70s and 80s, following the Vietnam War. That could be interpreted to mean the United States is fifty years behind England in the decline of the church.

2. In Croft, Mobsby, and Spellers, eds., *Ancient Faith, Future Mission*, 35.

3. Quoted in John Bowen, "A Beginner's Guide to Fresh Expressions," a paper, p. 9. (http://wycliffecollege.ca/documents/A%20Beginners%20Guide%20to%20Fresh%20Expressions.pdf)

4. The term "fresh expressions" originally was taken from the ordination vows in the Church of England where candidates for ordination pledge to proclaim the gospel afresh in every generation.

5. "The Methodist Church contributed a member to the Mission-shaped Church working party and approached the Archbishop of Canterbury in early 2004 about a structured relationship in what became the national Fresh Expressions initiative. At the Methodist Conference in 2004 the church adopted a new set of five focus areas including 'the encouragement of

fresh expressions ways of being church'" (Croft *Mission-Shaped Questions*, 5).

6. Address to church leaders, Fresh Expressions US National Gathering, April 27, 2014.

7. "The House of Bishops approved a set of guidelines for a new focus on ordained ministry in January 2006 given the designation 'ordained pioneer.'. . . The guidelines introduce the flexibility for ordinands training for this ministry to train primarily in context alongside their leadership of a fresh expression of church. Training is being overseen by existing training institutions with two new centres emerging in London with a major focus on this ministry. . . . Finally, and perhaps even more significantly, in January 2007 the House of Bishops approved a parallel set of guidelines for the recognition, training and support of lay pioneer ministry. This pays a particular and due regard to the ministry of Church Army Evangelists. Church Army have increasingly focused their mission and resources in the area of beginning fresh expressions of church and represent a very significant resource and well of expertise for the whole Church in the United Kingdom" (Steven Croft, *Mission-Shaped Questions*, 7).

8. A summary of this report, *From Anecdote to Evidence*, was released in January 2014 and is available at www.churchgrowthresearch.org.uk.

9. *Report on Strand 3b* (Church Army's Research Unit, October, 2013), 6.

10. This is the list of the ten parameters, from the report:

1. Was something Christian and communal brought to 'birth' that was new and further, rather than an existing group modified?

2. Has the starting group tried to **engage with non-churchgoers**? There was intention to create a fresh expression of Church, not begin an outreach project from an existing church. The aim was for the Christians to change, to fit a culture and context, not make the local/indigenous people change, to fit into an existing church context.

3. Does the resultant community meet **at least once a month**? In cases of monthly meetings further questions about how to deepen community, build commitment and increase discipleship follow.

4. Does it have **a name** that helps to give it an identity? An active search, not yet yielding a name, is allowed.

5. Is there **intention to be Church**? This could be from the start, or by discovery on the way. This admits the embryonic fxD (fx of developing community) and cases of fxE (fx of evangelism) and even some fxW (fx of worship). The key is that they are *not* seen as a bridge back to 'real church'.

6. Is it Anglican, or **an Anglican partner** in an Ecumenical project? 'Anglican' here means the bishop welcomes it as part of the diocesan family, not whether it only uses centrally authorised worship texts, or has a legal territory such as a parish.

7. There is some form of **leadership** recognised within, and also without.

8. At least the majority of members (who are part of the public gathering) see it as **their major expression** of being church.

9. There is **aspiration for the four creedal 'marks' of church, or ecclesial relationships:** 'up/holy, in/one, out/apostolic, of/catholic'. We question validity in an absence of 'mission/out'. (Our Church Army team see the two dominical sacraments as a given consequence of the life of a missional community which follows Jesus, but not the sole or even best measure of being church.)

10. There is **intent to become 'three self'** (self-financing, self-governing and self-reproducing). These factors need contextualisation, but are some marks of advancing maturity. They are not to be interpreted as indicators of congregationalist independency, or breakaway tendencies.

11. "The data . . . neither guarantees these young attenders will be retained, nor that they have all come to an active committed faith. It may be more realistic to see it as a promising beginning. Yet it needs to be added that one cannot retain what is not present in the first place. This high under 16s attendance figure could make the contribution of the fxC towards both the present and the future life of the Church of England yet more significant. . . . On average at the fxC, 41% of the attendees are under 16. This is significantly higher than in inherited church and is a promising beginning" (*Report on Strand 3b*, p. 45).

12. In Moynagh, *Being Church, Doing Life*.

13. *Report on Strand 3b*, 64.

14. Alan Roxburgh and Fred Romanuk, *The Missional Leader* (San Francisco: Jossey-Bass, 2006), xiii.
15. "78% are taking some steps to grow disciples, not just attract attenders" (Ibid., 6).
16. Quoted in Moynagh, *Church for Every Context*, xvi.
17. "The emerging church and the missional church movements are somewhat distinct" (Van Gelder and Zscheile, *Missional Church in Perspective*, 9).
18. See *Report on Strand 3b*, 78-79.

Chapter 16

1. Jonny Baker, in Jonny Baker and Cathy Ross, *The Pioneer Gift*, (London: Canterbury Press, 2014), 1.
2. https://www.freshexpressions.org.uk/pioneerministry.
3. Church Army Research Unit, Church Growth Research Project *Report on Strand 3b*: An analysis of fresh expressions of Church and church plants begun in the period 1992-2012, October 2013, 6.
4. See Stetzer and Bird, *Viral Churches*, 50-62; also Stetzer, *Planting Missional Churches*, 9-10; and Hirsch and Catchim, *Permanent Revolution*, 240. "The so-called circuit riders were a key factor in this success. These profoundly apostolic laypeople were passionate disciples who, with some rudimentary training, rode from town to town, planting churches as they went. They would then circle back to ensure that the churches were growing and healthy. Stark and Finke discovered that around 1850, the stunning growth turned into trended decline. They discovered that during this period, the more institutionally inclined Episcopalians and Presbyterians had relentlessly mocked the Methodists as being uncouth and not knowing Latin, Greek, and Hebrew. Under this barrage of insults, the Methodist leadership decided that the circuit riders should do rigorous seminary training at least equal to that of their antagonists. The circuit riders were then required to do four years of seminary training as a prerequisite for licensing to the ministry. Methodism in America has never regained a positive growth pattern lost in that fateful decision" (Hirsch and Catchim, *Permanent Revolution*, 240).
5. Stetzer and Bird, *Viral Churches*, 55-56.
6. Karlie Allaway, in Baker and Ross, *The Pioneer Gift*, 78.

7. For an in-depth understanding of this fivefold "APEST" model, see Alan Hirsch and Tim Catchim, *The Permanent Revolution* (San Francisco: Jossey-Bass, 2012).

8. Hirsch and Catchim, *The Permanent Revolution*, 92–93, 108.

9. Hugh Halter, *BiVo: A Modern-Day Guide for Bi-Vocational Saints* (Littleton, CO: Missio Publishing, 2013), 24–25.

10. Stetzer, *Planting Missional Churches*, 168–69.

11. Charlie Johnson, pioneer of a fresh expression in Ft. Worth, Texas, believes there are opportunities for pioneers to earn their living through the growing world of chaplaincy as hospice chaplains, corporate chaplains, and the like. Johnson noted: "The entire array of non-profits are seeking professionals to care for the spiritual health of their staff and clients. Addiction recovery, veterans re-entry, child abuse prevention and treatment, food security, and public education come immediately to mind, but I'm also hearing of artistic and environmental groups exploring partnerships with spirituality providers. Look at how evangelicals have embraced the issues of human trafficking and global warming . . . now Christian community groups are springing up in food banks, residential treatment centers, homeless shelters, and even educational and artistic contexts such as libraries and museums." Email dated 8/29/2014.

12. Halter, *BiVo*, 17.

13. Ian Mobsby, in *New Monasticism*, 12.

Chapter 17

1. Lois Barrett, quoted in David Bosch, *Transforming Mission*, 548.

2. Roxburgh and Romanuk, *The Missional Leader*, xv.

3. At a talk during a Pioneer Retreat in Richmond, VA.

4. *Listening for Mission: Mission Audit for Fresh Expressions*, The Archbishops' Council, 2006, 3.

5. See Branson and Warnes, *Starting Missional Churches*, 186, 191.

6. Houle, *Entering the Shift Age*, 52.

7. Ibid., 53–54.

8. Cray, Mobsby, and Kennedy, *Fresh Expressions and the Kingdom of God*, 173.

9. Bergquist and Karr, *Church Turned Inside Out*, 115.

10. Stetzer and Bird, *Viral Churches*, 4, 36.

11. Bob and Mary Hopkins's book, *Evangelism Strategies* (UK: ACPI Books, 2011) is an excellent resource for digging deeper into the concept of a person of peace.

Chapter 18

1. Hirsch and Catchim: "Front loading missional projects with detailed blueprints for action may well bolster confidence in the beginning, but this kind of planning assumes too much about the intricate cultural nuances of the target context and will be unlikely to generate innovation. Church planting and leading an apostolic movement have got to be more improvisatory. No one can know all the variables until they immerse themselves in that context and begin to act intentionally within it. It does not mean starting without a plan; it just means those plans need to be somewhat more open-ended and nimble" (*Permanent Revolution*, 193–94).
2. Most fresh expressions of church are not complicated. However, there are some fresh expressions that require the running of companion businesses, collecting fees besides regular offerings, and boards. If you anticipate something more involved than simple gatherings for discussion, you might find helpful a service like startchurch.com.
3. Cathy Ross, in *The Pioneer Gift*, 31.
4. Sparks, Soerens, and Friesen, *The New Parish*, 127, 137.
5. Branson and Warnes, *Starting Missional Churches*, 28.
6. "As we have seen, we might have been experts in our own culture, but when we are in a completely alien one, we have to start again. This can trigger the innovative spirit, because such displacement puts a person or an organization in the cultural intersection of an environment that creates the possibility of opportunity recognition, as well as in a place to go on a learning journey" (Hirsch and Catchim, *Permanent Revolution*, 191).
7. Halter and Smay, *The Tangible Kingdom*, 138–39.
8. Quoted in Baker and Ross, *The Pioneer Gift*, 33.
9. Michael Moynagh, *Church for Every Context* (London: SCM Press, 2012), 205–10.
10. Two great resources on this point are *Toxic Charity* by Robert D. Lupton (San Francisco: HarperOne, 2012) and *When Helping Hurts* by Steve Corbett and Brian Fikkert (Chicago: Moody Publishers, 2014).

11. Neil Cole, *Organic Church* (San Francisco: Jossey-Bass, 2005), 182; "People of peace are key people who are spiritually open, have good reputations, and have influence in the community" (Alan Hirsch, *Shaping of Things*, 88).
12. Hopkins, *Evangelism Strategies*, 73–74.
13. Ibid., 88.

Chapter 19

1. Bean, *How to Be a Christian*, 196; http://www.auroracommons.org.
2. Sparks, Soerens, and Friesen, *The New Parish*, 23; Darrell Guder said it this way: "Instead of separating the work of particular congregational communities or the church in general into mission and nurture, the total life of the 'people sent' makes a difference to its apostolic witness. How Christians behave toward one another, the testimony that their relationships make in the public square, and the character of their life together as a whole community are integral to their apostolic mission" (Guder, *Missional Church*, 128).
3. Manuscript of his chapter for *Messy Church* provided to me by Bob Hopkins.
4. The following, by Darrell Guder, helps us understand more fully the historic understandings of church: "The process of naming and defining the 'marks of the church' at Nicea in the fourth century was another example of missional connectedness at work. . . . The church that is faithful to the gospel tradition, the Nicene Creed proclaimed, will always be experienced as 'one, holy, catholic, and apostolic.' The Reformation responded to the crisis of the sixteenth century by supplementing these classic marks with its definition of the 'true church' in terms of its basic functions: wherever the Word is properly preached, the sacraments rightly administered, and (the Reformed tradition) Christian discipline practiced" (Guder, *Missional Church*, 254–45).
5. Stetzer and Bird, *Viral Churches*, 43.

Chapter 20

1. Bosch, *Transforming Mission*, 173.
2. See Charles Kraft, *Christianity in Culture: A Study in Biblical Theologizing in Cross-Cultural Perspective* (Maryknoll, NY: Orbis Books, 2005).

3. Williams Dillon, *God's Work in God's Way* (Brown Gold Publication, 1972).
4. David Hesselgrave also turned to 1 Corinthians 14 and found there a biblical model—five characteristics of a biblical worship service:
    1. "A heavy reliance upon revealed truth." (All activities listed, the psalm, the teaching, etc., originate with God.)
    2. "A total participation by believers." ("Each one has a psalm.")
    3. "Clarity of expression." (Prophecy is preferred above tongues for it is intelligible.)
    4. "Orderliness." ("A fitting and orderly way.")
    5. "Critical reception of the message." (The listeners judge what is said.)

    David Hesselgrave, *Planting New Churches Cross-Culturally: North America and Beyond* (Grand Rapids: Baker Academic, 2000), 90.
5. See Dee Hock, *Birth of the Chaordic Age* (San Francisco: Berrett-Koehler Publishers, 1999).
6. See Michael Moynagh, *Being Church, Doing Life*, 5–16.
7. Halter and Smay, *AND: The Gathered and Scattered Church* (Grand Rapids: Zondervan, 2010), 183.
8. See Bean, *How to Be a Christian*, 135ff.
9. Darrell Guder, *Missional Church*, 243.
10. Peyton Jones, *Church Zero*, 188–89, 196.
11. Kiva is "a non-profit organization with a mission to connect people through lending to alleviate poverty." (See www.kiva.org)

Chapter 21

1. "Our priority for pulpit-centered Christianity may actually be one of the most consumer-oriented aspects of evangelicalism today. . . . This may sound a bit crass, but here's the real deal: Most churches send the majority of their staff time and financial resources paying for and preparing to deliver a sixty-minute program, which prioritizes preaching. All of this, even though within twenty minutes most adults have forgotten 95% of what they just heard. If the church were like a business, that would be like putting 90% of your investment portfolio into a product that has not produced growth for the past 40 years. . . . The church service with a sermon has and always will be necessary and helpful but if used as the main way of making missional disciples, it falls short" (Halter and Smay, *AND*, 183–84).

2. Alan Hirsch, in Frost and Hirsch, *The Shaping of Things to Come*, 189.

3. J. C. Hoekendijk, *The Church Inside Out* (Philadelphia: Westminster Press, 1966), 178.

4. Hugh Halter, *BiVo*, 100.

5. Harley Shreck and David Barrett, *Unreached Peoples: Clarifying the Task* (CA: MARC, 1987), 174–75.

6. Quoted in *Fresh Expressions and the Kingdom of God*, 178.

7. Steven Croft, in *Mission-Shaped Questions*, 35.

8. *By Water and the Spirit*, http://www.umc.org/what-we-believe/this-holy-mystery; See also http://www.umc.org/what-we-believe/may-a-person-who-has-not-been-baptized-participate-in-holy-communion, where this is found: "Yes, our church does not seek to close God's Table, although the historic and normal Christian order of the sacraments is baptism first—as birth into the family—and communion following, as continuing nurture at the family table. Pastors and congregations reach out and encourage those who partake at the Table to share fully in the life of God's people, including coming to the font after appropriate preparation."

9. Croft, *Mission-Shaped Questions*, 59.

10. Ibid., 29, 35, 41.

11. Quoted in John Bowen, "A Beginner's Guide to Fresh Expressions," a paper, 6. http://wycliffecollege.ca/documents/A%20Beginners%20Guide%20to%20Fresh%20Expressions.pdf.

Chapter 22

1. "Fresh expressions of church . . . are in the process of becoming, and it will be through the stories and emerging praxis of fresh expressions that criticisms are either answered or ignored. . . . Fresh expressions, whatever their perceived faults and failings, are . . . very young indeed, and will take time to find their true place within the wider economy of the Church" (Cray, Mobsby, and Kennedy, *Fresh Expressions and the Kingdom of God*, 135, 139).

2. Quoted in Moynagh, *Church for Every Context*.

3. "In a sense, *Mission-shaped Church* (2004) is a hypothesis. The assumed hypothesis is that the secularization thesis is wrong; social change does not make church demise inevitable; the problem has been the church's failure to adapt; new contextual churches are the Spirit's means of reversing decline. As yet there

is insufficient evidence to confirm this hypothesis, but the new types of church championed by *Mission-shaped Church* are starting to provide pointers. In time, the fruitfulness or otherwise of these new churches will show whether the hypothesis is right" (Moynagh, *Church for Every Context*, 81).

4. "While some people think (the missional church) is just another fad or strategy, people like Craig Van Gelder have helped us to understand that the missional church has a rich history and has been in the making over the last century. One important development has been the refusion of church and mission, ecclesiology and missiology" (J. R. Woodward, *Creating a Missional Culture* [Downers Grove: IVP, 2012], 21). Hirsch wrote that whether this movement is a fad depends on whether these new forms of church truly become missional: "The absolutely vital issue for newer emerging churches will be their capacity to become genuinely missional. If they fail to make this shift, then they too will be another readjustment of Christendom. A mere fad" (Hirsch, *The Forgotten Ways: Reactivating the Missional Church* [Grand Rapids: Brazos Press, 2006], 71-72).

5. In Louise Nelstrop and Martyn Percy, *Evaluating Fresh Expressions* (Norwich, UK: Canterbury Press, 2008), 140.

6. Cole, *Church 3.0*, 213, 218.

Chapter 23

1. In *Evaluating Fresh Expressions*, 36.
2. Croft, *Mission-Shaped Questions*, 87.
3. See 1 Corinthians 3.
4. In *Evaluating Fresh Expressions*, 23.
5. See Bean, *How to Be a Christian Without Going to Church*, 168-69.
6. Ibid., 168.
7. Michael Moynagh with Andy Freeman, *How Can We Be Sustainable?* (Warwick: Fresh Expressions UK, 2011), 5.
8. We would be hard pressed to find many inherited churches that have overcome the human tendency to flock with birds of a feather. Thus fresh expressions of church are neither better nor worse by design than inherited churches at overcoming barriers.
9. Donald McGavran, *Understanding Church Growth* (Grand Rapids: Erdmans, 1970), 223.
10. Ibid., 224.
11. Ibid., 227, 230.

12. Rene Padilla, *Mission Between the Times* (Grand Rapids: Wm. B. Erdmans Publishing, 1985), 166.
13. Ibid., 167.
14. See Michael Moynagh, *Being Church, Doing Life*, 76, and *Church for Every Context*, 21.
15. "Overall, a church multiplication movement will mean more . . . communities and networks of healthy and Gospel-focused churches completely different from ours. To truly reach our world, churches need to multiply among every thin slice of society: suburban, urban, rural, cowboy, artistic, senior adult, collegiate—and on the list goes. These groups each have their own language, culture, values, and perspectives. If a biblical church effectively reaches any of the varied members of the human race, we're in favor of it" (Stetzer and Bird, *Viral Churches*, 36).
16. Bosch, *Transforming Mission*, 138.

A Fresh Expressions Story: At the Intersection of Grace and Main

1. You can read more about Grace and Main on their website, graceandmain.org, and read stories about their work at ThirdChanceMinistries.com.

Chapter 24

1. Peyton Jones, *Church Zero*, 151.
2. Hirsch and Frost, *The Shaping of Things to Come*, 9.
3. Ibid., 9–10.
4. Leonardo Boff, *Church, Charism & Power* (New York: Crossroad, 1985), 9.
5. Steve Croft, *Mission-Shaped Questions*, 143.
6. Michael Moynagh, *Being Church, Doing Life*, 116.
7. Gordon MacDonald, *Who Stole My Church?* (Nashville: Thomas Nelson, 2007), 224.
8. Moynagh, *Being Church, Doing Life*, 278.

Chapter 25

1. Halter and Smay, *AND: The Gathered and Scattered Church*, 153.
2. Ibid., 156–57.
3. Roxburgh and Romanuk, *The Missional Leader*, 176.
4. Roxburgh and Boren, *Introducing the Missional Church*, 137.

5. There is a process that might be helpful to your congregation as you consider becoming more missional, and "experimenting around the edge." It is intended to discern how God is speaking to a congregation about an external orientation.

   The Missional Change Model (MCM) is a 13–24 month process that is similar to the Appreciative Inquiry model, yet has as its specific intent the development of a missional mindset in a congregation. It was developed by Alan Roxburgh and may be found in *Introducing the Missional Church* and *The Missional Leader*.

   A key assumption of the MCM is that missional transformation cannot be introduced by a leader or leaders, but must emerge from among the congregation in order to be owned. The role of leaders is to create the environment in which that can happen.

   A majority of the congregation is not likely to work through the MCM; it is those who have a missional heart who are the most likely to make it all the way through. But the people who are committed to being a missional church will influence others until a majority of the church is engaged.

   In the Missional Change Model the first step is to create opportunities for people to talk about the radical societal changes going on around them, including the world of faith, and their feelings about those changes. Facilitators lead the church through safe dialogue and discussion about any feelings of discomfort and confusion.

   From there, the congregation expresses what they believe, to that point, God is leading them to do in their world. People are encouraged to discern, to pray, and to experiment.

   Eventually, people begin to think differently and missional thinking begins to bud in the congregation. The church starts trending toward a missional mindset and is prepared for talks concerning the sort of structural and programmatic changes that would be necessary to live into their new paradigm.

   This summary here is an inadequate representation of the MCM process. I encourage you to read *Introducing the Missional Church* for a full explanation.

6. Houle, *Entering the Shift Age*, 201.

Chapter 26

1. Halter and Smay, *AND: The Gathered and Scattered Church*, 141.
2. Alan Hirsch, *The Forgotten Ways*, 30. See also Ed Stetzer and Warren Bird, *Viral Churches*, 49.
3. Croft, *Mission-Shaped Questions*, 22.
4. Reggie McNeal, *Missional Renaissance*, 64.
5. Jim Kitchins, *Postmodern Parish*, 39.
6. Bergquist and Karr, *Church Turned Inside Out*, 4–5.
7. Leonard Sweet has a powerful treatment of this theme in his book, *AquaChurch 2.0: Piloting Your Church in Today's Fluid Culture* (Colorado Springs, CO: David C. Cook Publishers, 2008).